ACCOUNTING, A MULTIPARADIGMATIC SCIENCE

ACCOUNTING, A MULTIPARADIGMATIC SCIENCE

Ahmed Riahi-Belkaoui

Q

Quorum Books
Westport, Connecticut • London

Library of Congress Cataloging-in-Publication Data

Riahi-Belkaoui, Ahmed.
    Accounting, a multiparadigmatic science / Ahmed Riahi-Belkaoui.
      p.   cm.
    Includes bibliographical references and index.
    ISBN 1–56720–048–6 (alk. paper)
    1. Accounting. 2. Accounting—Research. I. Title.
HF5635.R45   1996
657—dc20   96–2215

British Library Cataloguing in Publication Data is available.

Library of Congress Catalog Card Number: 96–2215
ISBN: 1–56720–048–6

First published in 1996

Quorum Books, 88 Post Road West, Westport, CT 06881
An imprint of Greenwood Publishing Group, Inc.

Printed in the United States of America

The paper used in this book complies with the
Permanent Paper Standard issued by the National
Information Standards Organization (Z39.48–1984).

10 9 8 7 6 5 4 3 2

To my family here and there

Contents

Exhibits
ix

Preface
xi

1. Accounting: Toward a Multiple Paradigm Science
1

2. The Anthropological/Inductive Paradigm
35

3. The True Income/Deductive Paradigm
65

4. The Decision Usefulness/Decision Model Paradigm
93

5. The Decision Usefulness/Decision Maker/Aggregate Market Behavior Paradigm
121

6. The Decision Usefulness/Decision Maker/Individual User Paradigm
147

Index
185

Exhibits

1.1	Accounting Research Framework	10
1.2	Jungian Typology of Researchers	26
2.1	Summary of the Papers Reviewing Watts and Zimmerman	56
3.1	Qochinski Company Income Statements for the Year Ending December 31, 19X3	72
3.2	Qochinski Company Balance Sheets for the Year Ending December 31, 19X3	73
3.3	Qochinski Company General Price Level Income Statements for the Year Ending December 31, 19X3	77
3.4	Qochinski Company General Price Level Balance Sheets for the Year Ending December 31, 19X3	78
3.5	Qochinski Company General Price Level Gain or Loss for the Year Ending December 31, 19X3	79
3.6	Error-Type Analysis	82
6.1	List of Propositions and Corollaries	152
6.2	The U-Curve Hypothesis	164

Preface

Accounting was once considered an intruder in the halls of academia. It has since grown into a full-fledged social science and field of inquiry, dominated by the fierce competition among different paradigms. These accounting paradigms, striving for primacy through books, journals, conferences, seminars, and other means of defense, are mainly characterized by their exemplars, their images of the subject matter, their theories, and finally the methods they use. They have given to accounting a new "cachet" and image appropriate to a field whose findings could one day be displayed in the salon and the national academy and discussed by realists, idealists, and phenomenalists.

This book provides a critical examination of each of these accounting paradigms as a guide to researchers and policy makers in need of a proper interpretation and positioning of the products of accounting research.

The book consists of six chapters covering the nature of accounting as a multiparadigmatic science and each of the paradigms: (1) the anthropological/inductive paradigm, (2) the true income/deductive paradigm, (3) the decision usefulness/decision model paradigm, (4) the decision usefulness/decision maker/aggregate market behavior paradigm, and (5) the decision usefulness/decision maker/individual user paradigm.

Each chapter examines the paradigms in terms of their exemplars, the image of the subject matter, theories, and methods. The book serves two purposes: first, as a guide to the accounting literature and for a better understanding of the principles differentiating the researchers in accounting, and second, as a textbook to be used in research methodology and accounting theory courses.

No book can be written without the help of numerous individuals and organizations. A special note of appreciation is extended to my teaching and research assistants Dimitra Alvertos, Pearl W. Zhang, and Debbie Reed. I also want to thank Eric Valentine and Bridget M. Austiguy-Preschel from Greenwood Publishing for their continuous and intelligent support, and Pat Steele, who copyedited the manuscript.

ACCOUNTING, A MULTIPARADIGMATIC SCIENCE

1 Accounting: Toward a Multiple Paradigm Science

INTRODUCTION

Not long ago, accounting within and outside the university was viewed with contempt. The situation was described as follows:

I am sure that all of our colleagues look upon accounting as an intruder, a Saul among the prophets, a pariah whose very presence detracts somewhat from the sanctity of the academic walls. It is true that we ourselves speak of the science of accounts, or the art of accounting, even of the philosophy of accounts. But accounting is, alas, only a pseudo-science unrecognized by J. McKeen Cattel; its products are displayed neither in the salon, nor in the national academy; we find it discussed by neither realist, idealist, nor phenomenalist. The humanists look down on us as beings who dabble in the sordid figures of dollars and cents instead of toying with infinities and searching for the illusive soul of things; the scientists and technologists despise us as able only to record rather than to perform deeds.[1]

Fortunately, as this chapter will show, the field has drastically changed toward becoming a true, full-fledged "normal science" with competing paradigms striving for dominance.

ACCOUNTING AS A SOCIAL SCIENCE

At one point in time, the accounting literature developed a long drawn out debate about whether accounting is a service.[2,3] Those who argue that accounting is an art or a trade suggest that the accounting skills necessary to be a good tradesman should be taught, and that a "legalistic" approach to accounting is warranted. The advocates of accounting as a science suggest instead the teaching of the accounting model of measurements to give the accounting students more conceptual insight in what conventional accrual accounting is attempting to do to meet the general objectives of serving users' needs; and to provoke critical thought about the field and the dynamics of change in accounting.[4] How accounting is taught, as a trade or as a science, will affect the views of the field and the preparedness of those students electing to major in accounting and to ultimately join the ranks of the accounting profession. Theory, in both the normative and positive senses, and the science of accounting, placed at the front and not only at the back of the curriculum may prepare students to better understand accounting practices, to be prepared for changes in these practices, and ultimately to make better policy decisions. This last argument fits perfectly to the now widely held view that accounting is a full-fledged social science. This argument was eloquently made by Mautz as follows:

Accounting deals with enterprises, which are certainly social groups; it is concerned with transactions and other economic events which have social consequences and influence social relationships; it produces knowledge that is useful and meaningful to human beings engaged in activities having social implications; it is primarily mental in nature. On the basis of the guidelines available, accounting is a social science.[5]

The questions of whether accounting is a science has never been adequately answered. A good definition is "A classified and systematized body of knowledge . . . organized around one or more central theories and a number of general principles . . . usually expressed in quantitative terms . . . knowledge which permits the prediction and, under some circumstances, the control of future events."[6]

Accounting meets the preceding criteria. It has a distinct subject matter and includes underlying uniformities and regularities conducive to empirical relationships, authoritative generalizations, concepts, principles, laws, and theories. It definitely can be considered a science. If one subscribes to the unity-of-science argument, a single scientific method is equally applicable to accounting and other sciences. As Carl Hempel observed:

The thesis of the methodological unity of science states, first of all, that, notwithstanding many differences in their techniques of investigation, all branches of empirical science test and support their statements in basically the same manner, namely by deriving from them implications that can be checked intersubjectively and by performing for those implications the appropriate experimental or observational tests. This, the unity of method thesis holds, is true also of psychology and the social and historical disciplines. In response to the claim that the scholar in these fields, in contrast to the social sciences, often must rely on empathy to establish his assertions, logically-empiricist writers stressed that imaginative identification with a given person often may prove a useful heuristic aid to the investigator who seeks to guess at a hypothesis about that person's beliefs, hopes, fears, and goals. But whether or not a hypothesis they arrived at is factually sound must be determined by reference to objective evidence: the investigator's emphatic experience is logically irreverent to it.[7]

There is, therefore, a common acceptance by all sciences of a methodology for the justification of knowledge. That methodology rests in determining whether a true value can, in principle, be assigned to a hypothesis—that is, whether it can be refuted, confirmed, falsified, or verified, respectively. Confirmation is the extent to which a hypothesis is capable of being shown to be empirically untrue, that is, of failing to describe the real world accurately. Falsification is the extent to which a hypothesis is capable of being shown to be empirically untrue, that is, of failing to describe the real world accurately. Confirmation of hypotheses does not necessarily imply that they are falsifiable, and vice versa. In fact, hypotheses that are naturally grounded in theory can be either purely confirmable, purely refutable, or both confirmable and refutable. Purely confirmable hypotheses come from existential statements, that is, statements that propose the existence of some phenomenon. For example, the hypothesis "There are CPAs within public accounting firms who view inflation accounting as useless" is a purely confirmable hypothesis.

Purely refutable hypotheses come from universal laws, that is, statements that take the form of universal generalized conditionals. An example of such a hypothesis is "All accountants are CPAs." If the hypothesis is stated as "There are accountants who are CPAs," it becomes an existential statement, which is purely confirmable. Therefore, it appears that universal laws are basically negative existential statements that are purely refutable or falsifiable.

Both confirmable and refutable hypotheses come from singular statements, that is, statements that refer only to specific phenomena that are bound in time and space. For example, the hypothesis "All individuals tolerant of ambiguity process more information cues than those who are intolerant of ambiguity'' can be both confirmed and refuted. However, there are hypotheses that are neither strictly confirmable nor strictly refutable.

They are hypotheses arising from statistical or tendency laws, that is, statements specifying a ''loosely specified'' statistical relationship between a phenomenon and a large number of variables. Most accounting hypotheses fall within this category, which makes them neither strictly confirmable nor strictly falsifiable. The market model, the accounting predictive models of economic events, the positive theory of accounting, the human information-processing models, and most empirical accounting research fit the description. If the data contradict the hypothesis derived from these theories or models, defenders can always claim different excuses, including contamination of the data, or small or biased sample size. The retoric of research plays a crucial role in challenging whatever results are provided by the data. Is this a cause for alarm, given that statistical laws abound in accounting research? Bunge suggested that this would be a mistake:

Some die-hard classical determinists claim that stochastic statements do not deserve the name of law and are to be regarded, at their best, as contemporary devices. This anachronistic view has no longer currency in physics, chemistry, and certain branches of biology (notably genetics), especially ever since these sciences found that all major laws within domains are stochastic laws deducible (at least in principle) from laws concerning single systems in conjunction with definite statistical hypotheses regarding, e.g., the compensation of random deviations. Yet the prejudice against stochastic laws still causes some harm in psychology and sociology, where it serves to attack the stochastic approach without compensating for its loss by a scientific study of individuals.[8]

The refutation or confirmation is done by repeated testimony and new evidence.

ALTERNATIVE FOUNDATIONS OF ACCOUNTING

The accounting foundations have been identified in the literature, namely, the marginal-economics-based accounting and the political-economy accounting.

Marginal-Economics-Based Accounting

Neoclassical marginal economics has had a paramount influence on accounting practice, theory, and research. Various recurring themes are good evidence of such influence.

Accounting's commitment to marginalism is best illustrated by two enduring emphases, namely, on individualism and on preserving objectivity and independence. The first emphasis included both a view of the sovereignty of individual owners, which ignored the separation of ownership and management, and a view that explicitly recognizes the separation of ownership and management but also considers the firm as a "legal" person having the right to maintain command over a given level of resources.[9] The second emphasis put the accountant in the position of historian and accounting in the position of an impartial record of historical exchanges with objectivity as a paramount objective.

Both emphases improved constraints on the practice and teachings of accounting. As noticed by Anthony Tinker and his associates, the first emphasis preempted questions about the class affiliations of individuals and the part played by accountants in class conflicts, and the second emphasis led to shunning subjective questions of value and confirming accounting data to objective market prices.[10] The motivation behind the role of historian is explained as follows:

This image of the accountant—often as a disinterested, innocuous "historian"—stems from the desire to deny the responsibility that accountants bear for shaping subjective expectations which, in turn, affect decisions about resources allocation and the distribution of income between and within classes. This attachment to historical facts provides a veneer of pseudo-objectivity that allows accountants to claim that they merely record—not partake in—social conflicts.[11]

In marginal economics and conventional accounting, as based on its related economics, value and profit are linked to the worth of future consumption possibilities as assessed by the present value of some of the accounting assets on the basis-value concept and for comparing projects on the basis of their present values. Tinker, however, showed that in comparing alternative capital investment projects, marginal-economics-based accounting does not yield a unique solution.[12] The comparison depends on the choice of the interest rate. The most desirable project for a society can be ascertained only for a given interest rate, which works well for a given firm using its cost of capital as the interest rate. Given the difference in the cost of capital between firms, however, the calculations are indeterminate. This argues for using a given market rate of interest to conclude that one project is socially preferable to another. This solution, however, is challenged by what are known as the Cambridge Controversies. Basically, it is pointed out that the marginalist explanation is tautological. It is summarized as follows:

> We begin by asking how the rate of profit is determined and answer it with reference to the quantity of capital and its marginal revenue product. We then ask how these are determined and the reply is by assuming a division of future income and discounting the returns to capital with the market rate of interest. All that has been said is that the market rate of interest is a function of the market rate of interest (and an assumed income distribution).[13]

Similarly, D. J. Cooper pointed out that the market rate of interest depends on the supply and demand for monetary capital, which, in turn, depends on the market rate of interest.[14] In short, marginal economics is shown as either tautological or indeterminate.

Political-Economy Accounting

Political-economy accounting was spurred by the limitations of marginal economics and the merits of political economy. For example, unlike marginalism, political economy recognizes two dimensions of capital: one as (physical) instruments of production and one as man's relationship to man in a social organization.[15] Different kinds of society (feudal, slave, capitalist, and so on) exist and are characterized by different social institutions (e.g., legal, state, educations, religious, law and order, political-government administration). In each of these societies, contradicting groups exist with different powers striving for dominance, which may lead to forms of exploitation, alienation, and inequalities. Therefore, unlike the situation in marginalism, here accounting is to serve an ideological role in legitimizing the ideology of the basis organizing principal and in mystifying relationships among classes in society and reinforcing unequal power distributions.[16] Accounting as an ideology is within the realm of the political-economy accounting.

As another example, the research based on marginalism and assessing the usefulness of corporate reports for users has implications for only the private value of information with a bias for the shareholder and manager classes in society and is therefore not helpful in either the design or choice of alternative accounting reports aimed at informing the social welfare. The impact of corporate accounting reports on social welfare is also within the realm of the political-economy accounting.

Besides its alleged interest in ideology and social welfare, political-economy accounting is an alternative accounting approach aimed at looking at the accounting functions within the broader structural and institutional environment in which it operates. A good definition is as follows:

A Political Economy of Accounting (PEA) is thus a normative, descriptive and critical approach to accounting research. It provides a broader, more holistic, framework for analyzing and understanding the value of accounting reports within the economy as a whole. A PEA approach attempts to explicate and interpret the role of accounting reports in the distribution of income, wealth, and power in society. In so doing, a PEA approach models the institutional structure of society that helps fashion this role and provides a framework for examining novel sets of institutions, accounting and accounting reports.[17]

In fact, D. J. Cooper and M. J. Sherer presented three features of the political-economy accounting.[18]

1. It should recognize power and conflict in society and consequently should focus on the effects of accounting reports on the distribution of income, wealth, and power in society. This feature directly contradicts the pluralist concept in favor of the views that either society is controlled by a well-defined elite or there is continuous societal conflict between essentially antagonistic classes.[19]

2. It should recognize the specific historical and institutional environment of the society in which it operates, namely, that (a) the economy is dominated by large corporations; (b) disequilibrium is a permanent feature of the economy; and (c) the state plays a paramount role in managing the economy, in failing to control its spending levels, in protecting commercial interest and large firms, in preserving social harmony and its own legitimacy, and at the same time in intervening in the determination of accounting policies.

3. It should adopt a more emancipated view of human motivation and the role of accounting. Accounting should be recognized as an influencing agent causing either motivation or even alienation at work and the pursuit of self-interest and playing a socially active rather than passive function.[20]

For example:

In the same way as the medical profession may have a legitimate concern with housing, social conditions and public health of the community, so the accounting profession may have legitimate concerns in relation to its immediate environment (e.g. the commercial and financial sectors of the economy). Attempts to resolve technical issues without consideration of this environment may result in an imperfect and incomplete resolution due to the acceptance of current institutions and practices.[21]

ALTERNATIVE APPROACHES TO ACCOUNTING RESEARCH

Framework of the Nature of Accounting Research

Burrell and Morgan[22] made two main sets of assumptions about social science and about society.

The assumptions about social science relate to the ontology of the social world, epistemology, human nature, and methodology. These assumptions can also be thought of in terms of the subjective-objective dimension.

First, the ontological assumption, concerning the very essence of the accounting phenomenon, involves nominalism-realism differences. The debate is whether the social world external to individual cognition is a compound of pure names, concepts, and labels that give a structure to reality, as in normalism, or whether it is a compound of real, factual, and tangible structures, as in realism.

Second, the epistemological debate, concerning the ground of knowledge and the nature of knowledge, involves the antipositivism-positivism debate. This debate focuses on the utility of a search for laws or underlying regularities in the field of social affairs. Positivism supports the utility. Antipositivism refutes it and argues for individual participation as a condition of understanding the social world.

Third, the human-nature debate, concerning the relationship between human beings and their environment, involves the voluntarism-determinism debate. This debate focuses on whether humans and their activities are determined by the situation or environment, as in determinism, or are the result of their free will, as in voluntarism.

Fourth, the methodology debate, concerning the methods used to investigate and learn about the social world, involves the ideographic-nomothetic debate. This debate focuses on whether the methodology involves the analysis of the subjective accounts obtained by participating or getting inside the situation, as in the ideographic method, or whether the methodology involves a rigorous and scientific testing of hypotheses, as in the nomothetic method.

The assumption about the nature of society relates to the order-conflict debate or, more precisely, the regulation-radical change debate.

The sociology of regulation attempts to explain the society by focusing on its unity and cohesiveness and the need for regulation. The sociology of radical change, in contract, seeks to explain society by focusing on the radical change, deep-seated structural conflict, modes of domination, and the structural contradictions of modern society. As highlighted by Burrell and Morgan, the sociology of regulation is concerned with status quo, social order, consensus, social integration and cohesion, solidarity, need satisfaction, and actuality, whereas the sociology of radical change is concerned with structural conflict, models of domination, contradiction, emancipation, deprivation, and potentiality.

Any social science discipline, including accounting, can be analyzed along metatheoretical assumptions about the nature of science, the subjective-objective dimension, and about the nature of society, the dimension of regulation-radical change. Using these two dimensions, Burrell and Morgan were able to develop a coherent scheme for the analysis of social theory, in general, and organizational analysis, in particular.[23] The scheme consists of four distinct paradigms, labeled as

1. the radical humanist paradigm, characterized by the radical change and subjective dimensions;
2. the radical structuralist paradigm, characterized by the radical change and objective dimensions;
3. the interpretive paradigm, characterized by the subjective and regular dimensions; and
4. the functionalist paradigm, characterized by the objective and regulation dimensions.

The framework is illustrated in Exhibit 1.1. It comprises of four views of reality to be used in analyzing a wide range of social theories, including accounting. As Burrell and Morgan stated:

Given the cross linkages between rival intellectual traditions, it becomes clear to us that our two sets of assumptions could be counter-posed to produce an analytical scheme for studying social theories in general: the two sets of assumptions de-

Exhibit 1.1
Accounting Research Framework

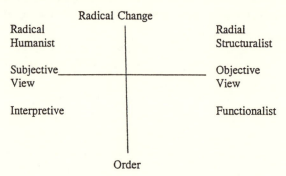

fined four basic paradigms reflecting quite separate views of social theory. On attempting to relate this scheme to the social science literature we found that we posed an extremely powerful tool for negotiating our way through different subject areas, and one which made sense of a great deal of the confusion which characterizes much contemporary debate within the social science.[24]

This framework is very much applicable to accounting, to explain four accounting paradigms—the functionalist, interpretive, radical humanist, and radical structuralist. Various attempts were made to classify accounting literature using the Burrell and Morgan framework.[25]

The Situation in Accounting

Accounting theories and research have been based predominantly on the functionalist view, although modest attempts have been made to move to the interpretive, radical humanist, and radical structuralist paradigms.

The Functionalist View in Accounting

The *functionalist view* in accounting focuses on explaining the social order, in which accounting plays a role, from a realist, positivist, determinist, and nomothetic standpoint. It is concerned with effective regulation on the basis of objective evidence.

The functionalist paradigm in accounting views accounting phenomena as concrete real-world relations possessing regularities and causal relationships that are amendable to scientific explanation and prediction.

In addition, the social order, as defined by extant structures of market and firm, is taken for granted, and no reference to domination or conflict is made. Both views of accounting phenomena and the social world are used to develop theories assumed to be value free rather than historically relative.

1. As in structural functionalism, the functionalist paradigm in accounting focuses on establishing the functions of accounting needed for an efficient functioning of organizations. These functions are the "functional prerequisites" or "functional imperatives" of adaptation, goal attainment, integration, and latency or pattern maintenance. To serve these imperatives, the structures or elements of accounting are defined.

2. As in system theory, the functionalist paradigm in accounting focuses on both the search for analogical representation of the accounting system and a system analysis.

3. Interactionism with its focus on human association and interaction is expressed in the form of behavioral accounting.

4. Objectivism, with its commitment to the models and methods used in the natural sciences, is the predominant avenue in accounting theorizing and research. In fact, abstract empiricism as a label fits perfectly most of the published empirical accounting research. There is a definite urge to develop rigorous models of the accounting phenomena in the absence of confounding variables and a methodological reliance on hypothetic-deductive methods.

The Interpretive View in Accounting

The *interpretive view* in accounting would focus on explaining the social order from a nominalist, antipositivist, voluntarist, and ideographic standpoint. If it existed in accounting, it would aim to understand the subjective experience of individuals involved in the preparation, communication, verification, or use of accounting information. Hermeneutics, if applied in accounting, would focus on the study of the accounting objectification, such as accounting institutions, accounting ideologies, using the method of verstehen, that is, to understand through reenactment. Phenomenology, if applied to accounting, would attempt to make explicit the "essences" that cannot be revealed by ordinary positivist observations. The interpretive paradigm in accounting, although in its infancy, has focused on (1) the ability of information to "construct reality,"[26] (2) the role of accounting as a "linguistic" tool,[27] and (3) other roles and images that accounting may take.[28]

To the interpretists, accounting is no more than names, concepts, and labels used to construct social reality. It can be understood only from the point of view of those directly involved in its preparation, communication, or use. Methodologically, ideographic methods rather than hypothetic-deductive methods are needed to reenact the actor's definition of the problem.

Although the interpretive paradigm is not predominant in accounting, it suffers from three major limitations: (1) it assumes that a "quasi-divine" observer can understand social action through sheer subjectivity and without interference; (2) it creates the illusion of pure theory by using a monological line of reasoning; and (3) it fails to be an inquiry of change.[29]

The Radical Humanist View in Accounting

The *radical humanist view* in accounting focuses on explaining the social order from a nominalist, antipositivist, voluntarist, and ideographic perspective and places emphasis on forms of radical change. It respects any research that reduces philosophical critique to some normative methodology. In the form of critical theory, it requires two forms of analysis: "(a) a taxonomic analysis of the ontological, epistemological, and methodological concerns underlying organization science; and (b) a critique (based on this analysis) of the dynamic interplay between organizational research, theory and practice."[30] It will expand its epistemic critique to include: "(a) a discussion of the limitation of alternative modes of inquiry; (b) an analysis of the relationship between the community of organizational researchers and organization between the community of organizational researchers and organizational practitioners and members; and (c) the acknowledgment of the practical aim of any particular mode of research."[31]

Critical theory in accounting will assume that theories, bodies of knowledge, and facts are mere reflections of realistic world views. It will view accountants, accounters, and accounts as prisoners of a mode of consciousness that is shaped and controlled through ideological processes. All aspects of accounting will be scrutinized for their alienating properties. In short, accounting will be viewed as creating a "psychic prison" where organizational realities become confirming and dominating. The argument is that accounting systems encourage and sustain alienation and conflict.[32] This view would suggest that accounting should help people realize their potential by helping them realize their needs or would direct it to avenues in line with Jurgen Habermas's concern with communicative competence and Antonio Gramsci and George Lukacs's concern with ideology and false consciousness.[33]

Gramsci, in particular, addressed the problem of false consciousness by examining the position of intellectuals in contemporary society. Although he argued that all humans are intellectual beings, not everyone under capitalism performs intellectual functions. He further distinguished between traditional intellectuals, who historically have been autonomous of class interests, and organic intellectuals, who are ideologically aligned with class interests. In contemporary capitalism, most intellectuals are organically tied to the bourgeoisie. Because of the ideological hegemony of capitalism, few intellectuals articulate the interest of the subordinate class. This type of radical humanist interpretation applied to the field of accounting suggests that until an "organic" elite emerges of accountants who are not tied ideologically to the capitalist class, the discipline of accounting will continue to reproduce the interests and the ideology of capitalism. Classical or functionalist accountants will be, however, very quick to accuse the humanist of being partisan and nonacademic. As Burrell and Morgan discussed, humanists are often labeled as "radicals hellbent upon fanning the flames of revolutionary consciousness, or as mindless existentialists who will nor or cannot adjust to the world of everyday 'reality' and accept the inevitable march of 'progress.' "[34]

The Radical Structuralist View in Accounting

The *radical structuralist view* in accounting would challenge the social order from a realist, positivist, deterministic, and nomothetic standpoint. It would seek radical change, emancipation, and potentiality using an analysis emphasizing structural conflict, modes of domination, contradiction, and deprivation. This paradigm would generate accounting theories based on metaphors such as the instrument of domination, schismatic system, and catastrophe. The role of accounting in Weber's classic analysis of bureaucracy as a mode of domination, in Robert Michels's analysis of the "iron law of oligarchy," and in Marxists' analyses of organization will emerge as a powerful instrument of domination to be understood as an essential part of a wider process of domination within society as a whole.[35] As stated by David Cooper:

From the point of view of these radical structuralists, organizations are instruments of social forces concerned to maintain the division of labor and distribution of wealth and power in society. To these researchers, whose perspective seems almost completely missing in current accounting research, there is an actuality of organizations that includes sexual and racial discrimination, patterns of social stratification and unequal distributions of wealth, power and rewards. . . .The failure to acknowledge these characteristics and consider the relationship of accounting practices to them seems a curious omission for studies that explicitly seek to account for accounting.[36]

Structuralist accountants will hold an objective view of the social world but focus on contradictions and crisis tendencies created by the accounting process. Unlike the radical humanists with their emphasis on super-structural phenomena such as ideology and distorted consciousness, the radical structuralists in accounting will focus on the link between accounting and the economic and political relations of domination.

Marxist structuralists such as Louis Althusser and Nicos Poulantzas have stressed the relative autonomy of political and ideological structures from the underlying economic base as a connective to the overly deterministic models of classical Marxism. With respect to the accounting enterprise, this approach would focus on the relative independence of accounting practices, policies, and theories from overt, economic, and political forces. The development of accounting could be seen as a ''sui generis'' process, defined from within. A similar agenda for accounting within the radical structuralist school has been eloquently stated as follows:

Radical theories may also be applied to more specific accounting questions: What underlies major shifts in the regulatory practices of the state and how much importance should accountants attribute to these changes? What determines the state's level of autonomy vis-à-vis advantaged and disadvantaged groups and, in this regard, how much credence may be attached to the view of writers, such as Benston, that disclosure regulations are captive of vested interest? Does the degree of state autonomy vary across regulatory spheres of interests? What stance should the accounting profession take in relation to the ''contested terrain'' of state regulation? Who are the sides in the struggle for control over the state's regulatory apparatus, and how should accountants choose a side to support? The continued dominance of neoclassical thought serves to exclude such questions from the accounting research agenda. This situation will persist as long as academic accounting falls short of the scholarly ideal that everything should be open for discussion in an intellectual community.[37]

Ideography versus Nomothesis

The widely accepted view of the role of accounting research is that it functions to ''establish general laws covering the behavior of empirical events or objects with which the science is concerned, and thereby enable us to connect together our knowledge of separately known events and to make reliable predictions of events yet unknown."[38]

To accomplish these functions, the natural science model, including careful sampling, accurate measurement, and good design and analysis of theory-supported hypotheses, is generally adopted as the model supporting good research.[39] This now has met with objections leading to the ideographic-versus-nomothetic-methodology debate. The distinction between the two methodologies was first made by Gordon Allport as follows:

The nomothesis approach . . . seeks only general laws and employs only those procedures admitted by the exact sciences. Psychology in the main has been striving to make itself a completely nomothetic discipline. The ideographic sciences . . . endeavor to understand some particular event in nature or in society. A psychology of individuality would be essentially ideographic.[40]

The debate persisted over the years, sometimes with other labels such as "qualitative versus quantitative research" or "inquiry from the inside versus inquiry from the outside" or "subjective versus objective research." The difference between nomothesis and ideography stems from differences in the underlying assumptions of social science knowledge. The subjective approach to social science features a nominalism assumption for ontology, an antipositivism assumption for epistemology, a voluntarism assumption of human nature, and finally, an ideographic assumption for methodology. The objective approach, however, features a realistic ontology, a positivist epistemology, a deterministic assumption of human nature, and a nomothetic methodology.[41] In fact, Gibson Burrell and Gareth Morgan gave an exhaustive definition of both nomothesis and ideography. The ideographic approach

is based on the view that one can only understand the social world by obtaining firsthand knowledge of the subject under investigation. It thus places considerable stress upon getting close to one's subject and . . . emphasizes the analysis in the subjective accounts which one generates by "getting inside" situations and involving oneself in the everyday flow of life—the detailed analysis of the insights generated by such encounters with one's subject and the insights revealed in impressionistic accounts found in diaries, biographies and journalistic records.[42]

On the other hand, the nomothetic approach

is basing research upon systematic protocol and technique. It is epitomized in the approach and methods employed in the natural sciences. . . . It is preoccupied with the construction of scientific tests and the use of quantitative techniques for the analysis of data. Surveys, questionnaires, personality tests and standardized research instruments of all kinds are prominent among the tools which comprise nomothetic methodology.[43]

The approach, nomothesis versus ideography or inquiry from the outside versus inquiry from the inside, differs in terms of the mode of inquiry, the type of organizational action, the type of organizational inquiry, and the role of the researcher and in terms of a number of analytic dimensions.[44] One noticeable difference is associated with different types of knowledge. The ideographic method is interested in the knowledge of the particular as a condition for praxis, which is "a knowledge of how to act appropriately in a variety of particular situations."[45] The nomothetic method is interested in the development of universal knowledge theory.[46]

The difference between the two modes of inquiry is best translated in other languages by the use of two separate verbs to distinguish the two ways of knowing: knowledge about and acquaintance with. French uses *savoir* and *connaitre;* German uses *wissen* and *kennen;* and Latin uses *scire* and *nosere.*

Although both approaches have been debated in the literature, it is not an exaggeration to state that nomothesis has dominated accounting research with its search for general laws, universal variables, and a large number of subjects. The concern has been for methodological precision, rigor, and credibility, even if often irrelevant to the reality of organizations and accounting. Accounting researchers should pay attention to more of the objections raised against natural science in particular and nomothesis in general. For example, Orlando Behling raised five key objections to the use of the natural science model used in social science research and applicable to accounting research, namely,

1. *Uniqueness.* Each organization, group, and person differs to some degree from all others; the development of precise general laws to organizational behavior and organization theory is thus impossible.

2. *Instability.* The phenomena of interest to researchers in organizational behavior and organization theory are transitory. Not only do the "facts" of social events change with time, but the "laws" governing them change as well. Natural science research is poorly equipped to capture these fleeting phenomena.

3. *Sensitivity.* Unlike chemical compounds and other things of interest to natural science researchers, the people who make up organizations, and thus organizations themselves, may behave differently if they become aware of research hypotheses about them.

4. *Lack of Realism.* Manipulating and controlling variables in organizational research change the phenomena under study. Researchers thus cannot generalize from their studies because the phenomena observed inevitably differ from their real world counterparts.

5. *Epistemological Differences.* Although understanding cause and effect through natural science research is an appropriate way of "knowing," not tapped by this approach is more important in organizational behavior and organizational theory.[47]

F. T. Luthans and T. R. Davis questioned the "sameness assumption" implied by nomothesis, namely, the selective examination of many subjects under the theoretical assumption that there are more similarities than differences among individuals.[48] Based on an interactive theoretic assumption of behavior-person-environment, of real people interacting in real organizations, ideography is suggested as a useful approach using intensive single-case experimental designs and direct observational measures.[49] Luthans and Davis stated:

Central to an ideographic approach to interactive organizational behavior studies in natural settings that intends to examine and make conclusions and test specific hypotheses are intensive single case experimental designs and direct methods such as systematic participant observations. When understood and on close examination, it turns out that these designs and methods hold up as well (and some ideographic researchers would argue better) to the same evaluative criteria for scientific research that currently are being used by nomothetically-based researchers.[50]

Among the qualitative or ideographic methodologies used, ethnography and phenomenology have gained a solid place. Ethnography is used by anthropologists immersing themselves in other people's realities. It has reached the level of a paradigm as indicated by the following:

Paradigmatic ethnography begins when the observer, trained in or familiar with the anthropological approach, gets off the boat, train, plane, subway or bus prepared for a lengthy stay with a suitcase full of blank notebooks, a tape recorder, and a camera. Paradigmatic ethnography ends when the masses of data that have been recorded, filed, stored, checked, and rechecked are organized according to one of several interpretive styles and published for a scholarly or general audience.[51]

Accounting researchers interested in the ethnographic method would have to have a lengthy, continuous firsthand involvement in the organizational setting under study. They would require field observations to examine the deep structure as well as the surface behavior of those in it. As suggested by John Van Maanen, they would need to (1) separate the first-order concepts or theories used by the analyst to organize and explain these facts; (2) distinguish between presentational data that document "the running stream of spontaneous conversations and activities engaged in and observed by the ethnographer while in the field" and presentional data that "concern those appearances that informants strive to maintain (or enhance) in the eyes of the field worker, outsiders and strangers in general work colleagues, close and intimate associates, and to varying degrees themselves"; and (3) continuously assess the believability of the talk-based information to uncover lies, areas of ignorance, and the various taken-for-granted assumptions.[52]

Phenomenology goes beyond participant observation and ethnography by emphasizing the search for reality as it is "given" in the structures of consciousness universal to humankind. Herbert Spiegelberg described the following seven steps in phenomenology to guide the researcher:

1. To investigate particular phenomena,
2. To investigate general essences,
3. To grasp essential relationships among essences,
4. To watch modes of appearing,
5. To watch the constitution of phenomena in consciousness,
6. To suspend belief in the existence of phenomena, and
7. To interpret the meaning of phenomena.[53]

Although the debate of ideography versus nomothesis will go on in various social science literatures, there is an established school of thought that recommends the use of multiple methods. It is generally described as one of convergent methodology, multimethod/multitrait, convergent validation, or what has been called "triangulation."[54] In fact, the originator of the debate, Allport, proposed that the ideographic and nomothetic methods were "overlapping and contributing to one another."[55] The use of both methods can (a) lead to more confidence in the results, (b) help to uncover the deviant or off-quadrant dimension of a phenomenon, (c) lead to a synthesis or integration of theories, and (d) serve as a critical test.[56]

A thread linking all of these benefits is the important part played by qualitative methods in triangulation. The research is likely to sustain a profitable closeness to the situation which allows greater sensitivity to the multiple sources of data. Qualitative data and analysis function as the glue that cements that interpretation of multi-method results. In one respect, qualitative data are used as a critical counterpoint to quantitative methods. In another respect, the analysis benefits from the perceptions drawn from personal experiences and firsthand observations. Thus enters the artful researcher who uses the qualitative data to enrich and enlighten the portrait.[57]

What all of this implies for research practice is an eventual choice between the following three options:[58]

1. Pursue both nomothetic and ideographic research and then aggregate.

2. Alternate between nomothetic and ideographic research, running back and forth between the two methods to capitalize on the strengths of one method in certain cases and overcome the deficiencies of the other method in the same cases.

3. Develop a new science described eloquently as follows: "The new science (human action science) that is gradually emerging is likely to be more actor based, experientially rooted, praxis-oriented, and self-reflective than the current image of (positivistic, objective) science. It is likely to incorporate both the American 'pragmatic' thinking of Pierce, James, Dewey, and Mead and the German 'critical' thinking of Marx, Dilthey, Husserl, Weber, Heidegger, Gadamer, and Habermas. It will probably develop from the inside and bridge toward the precision and generalizability of inquiry from the outside."[59]

A GENERAL THEORY OF SCIENTIFIC REVOLUTIONS

A theory of scientific revolutions will focus on the progress of knowledge and the motivation for such progress. Thomas Kuhn's work focused on the progress of knowledge in a particular discipline or normal science.[60] This thesis of scientific revolutions rests on the concept of paradigm. After criticisms were raised about the different and inconsistent use of the term, Kuhn refined it for the second edition of his book:

In much of the book the term "paradigm" is used in two different senses. On the one hand, it stands for the entire constellation of beliefs, values, techniques that are shared by the members of a given community. On the other, it denotes one sort of element in that constellation, the concrete puzzle-solutions which, employed as models or examples, can replace explicit rules as a basis for the solution of the remaining puzzles of normal science.[61]

These paradigms do not remain forever dominant. Anomalies are first recognized. The anomaly is incorrigible. A period of insecurity and crisis arises with a dispute between those who see the anomaly as a counter-example and those who do not: "Normal science repeatedly goes astray. And when it does—when, that is, the profession can no longer evade anomalies that subvert the existing tradition of scientific practice—then begins the extraordinary investigation that leads the profession at last to a new set of commitments, a new basis for the practice of science."[62]

The crisis continued with the emergence of alternative sets of ideas and clear identification of schools of thoughts. What actually goes on in the crisis period is not well known. H. Gilman McCann suggested the following characteristic levels of theoretical and quantitative work associated with the initial and final periods of a normal science:

1. The level of theoretical work will rise as the revolution develops. The rise is composed of (a) an increase in the level of theoretical work among followers of the given paradigm and (b) an initially high level of theoretical work by the followers of the new paradigm, followed by a decline once the success of the new paradigm is assured.

2. The shift to the new paradigm will occur earlier among theoretical papers than among others.

3. The level of quantitative work will rise as the revolution develops. The rise is composed of (a) an increase, possibly followed by a decline, in the level quantitative work among the followers of the given paradigm and (b) an initially high level of quantitative work among supporters of the new paradigm, possibly followed by a decline as the new paradigm succeeds and new problems come to light.

4. The shift to the new paradigm will occur earlier among quantitative papers than among others.

5. The rise in the level of quantitative work will be most pronounced among theoretical papers.

6. There will be an increase in the number of authors as the revolution develops.

7. There will be an increase in the productivity of authors as the revolution progresses.

8. The shift to the new paradigm will occur earlier among papers of younger authors than among papers of older ones.

9. The supporters of the new paradigm will be younger than the defenders of the old one.

10. There will be few neutral papers.

11. The proportion of citations to authors supporting the new paradigm will increase during the revolution.[63]

All laws and propositions become subject to empirical testimony. The final rejection of one paradigm for another does not, however, rest exclusively on empirical evidence. Nonlogical factors, including metaphysical views, philosophical positions, ethnocentrism, and nationalism, and the social characteristics of the scientific community may have a bearing on the decision.[64] Domination of the new paradigm is accompanied by recognition bestowed on its proponents. It is this recognition, rather than money or power, that will become the motivating factor for researchers in a given paradigm and in a given scientific community. Basically, researchers will exchange recognition for information. As stated by W. O. Hagstrom: "Manuscripts submitted to scientific periodicals are often called 'contributions,' and they are, in fact, gifts."[65]

In general, the acceptance of a gift by an individual or a community implies a kind of recognition of the status of the donor and the existence of certain kinds of reciprocal rights . . . in science, the acceptance by scientific journals of contributed manuscripts establishes the donor's status as a scientist—indeed, status as a scientist can be achieved only by mush gift-giving—and it assures him of prestige within the scientific community.[66]

Although it may be difficult to disagree with the notion that recognition is the primary motivation for research in any discipline, it is tempting to argue that the driving force is the satisfaction of a job well done. R. K. Merton argued the case as follows:

Recognition of originality becomes socially validated testimony that one has successfully lived up to the most exacting requirements of one's role as a scientist. The self-image of the individual scientist will also depend greatly on the appraisals by his scientific peers of the extent to which he has lived up to this exacting and crucially important aspect of his role.[67]

There is, nevertheless, a gem of psychological truth in the suspicion enveloping the drive for recognition in science. Any intrinsic reward—game, money, position—is morally ambiguous and potentially subversive of culturally esteemed values. For as rewards are meted out, they can displace the original motive: concern with recognition can displace concern with advancing knowledge.[68]

With recognition as either a goal or a sign of a job well done, the researchers in the dominant paradigm, and the other still struggling paradigms ("the resisters"), communicate their information either in formal channels of communication for institutional recognition or indirect communication for elementary recognition.[69]

ACCOUNTING AS A MULTIPLE PARADIGM SCIENCE

Central to the general theory of scientific revolutions is the proper definition of the concept of a paradigm. Kuhn's use of the term is different and inconsistent. The narrow definition provided in the epilogue to the second edition of his book was still found to be vague.[70] It did not alleviate the major criticisms directed toward Kuhn's change of view that paradigms rise and fall as a result of political factors to the view that one paradigm wins over another for good reasons, including "accuracy, scope, simplicity, fruitfulness, and the like."[71] George Ritzer, for example, argued in favor of the first view and maintained that the emergence of a paradigm is essentially a political phenomenon.[72] He stated:

One paradigm wins out over another because its supporters have more power than those who support competitors. For example, the paradigm whose supporters control the most important journals in a field and thereby determine what will be published is more likely to gain pre-eminence than paradigms whose adherents lack access to prestigious outlets for their works. Similarly, positions of leadership in a field are likely to be given to supporters of the dominant paradigm, and this gives them a platform to enunciate their position with a significant amount of legitimacy. Supporters of paradigms that are seeking to gain hegemony within a field are obviously at a disadvantage, since they lack the power outlined above. Nevertheless, they can, by waging a political battle of their own, overthrow a dominant paradigm and gain that position for themselves.[73]

Phillips was in agreement with Ritzer's arguments about the first view and also argued that the reasons advanced in the second view are paradigm dependent.

With the view that paradigms are politics dependent, Ritzer offered the following definition of a paradigm.

A paradigm is a fundamental image of the subject matter within a science. It serves to define what should be studied, what questions should be asked, how they should be asked, and what rules should be followed in interpreting the answer obtained. The paradigm is the broadest unit of consensus within a science and serves to differentiate one scientific community (or subcommunity) from another. It subsumes, defines and interrelates the exemplars, theories, methods, and instruments that exist within it.[74]

The basic components of a paradigm emerge from Ritzer's definition:

1. an exemplar, or a piece of work that stands as a model for those who work within the paradigm,
2. an image of the subject matter,
3. theories, and
4. methods and instruments.

Ahmed Belkaoui used Ritzer's definition to analyze scientific communities or subcommunities in accounting with the assumptions that (1) accounting lacks a single comprehensive paradigm and is a multiparadigm science and (2) each of these accounting paradigms is striving for acceptance, even domination within the discipline.[75] Although stated in terms of competing theories, the following statement could be used to argue for competing paradigms:

While the value of the prediction of a theory to users influences its use, it does not solely determine its success. Because the costs of errors and the implementation vary, several theories about the phenomena can exist simultaneously for predictive purposes. However, only one will be greatly accepted by theorists. In accepting one theory over another, theorists will be influenced by the intuitive appeal of the theory's explanation for phenomena and the range of phenomena it can explain and predict as well as by the usefulness of its predictions to users.[76]

Following suggestions made by M. C. Wells and the 1977 American Accounting Association's publication of its *Statement on Accounting Theory and Theory Acceptance,* the following paradigms were suggested[77]

1. the anthropological/inductive paradigm,
2. the true income/deductive paradigm,
3. the decision usefulness/decision model paradigm,
4. the decision usefulness/decision maker/aggregate market behavior paradigm, and
5. the decision usefulness/decision maker/aggregate market behavior paradigm.

Each of these paradigms is examined in the remaining chapters with a particular focus on the four components: exemplar, image, theories, and methods.

TOWARD A PROFESSIONAL VALUE SYSTEM

A professional value system of academic accountants is a conceptual net not only encompassing their definitions of accounting—what it is, what it has been and will be, and what it should be—but also revealing their implicit and basic assumptions concerning their discipline as a science and occupation. Several value dimensions are compatible with this interpretation as follows:

1. *Worldviews.* The diverse accounting paradigms are due to differences in fundamental metaphonical assumptions that accounting theorists hold about human behavior. Social philosophers and scientists similarly disagree about whether human behavior is simple or complex, predictable or unpredictable, rational or irrational, and whether the social and economic system is basically stable or unstable. They also differ in their orientation toward social and economic changes and attitudes toward deliberate interventions to solve societal problems.

2. *Pure Accounting Theory.* This dimension of the professional value system deals with the value of theory construction and verification as the proper work of the accounting researcher, the problem of codifying empirical findings, the difference between theory and research, the role of the historical approach, the importance of ingenuity in theory and development, and the usefulness of true accounting theory.

3. *Societal Role.* Given the increased interest in the societal role of accountants,

this dimension of the professional value system deals with the role of the academic accountant as an intellectual social critic, the dilemma between possibly studying and actively attempting to solve problems, and the social utility of accounting knowledge.

4. *Scientific Method.* The emphasis on the scientific method is a professional value that may divide academic accountants into different camps. This value dimension treats the contrast between rigorous, statistical methods and experimental and laboratory methods, on the one hand, and direct observation, participant observation, inventiveness, and intuition, on the other hand.

5. *Value Freeness.* This value dimension treats of the principle of ethical neutrality, value freeness as a central scientific canon, the possible bias created by the external support, the relation between the value-free ideal and the autonomy of accounting researchers, and the political implications of external support for the accounting value system.

6. *Professionalization.* This value dimension treats of the attitudes toward the social organization and control, the requirements for membership in accounting organizations, the adoption of a code of ethics, the issue of licensing of academic accountants, and the relation of accounting to other disciplines.

7. *Self-Image.* This value dimension deals with the intellectual and philosophical content of accounting, its importance to society's goal, and the way accountants are remunerated.

8. *Criteria for Prestige.* This value dimension deals with the importance of scholarly publications, the systems of evaluating personnel on the basis of their publications, and the relative importance of research vis-à-vis teaching.

9. *Beliefs about People and the Public.* This value dimension covers the academic accountant's ways of dealing with practioners and others and the need to communicate to a larger audience.

These value dimensions depict only general themes of accountants' value and belief systems. The difference between individuals on these dimensions may determine their preferential research behavior.

HOW TO CLASSIFY ACCOUNTING RESEARCHERS

Given the proliferation of images, foundations, approaches, and paradigms in accounting, the question remains how to classify scientists in general and accounting researchers in particular. Various frameworks are possible for the classification of researchers in general, including (a) the typology of Liam Hudson,[78] the typology of Gerald Gordon,[79] the typology of Mitroff's survey of the Apollo Scientists,[80,81] the typology of

Exhibit 1.2
Jungian Typology of Researchers

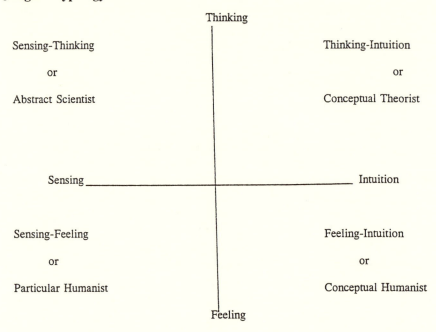

Abraham Maslow,[82] and the typology of C. G. Jung.[83] It is, however, the typology of C. G. Jung that seems the most useful in classifying scientists in general[84] and accounting researchers in particular.[85] Basically, Jung classified individuals depending on (a) sensation or intuition and (b) the way they reach decisions by thinking or feeling. The definitions of these components of the Jungian dimensions follow:

Sensation involves receiving information through the senses, focusing on detail, emphasizing the here and now and the practical. Intuition, in contrast, involves input of information through the imagination, emphasizing the whole on gestalt, dwelling in idealism, in hypothetical possibilities, and taking an interest in the long term. . . . Thinking is concerned with the use of reasoning which is impersonal and formal to develop explanations in scientific, technical and theoretical terms. Feeling, on the other hand, relates to the reaching of decisions on the basis of highly personal value judgements and focusing on human values, moral and ethical issues.[86]

The combination of the two dimensions, as shown in Exhibit 1.2, results in four personality types: (1) sensing-thinking (STs), (2) sensing-feeling (SFs), (3) intuition-feeling (IFs), and (4) intuition-thinking (ITs). This typology was used by Mitroff and Kilman[87] to produce a classification of researchers: the analytical scientist (AS), the conceptual theorist (CT), the conceptual humanist (CH), and the particular humanist (PH).

The analytical scientist, a sensing-thinking person, is motivated by the conduct of inquiry along a precise methodology and logic, with a focus on certainty, accuracy, and reliability, and a reliance on a simple, well-defined consistent paradigm. As stated by Mitroff and Kildman:

To know is to be certain about something. Certainty is defined by the ability to "phrase" or enumerate the components of an object, event, person, or situation in a precise, accurate, and reliable fashion. Therefore knowledge is synonymous with precision, accuracy, and reliability. Any endeavor that cannot be subjected to this formula or line of reasoning is either suppressed, devalued, or set aside as not worth knowing or capable or being known.[88]

The conceptual theorist, a thinking-intuition person, attempts to generate multiple explanations or hypotheses for a phenomena with a focus on discovery rather than testing. As stated by Mitroff and Kilman:

Whereas the AS attempts to find the single schema that best represents the world, the CT is interested in exploring, creating, and inventing multiple possible and hypothetical representations of the world—even hypothetical worlds themselves. Further, the CT's emphasis is on the large-scale differences between these different representations rather than the details of any single schema. A potential danger for the AS is getting bogged down in infinite details; a potential danger for the CT is ignoring them altogether for the sake of comprehensiveness. ASs tend to suffer from "hardening of the categories"; CTs tend to suffer from "loosening of the wholes."[89]

The particular humanist, a sensing-feeling person, is concerned with the uniqueness of particular individual human beings. Everyone is a unique means rather than an abstract, theoretical end.

The conceptual humanist, an intuition-feeling person, focuses on human welfare, directing his personal conceptual inquiry toward the general human good.

NOTES

1. Henry Rand Hatfield, "A Historical Defense of Bookkeeping," *Journal of Accounting* (April 1924): 241–53.

2. R. R. Sterling, "Toward a Science of Accounting," *Financial Analysts Journal* (September–October 1975): 28–36.

3. R. R. Sterling, *Toward a Science of Accounting* (Lawrence, KS: Scholars Book Co., 1979).

4. John C. Burton, "Intermediate Accounting from a User Perspective," in *The Impact of Rule-Making on Intermediate Financial Accounting Textbooks,* D. L. Jensen, ed. (Columbus, OH: College of Administrative Sciences, 1982): 116.

5. R. K. Mautz, "Accounting as a Social Science," *The Accounting Review* (April 1963): 319.

6. Robert D. Buzzell, "Is Marketing a Science?" *Harvard Business Review* (January–February 1963): 37.

7. C. G. Hemmpel, "Logican Positivism and the Social Sciences," in *Legacy of Logical Positivism,* P. Achinstein and S. F. Barker, eds. (Baltimore: Johns Hopkins University Press, 1969), 151.

8. Marie Bunge, *Scientific Research I: The Search for System* (New York: Spring, 1967), 336.

9. For the first review, see Charles E. Sprague, *Accounting Principles for Business Enterprises,* Accounting Research Study No. 3 (New York: American Institute of Certified Public Accountants, 1963); Henry Rand Harfield, *Modern Accounting: Its Principles and Some of Its Problems* (New York: D. Appleton, 1909); John Canning, *The Economics of Accountancy* (New York: Ronald Press, 1929). For the second review, see William Paton, and Russell Stevenson, *Principles of Accounting* (New York: Macmillan, 1918); id., *Accounting Theory* (New York: Ronald Press, 1922); Henry W. Sweeney, "Maintenance of Capital," *Accounting Review* (December 1930): 277–87.

10. Anthony M. Tinker, Barbara D. Merino, and Marilyn Dale Neimark, "The Normative Origins of Positive Theories: Ideology and Accounting Thought," *Accounting Organizations and Society* (May 1982): 188.

11. Ibid.

12. Anthony M. Tinker, "Towards a Political Economy of Accounting: An Empirical Illustration of the Cambridge Controversies," *Accounting, Organizations and Society* (June 1980): 150.

13. Ibid., 151–52.

14. D. J. Cooper, "Discussion of Towards a Political Economy of Accounting," *Accounting, Organizations and Society* (June 1980): 161–66.

15. Tinker, "Towards a Political Economy of Accounting," 153.

16. S. Burchell, C. Clubb, A. Hopwood, J. Hughes, and J. Nahapiet, "The Roles of Accounting in Organizations and Society," *Accounting, Organizations and Society* 5 (1980): 5–27.

17. D. J. Cooper, and M. J. Sherer, "The Value of Corporate Accounting Reports: Arguments for a Political Economy of Accounting," *Accounting, Organizations and Society* (June 1984): 222.

18. Ibid., 218–19.

19. P. Stanworth, and A. Giddens, eds., *Elites and Power in British Society* (Cambridge: Cambridge University Press, 1974); R. Miliband, *The State in Capitalist Society* (London: Weindenfield and Nicholson, 1969).

20. A. B. Cherns, "Alienation and Accountancy," *Accounting, Organizations and*

Society (1978): 105–14; K. B. Peasnell, "Statement of Accounting Theory and Theory Acceptance," *Accounting and Business Research* (Summer 1978): 217–25.

21. Cooper and Sherer, "The Value of Corporate Accounting Reports," 219.

22. G. Burrell, and G. Morgan, *Sociological Paradigms and Organizational Analysis* (London: Heinemann, 1979).

23. Ibid., 2.

24. Ibid., 75.

25. Ahmed Belkaoui, *Inquiry and Accounting: Alternate Methods and Research Perspective* (Westport, CT: Quorum Books, 1987), Ch. 2; Wai Fong Chua, "Radical Developments in Accounting Thought," *The Accounting Review* (October 1986): 601–32; D. J. Cooper, "Tidiness, Muddle, and Things: Commonalities and Divergences in Two Approaches to Management Accounting Research," *Accounting, Organizations, and Society* 8 (1983): 1–21.

26. R. J. Boland, Jr., and L. R. Pondy, "Accounting in Organizations: A Union of Natural and Rational Perspectives," *Accounting, Organizations and Society* 5 (1980): 223–34; S. Burchell et al., "The Roles of Accounting in Organizations and Society," 5–27; I. Colville, "Reconstruction 'Behavioral Accounting,' " *Accounting, Organizations and Society* 2/3 (1983): 269–86; C. R. Tomkins, and R. Groves, "The Everyday Accountant and Researching His Reality," *Accounting, Organizations and Society* 4 (1983): 361–74.

27. Ahmed Belkaoui, "Linguistic Relatively in Accounting," *Accounting, Organizations and Society* (October 1978): 97–194.

28. D. C. Hayes, "Accounting for Accounting: A Study About Managerial Accounting," *Accounting, Organizations and Society* 2–3 (1983): 241–50.

29. Steffy and Grimes, "A Critical Theory of Organizational Science," *Academy of Management Review* 2 (1986): 322–36.

30. Ibid.

31. Ibid., 325.

32. R. Likert, *New Patterns of Management* (New York: McGraw-Hill, 1961); A. B. Cherns, "Alienation and Accounting," *Accounting, Organizations and Society* 3 (1978): 103–14.

33. J. Habermas, *Toward a Rational Society* (London: Heineman, 1971); A. Gramsci, *Prison Notebooks* (New York: International Publishers, 1971); G. Lukacs, *History and Class Consciousness* (London: Merlin Press, 1971).

34. Burrell, and Morgan, *Sociological Paradigms and Organizational Analysis,* 307.

35. Max Weber, *The Theory of Social and Economic Organization* (Glencoe, IL: Free Press, 1974); Robert Michels, *Political Parties* (Glencoe, IL: Free Press, 1949); Paul Baran, and Paul M. Sweezy, *Monopoly Capital* (New York: Monthly Review Press, 1966); Harry Braverman, *Labor and Monopoly Capital* (New York: Monthly Review Press, 1974); J. Kenneth Benson, "Organizations: A Dialectical View," *Administrative Science Quarterly* 22 (1977): 1–21.

36. David Cooper, "Tidiness, Muddle, and Things: Commonalities and Divergences in Two Approaches to Management Accounting Research," *Accounting, Organizations and Society* 8 (1983): 277.

37. Anthony Tinker, "Theories of the State and the State of Accounting: Economic

Reductionism and Political Voluntarism in Accounting Regulation Theory," *Journal of Accounting and Public Policy* (Spring 1984): 71.

38. R. Braithwaite, *Scientific Explanation* (Cambridge: Cambridge University Press, 1973), 1.

39. T. D. Coole, and D. T. Campbell, "The Design and Conduct of Quasi-Experiments and True Experiments in Field Settings," in *Handbook of Industrial and Organizational Psychology*, M. D. Dunnette, ed. (Chicago: Rand McNally, 1976); A. R. Abdel-Khalik, and B. B. Ahinkya, *Empirical Research in Accounting: A Methodological Viewpoint* (Sarasota, FL: American Accounting Association, 1979); D. T. Campbell, and J. C. Stanley, *Experimental and Quasi-Experimental Design for Research* (Chicago: Rand McNally, 1963).

40. Gordon W. Allport, *Personality: A Psychological Interpretation* (New York: Henry Holt, 1937), 22.

41. G. Burrell, and G. Morgan, *Sociological Paradigms and Organizational Analysis.*

42. Ibid., 6.

43. Ibid., 6–7.

44. Roger Evered and Meryl Reis Louis, "Alternative Perspectives in the Organizational Sciences: 'Inquiry from the Inside' and 'Inquiry from the Outside,' " *Academy of Management Review* 6, no. 3 (1981): 385–95.

45. Ibid., 390.

46. J. Habermas, *Knowledge and Human Interest* (Boston: Beacon, 1971).

47. Orlando Behling, "The Case for the Natural Science Model for Research in Organizational Behavior and Organizational Theory," *Academy of Management Review* 5, no. 4 (1980): 484–85.

48. F. T. Luthans, and T. R. Davis, "An Ideographic Approach to Organizational Behavior Research: The Use of Single Case Experimental Designs and Direct Measures," *Academy of Management Review* 7, no. 3 (1982): 382.

49. Ibid., 380.

50. Ibid.

51. Peggy Reeves Sanday, "The Ethnographic Paradigm(s)," *Administrative Science Quarterly* 24 (December 1979): 529.

52. John Van Maanen, "The Fact of Fiction in Organizational Ethnography," *Administrative Science Quarterly* (December 1979): 539–50.

53. Herbert Speigelberg, "The Essentials of the Phenomenological Method," in *The Phenomenological Movement: A Historical Introduction*, 2d ed., Vol. 2 (The Hague: Martinas Nijhoff, 1965), 655–57.

54. O. T. Campbell, and D. W. Fiske, "Convergent and Discriminant Validation by the Multitrait-Multimethod Matrix," *Psychological Bulletin* 56 (1959): 81–105; E. J. Webb et al., *Unobtrusive Measures in the Social Sciences* (Chicago: Rand McNally, 1966).

55. Allport, *Personality,* 22.

56. Todd D. Jick, "Mixing Qualitative and Quantitative Methods: Triangulation in Action," *Administrative Science Quarterly* 24 (December 1979): 609.

57. Ibid.

58. Evered and Louis, "Alternative Perspectives in the Organizational Sciences," 392–94.

59. Ibid., 394.

60. T. S. Kuhn, *The Structure of Scientific Revolution* (Chicago: University of Chicago Press, 1962 [1st ed.], 1970 [2d ed.]).

61. Ibid., 2d ed., 175.

62. Ibid., 1st ed., 6.

63. H. Gilman McCann, *Chemistry Transformed: The Paradigmatic Shift from Phlogiston to Oxygen* (Norwood, NJ: Alex Publishing Corp., 1978), 21.

64. Ibid., 13.

65. W. O. Hagstrom, *The Scientific Community* (New York: Basic Books, 1965), 17.

66. Ibid., 13.

67. R. K. Merton, "Priorities in Scientific Discovery: A Chapter in the Sociology of Science," *American Sociological Review* 22 (1957): 640.

68. R. K. Merton, "Behavior Patterns of Scientists," *American Scientist* 57 (1969): 17–18.

69. Hagstrom, *The Scientific Community*, 23.

70. Ahmed Belkaoui, *Accounting Theory* (San Diego: Harcourt Brace Jovanovich, 1985), 452.

71. Thomas S. Kuhn, "Reflections on My Critics," in *Criticism and the Growth of Knowledge*, Imre Lakatos and Alan Musgrave, eds. (Cambridge: Cambridge University Press, 1970), 231–78.

72. George Ritzer, "Sociology: A Multi-Paradigm Science," *The American Sociologist* (August 1975): 156–57.

73. Ibid., 156.

74. Ibid., 157.

75. Belkaoui, *Accounting Theory*, 451.

76. Ross, L. Watts, and Jerold L. Zimmerman, *Positive Accounting Theory* (Englewood Cliffs, NJ: Prentice-Hall, 1986), 12.

77. M. C. Wells, "A Revolution in Accounting Thought," *Accounting Review* (July 1976): 471–82; American Accounting Association, *Committee on Concepts and Standards for External Financial Reports: Statement on Accounting Theory and Theory Acceptance* (Sarasota, FL: American Accounting Association, 1977).

78. L. Hudson, *Contrary Imaginations* (New York: Scholer Books, 1966).

79. G. Gordon, "A Contingency Model for the Design of Problem Solving Research Programs: A Perspective or Diffusion Research," *Milbank Memorian Fund Quarterly* (Spring 1974): 185–220.

80. I. I. Mitroff, "Norms and Counter-Norms in a Select Group of the Apollo Moon Scientists: A Case Study of the Ambivalence of Scientists," *American Sociological Review* 39 (1974): 579–95.

81. I. I. Mitroff, *The Subjective Side of Science: An Inquiry into the Psychology of the Apollo Moon Scientists* (Amsterdam: The Netherlands Elsevier, 1974).

82. A. H. Maslow, *The Psychology of Science* (New York: Harper & Row, 1966).

83. G. G. Jung, *Collected Works*, Vol. 6, *Psychological Types* (Princeton, NJ: Princeton University Press, 1971).

84. I. I. Mitroff, and R. H. Kilmann, *Methodological Approaches to Social Science* (San Francisco: Jossey-Bass Publishers, 1978).

85. Choudhury, Nandan, "Starting Out in Management Accounting Research," *Accounting and Business Research* (Summer 1987): 205–20.

86. Ibid., 206.

87. I. I. Mitroff, and R. H. Kilman, *Methodological Approaches to Social Science.*
88. Ibid., 33.
89. Ibid., 68.

REFERENCES

American Accounting Association. *Committee on Concepts and Standards for External Financial Reports: Statement on Accounting Theory and Theory Acceptance.* Sarasota, FL: American Accounting Association, 1977.

Arrington, C. E., and J. R. Francis. "Letting the Cat Out of the Bag: Deconstruction, Privilege, and Accounting Research." *Accounting, Organizations and Society* (January 1985): 1–88.

Belkaoui, Ahmed. *Socio-Economic Accounting.* Westport, CT: Quorum Books, 1984.

Belkaoui, Ahmed. *Public Policy and the Problems and Practices of Accounting.* Westport, CT: Quorum Books, 1985.

Belkaoui, Ahmed. *Inquiry and Accounting: Alternate Methods and Research Perspectives.* Westport, CT: Quorum Books, 1987.

Belkaoui, Ahmed. *The Coming Crisis in Accounting.* Westport, CT: Quorum Books, 1989.

Burrell, G., and G. Morgan. *Sociological Paradigms and Organizational Analysis.* London: Heinemann, 1979.

Choudbury, Nandan. "Starting Out in Management Accounting Research." *Accounting and Business Researcher* (Summer 1987): 205–20.

Chua, Wai Fong. "Radical Developments in Accounting Thought." *The Accounting Review* (October 1986): 601–32.

Chua, Wai Fong. "Interpretive Sociology and Management Accounting Research—A Critical Review." *Accounting, Auditing and Accountability* 1 no. 2 (1988): 59–79.

Cooper, D. J., and M. J. Sherer. "The Value of Corporate Accounting Reports: Arguments for a Political Economy of Accounting." *Accounting, Organizations and Society* (June 1984): 207–32.

Danos, Paul. "A Revolution in Accounting Thought? A Comment." *The Accounting Review* (July 1977): 746–47.

Derrida, J. *Writing and Difference.* Translated by A. Bass. Chicago: The University of Chicago Press, 1978.

Hakanson, Nils H. "Where We Are in Accounting: A Review of Statements on Accounting Theory and Theory Acceptance." *The Accounting Review* (July 1978): 717–25.

Hopwood, A. G. "On Trying to Study Accounting in the Contexts in Which It Operates." *Accounting, Organizations and Society* (June 1983): 361–74.

Hunt, Herbert G. III, and Raymond L. Hogler. "Agency Theory as Ideology: A Comparative Analysis Based on Critical Legal Theory and Radical Accounting." *Accounting, Organizations and Society* (August 1990): 437–54.

Kuhn, Thomas S. "The Structure of Science Revolutions." In *International Encyclopedia of Unified Science,* 2nd enlarged ed. Chicago: University of Chicago Press, 1970.

Laughlin, Richard C. "Accounting Systems in Organizational Contexts: A Case for Critical Theory." *Accounting, Organization and Society* (October 1987): 479–507.

Mitroff, I. I., and R. H. Kilman. *Methodological Approaches to Social Science.* San Francisco: Jessey-Bass Publishers, 1978.

Neimark, M. "The Kind is Dead. Long Live the King." *Critical Perspectives on Accounting* (March 1990): 103–14.

Peasnell, K. V. "Statement on Accounting Theory and Theory Acceptance: A Review Article." *Accounting and Business Research* (Summer 1978): 217–25.

Ritzer, George. "Sociology: A Multiple-Paradigm Science." *The American Sociologist* (August 1975): 156–57.

Ritzer, George. *Sociology: A Multi-Paradigm Science.* Boston: Allyn & Bacon, 1975.

Tinker, Tony. *Paper Prophets: A Social Critique of Accounting.* Westport, CT: Praeger, 1985.

Tomkins, C. R., and R. Groves. "The Everyday Accountant and Researching His Realities." *Accounting, Organizations and Society* 4 (Fall 1983): 361–74.

2 The Anthropological/Inductive Paradigm

INTRODUCTION

The anthropological/inductive paradigm, better known nowadays as the positive approach, focuses on the particular to make a case for a general theory of accounting. Basically, the approach attempts to develop a theory of accounting from an explanation of the particular actions and choices made in practice. It is examined next.

EXEMPLARS

Several studies qualify as exemplars of the anthropological/inductive paradigm—namely, the works of Gilman, Hatfield, Ijiri, Littleton, and Paton.[1] The authors of these studies share a concern for a descriptive-inductive approach to the construction of an accounting theory and a belief in the value of extant accounting practices. For example, Ijiri considers the primary concern of accounting to be the functioning of accountability relationships among interested parties. The objective measurement is the economic performance of the firm. On the basis of discussions concerning research methodology and the role of logic in theory construction and policy formulation in accounting. Ijiri presents accountability as a descriptive theory of accounting: "What we are emphasizing is that current accounting practice can be better interpreted if we view accountability as the underlying goal. We are also suggesting that unless accounting is viewed in this manner, much of the current practice would appear to be inconsistent and irrational."[2]

In defense of his paradigm refuting the criticisms of advocates of current-cost and current-value accounting, Iriji also presents an axiomatic model of existing accounting practice that evaluates the significance of historical cost in terms of accountability and decision making.

Littleton arrives at his accounting principles from observations of accounting practices. Such inductively derived principles, supported by the test of experience, incorporate the goals implicit in accounting practice. For example, Littleton states:

Teachers of bookkeeping and later of accounting and auditing found it necessary to supplement the accumulated rules and descriptions of procedure with explanations and justifications. This was done in order that study should be something more than the memorizing of rules. Hence, it is appropriate to say that both the methods of practice and the explanations of theory were inductively derived out of experience.[3]

Good theory is practice-created and, moreover, is practice conditioning. Finally, whenever evidence of integration among accounting ideals is found, it will strengthen the conviction that accounting doctrine contains the possibility of being built into a system of coordinated explanations and justifications of what accounting is and what it can become.[4]

Two other studies by Gordon and by Watts and Zimmerman[5] qualify as exemplars of the anthropological/inductive paradigm. Both studies argue that management will select the accounting rule that will tend to smooth income and the rate of growth in income. Gordon theorizes on income smoothing as follows:

Proposition 1:   The criterion a corporate management uses in selecting among accounting principles is the maximization of its utility or welfare. . . .

Proposition 2:   The utility of a management increases with

1. its job security
2. the level and rate of growth in the management's income, and
3. the level and rate of growth in the corporation's size. . . .

Proposition 3: The achievement of the management goals stated in Proposition 2 is dependent in part on the satisfaction of stockholders with the corporation's performance; that is, other things the same, the happier the stockholders, the greater the job security, income, etc., of the management. . . .

Proposition 4: Stockholders' satisfaction with a corporation increases with the average rate of growth in the corporation's income (or the average rate of return on its capital) and the stability of its income. This proposition is as readily verified as Proposition 2. Theorem: Given that the above four propositions are accepted or found to be true, it follows that a management would within the limits of its power, that is, the latitude allowed by accounting rules,

1. smooth reported income, and

2. smooth the rate of growth in income.

By "smooth the rate of growth in income," we mean the following: If the rate of growth is high, accounting practices that reduce it should be adopted, and vice versa.[6]

Several empirical tests in the income-smoothing literature leave Gordon's model unconfirmed. Also, Gordon's assumptions that shareholder satisfaction is solely a positive function of income and that increases in stock prices always follow increases in accounting income have been seriously contested. To avoid the pitfalls that may exist in Gordon's model, Watts and Zimmerman attempt to provide a positive theory of accounting by exploring the factors influencing management's attitudes regarding accounting standards.[7] At the outset, Watts and Zimmerman assume that management's utility is a positive function of the expected compensation of future periods and a negative function of the dispersion of future compensation. Their analysis shows that the choice of accounting standards can affect a firm's cash flow through taxes, regulation, political costs, information-production costs, and management-compensation plans: "The first four factors increase managerial wealth by increasing the cash flows and, hence, the share price. The last factor can increase managerial wealth by altering the terms of the incentive compensation."[8]

IMAGE OF THE SUBJECT MATTER

To those who adopt the anthropological/inductive paradigm, the basic subject matter is

1. existing accounting practices, and
2. management's attitudes toward those practices.

Proponents of this view argue, in general, either that the techniques can be derived and justified on the basis of their tested use or that management plays a central role in determining the techniques to be implemented. Consequently, the accounting-research objective associated with the anthropological/inductive paradigm is to understand, explain, and predict existing accounting practices. For example, Ijiri views the mission of this paradigmatic approach as follows:

This type of inductive reasoning to derive goals implicit in the behavior of an existing system is not intended to be pro-established to promote the maintenance of the status quo. The purpose of such exercise is to highlight where changes are most needed and where they are feasible. Changes suggested as a result of such a study have a much better chance of actually being implemented.[9]

THEORIES

Information/Economics

Exemplars of the information/economics paradigm are the works of Robert Crandall, Gerald Feltham, and Feltham and Joel Demski.[10] In his pioneering paper, Feltham provided a framework for determining the value of a change in the information system from the viewpoint of the individual making an informational decision (the decision maker). The framework relies on the individual components that are required to compute the expected payoff (or utility) for a particular information system. The components are (1) a set of possible actions at each period within a time horizon; (2) a payoff function over the events that occur during the periods; (3) probabilistic relationships between past and future events; (4) events and signals from the information system, including past and future signals; and (5) a set of decision rules as functions of the signals. The framework states that the value of changing from one information system to another is equal to the difference between the expected payoffs of the two alternatives.

Crandall examined the usefulness of the information/economics paradigm to the future development of accounting theory and offered the applied-information-economics approach as a new mainstream accounting theory. Simply, this approach consists of recognizing explicitly each component of the information/economics model and broadening the scope of accounting design to include all of these components.

The third exemplar, Feltham and Demski's "Use of Models in Information Evaluation," presents and discusses a model of information choice that views information evaluation in cost-benefit terms and as a sequential process. The entire process is summarized as follows:

Specification of a particular information system n results in a set of signals being supplied to the decision maker; the decision maker may then use the resulting information in selecting his or her action a; and this action may determine, in part, the events x of the subsequent period. The information evaluation must predict the relationship between each of the above elements: the signal-generation process, o (y/n); the decision maker's prediction- and action-choice process, a (y/n); and the relationship between the actions selected and the events that will occur, o (x/y, n, a). In addition, the decision maker must predict the gross payoff w(x) he or she will derive from the events of the subsequent period, as well as the cost of operating the particular information system w' (y,n).[11]

To those who adopt information/economics, the basic subject matter is (1) information is an economic commodity and (2) the acquisition of information amounts to a problem of economic choice. The value of information is viewed in terms of a cost-benefit criterion within the formal structure of decision theory and economic theory. Accounting information is evaluated in terms of its ability to improve the quality of the optimal choice in a basic-choice problem that must be resolved by an individual or a number of heterogeneous individuals. A single individual must select among different actions that have different possible outcomes. Assuming consistent, rational-choice behavior governed by the expected-utility hypothesis, the action with the highest expected payoff (or utility) is preferred by the individual. Information in this context is required to revise the probabilities of the original outcomes. Thus the individual may face a two-stage process: a first stage, during which the information system produces different signals, and a second stage, during which the observance of a signal results in a revision of probabilities and a choice of the conditional best action. The information system with the highest expected utility is preferred. The information required for a systematic probability-revision (Bayesian-revision) analysis, in turn, facilitates informational analysis on the basis of the subjective, expected-utility-maximization rule.

The information/economics draws its insight from various disciplines, including decision theory, game theory, information theory, and economics. Some of the analytical models proposed include the decision-theory model, the syndicate-theory model, the information-evaluation-decision-maker model, the team-theory model, and the demand-revelation model. Each of these frameworks, relying on a model of the firm, derives the demand for managerial accounting information. The usefulness of each model is based on the degree of congruence between the derived demand and the four observed uses of managerial accounting information, which are the belief-revision use, the performance-evaluation use (including b_1), the motivational use (and b_2), and the risk-sharing use.

1. The *decision-theory model,* as proposed by Feltham, presents a framework for determining the value of a change in an information system as the difference between the expected payoff of two alternative systems.[12] Its usefulness is limited to belief revision because it does not include performance evaluation.

2. The *syndicate-theory model* includes multiperson firms jointly choosing a set of actions in the presence of a sharing rule for the resulting uncertainty outcome. Exemplars include papers by R. B. Wilson, J. S. Demski and R. J. Swieringa, and Demski.[13] The situation in this model is explained as follows:

   > Each individual is interested in maximizing his own expected utility through the choice of the action and the sharing rule. The belief revision demand for information can again be derived. In addition, the choice of the action and the sharing rule will have an important effect on the total risk borne by the Syndicate and how that risk is allocated among its members. Since the sharing rule can be based only on jointly observed information, the Syndicate Theory model can be used to derive the risk-sharing use of information. The motivational use of information is still ignored because all motivational problems are assumed away. In particular, all information is assumed to be publicly available and the action is assumed to be jointly chosen and implemented.[14]

3. The *informational-evaluation-decision-maker model* keeps the multiperson characteristics and includes an owner or information evaluator delegating the action choice to one or more agents. Exemplars include the book by Demski and Feltham.[15] The situation in the model is evaluated as follows: "Since these models do not explicitly state the agent's utility function, the reader

does not know whether the agent is assumed to act in his own best interest. Therefore, any motivational implications derived from these models are suspect."[16]

4. The *team-theory model* includes a multiperson context and a sharing rule as in the syndicate-theory model.[17] The individuals are assumed to act in their own best interests using information available only to them and keeping the welfare of the team in mind. The situation in this model is evaluated as follows:

> The problem for the team is to choose the individual decision rule in order to maximize the team's welfare in the presence of decentralized information. Clearly, the belief revision use of information can be derived from the Team Model, but there is no motivational role for information in the Team Model since all individuals are assumed to have the same preferences. Each team member will therefore implement whichever decision rule is given to him. Further, the assumption of identical preferences implies that technological constraints are the only impediments to the full sharing and utilization of the privately acquired information. That is, when information can be transmitted in a Team setting, it is assumed to be transmitted honestly. In a more realistic setting, self-interest as well as technology may prevent the full and honest communication of information within the firm.[18]

5. The *demand-revelation model* is similar to the team-theory model with the additional issue of how to induce agents to reveal their private information honestly and to use it to maximize the profits of the organization. Exemplars are provided in the articles by M. Loeb, T. Groves, and Groves and Loeb.[19] The usefulness of the model is achieved by meeting both the belief-revision use and the motivational use.

The Analytical-Agency Paradigm

Two types of paradigms characterize the agency paradigm: an analytical or principal-agent paradigm, which is essentially mathematical, and a positive-agency paradigm, which is essentially empirical. The tension between them is evident in the following observations:

two almost entirely separate and valuable literatures that nominally address the same problem. . . . Each of the agency literatures has its strong and weak points, and on occasion a tension has surfaced between them. . . . Part is due to the "tyranny of journalism" that develops when mathematically inclined scholars take the attitude that if analytical language is not mathematics, it isn't rigorous, and if a problem cannot be solved with the use of mathematics, the effort should be abandoned. Part is due to the belief that the lack of the use of mathematics in the positive agency literature results in ex post factor theorizing that assumes the hypotheses will not be rejected. . . . However, some believe that so little is put in the current principal-agent models that there is little hope of producing results that will explain much of the rich variety of observed contracting practices . . . on the other hand, the methods of the positive agency literature justifiably seem unconstrained, and often perilously close to tautological to some.[20]

The analytical-agency paradigm traces its origin to the exemplar provided by R. H. Coase's seminal paper, which first referred to the nature of firm and the relationships of principal and agent.[21] He also put an emphasis on voluntary contracts that arise among various organizational parties as the efficient solution to these conflicts of interest. The analytical-agency paradigm evolved then to a view of the firm as a "nexus of contracts" with the statement by M. C. Jensen and J.W.H. Meckling that firms are "legal fictions which serve as a nexus for a set of contracting relationships among individuals."[22] E. F. Fama expanded this "nexus of contracts" view to include both capital markets and markets for managerial behavior.[23]

The agency relationship is said to exist when a contract between a person(s), a principal, and another person(s), an agent, to perform more service on the principal's behalf involves a delegation of the decision-making authority to the agent.[24] Both principal and agent are assumed to be motivated solely by self-interest, that is, to maximize their subjective utility, but also to be aware of their common interest. As Fama noted: "In effect, the firm is viewed as a team of individuals whose members act from self-interest but realize that their destinies depend to some extent on the survival of the team of in its competition with other teams."[25] The agent is striving to maximize the contractual fee he receives subject to the necessary effort levels. The principal is striving to maximize the returns from the use of his resources subject to the fee payable to the agent. These conflicts of interest are assumed to be brought into equilibrium by the agreed-on contracts. The contracts engage the members to agree to a set of cooperative behaviors, given implied self-interest motives.[26] Two reasons may lead to the divergence between self-interest and cooperative behavior, adverse selection and moral hazard, which are information-based problems.

Adverse selection, as an information problem, arises when the agent uses private information that cannot be verified by the principal to implement successfully an input-action rule different from that desired by the principal and thereby rendering the principal incapable of determining if the agent made the appropriate choice.

The *moral-hazard* problem, as an ex post information problem, arises when there are motivational problems and conflicts as a result of basing contracts on imperfect surrogates of behavior. Consider both the case of fire insurance and the problem in the Prisoner's Dilemma. As K. J. Arrow observed, ''The outbreak of a fire may be due to a contribution of ex- ogenous circumstances and individual choice, such as carelessness or, in the extreme case, arson. Hence, a fire insurance policy creates an incen- tive for an individual to change his behavior and ceases to be a pure insurance against an uncontrollable event.''[27] Then, as Stanley Baiman observed, ''The problem in the Prisoner's Dilemma presents a moral hazard: Both individuals would be better off if neither confessed. But such behavior is not enforceable because the two prisoners cannot write an enforceable contract between themselves based on their confessing behavior.''[28]

The basic agency problem is enriched by different options concerning

1. The initial distribution of information and beliefs (the basic agency problem assumes that neither individual has private precontract information, that is, one asymmetry of precontract information exists).

2. The description of the number of periods (the basic agency problem assumes a one-period world).

3. The description of the firm's production function in terms of
   a. the amount of capital supplied by the principal;
   b. the agent's level of effort, *e;*
   c. an exogenously determined, uncertain-state realization (weather, machine breakdown, competitors' behavior, and so on, which affects the agent's productivity.

4. The description of the feasible set of actions from which the agent chooses.

5. The description of the labor and capital markets.

6. The description of the feasible set of information system.

7. The description of the legal system that specifies the type of behavior that can be legally enforced and what is admissible evidence.

8. The description of the feasible set of payment schedules (the basic agency model assumes that the principal chooses the payment schedule and the monitoring system to reward and motivate the agent).

9. The description of the solution to the basic agency model. It consists of
   i) the employment contract, which incorporates . . .
      1. the payment schedule for the agent;
      2. the information system choices . . .
      3. specification of how the agent promises to act

ii) the agent's actual action."[29]
10. The role of self-interest.
11. The solution concept and the nature of optimality.

Income Smoothing/Earnings Management Hypotheses

Nature of Income Smoothing

Income smoothing can be viewed as the deliberate normalization of income in order to reach a desired trend or level. As far back as 1953, Heyworth observed that "more of the accounting techniques which may be applied to affect the assignment of net income to successive accounting periods . . . for smoothing or leveling the amplitude of periodic net income fluctuations."[30] What followed were arguments made by Monsen and Downs[31] and Gordon[32] that corporate managers may be motivated to smooth their income (or security), with the assumption that stability in income and rate of growth will be preferred over higher average income streams with greater variability. More specifically, Gordon theorized on income smoothing as follows:

Proposition 1: The criterion a corporate management uses in selecting among accounting principles is the maximization of its utility or welfare.

Proposition 2: The utility of a management increases with (1) its job security, (2) the level and rate of growth in the management's income, and (3) the level and rate of growth in the corporation's size.

Proposition 3: The achievement of the management goals stated in Proposition 2 is dependent in part on the satisfaction of stockholders with the corporation's performance; that is, other things being equal, the happier the stockholders, the greater the job security, income, and so forth, of the management.

Proposition 4: Stockholders' satisfaction with a corporation increases with the average rate of growth in the corporation's income (or the average rate of return on its capital) and the stability of its income. This proposition is as readily verified as Proposition 2.

Theorem: Given that the preceding four propositions are accepted or found to be true, it follows that a management would within the limits of its power, that is, the latitude allowed by accounting rules, (1) smooth reported income and (2) smooth the rate of growth in income. By "smooth the rate of growth in income," we mean the following: if the rate of growth is high, accounting practices that reduce it should be adopted, and vice versa.[33]

The best definition of income smoothing was provided by Beidelman as follows:

Smoothing of reported earnings may be defined as the intentional dampening of fluctuations about some level of earnings that is currently considered to be normal for a firm. In this sense smoothing represents an attempt on the part of the firm's management to reduce abnormal variations in earnings to the extent allowed under sound accounting and management principles.[34]

Given this definition, what needs to be explicated are the motivation of smoothing, the dimensions of smoothing, and the instruments of smoothing.

Motivations of Smoothing

As early as 1953, Heyworth claimed that motivations behind smoothing include the improvements of relations with creditors, investors and workers, as well as dampening of business cycles through psychological processes.[35] Gordon proposed that

1. The criterion a corporate management uses in selecting among accounting principles is to maximize its utility or welfare.
2. The same utility is a function of job security, the level and rate of growth of salary, and the level and growth rate in the firm's size.
3. Satisfaction of shareholders with the corporation's performance enhances the status and rewards of managers.
4. The same satisfaction depends on the rate of growth and stability of the firm's income.[36]

These propositions culminate the need to smooth as explained in the following theorem:

Given that the above four propositions are accepted or found to be true, it follows that a management should within the limits of its power, i.e., the latitude allowed by accounting rules, (1) smooth reported income and (2) smooth the rate of growth in income. By smooth the rate of growth in income we mean the following If the rate of growth is high, accounting practices which reduce it should be adopted and vice versa.[37]

Beidelman considers two reasons for management to smooth reported earnings.[38] The first argument rests on the assumption that a stable earnings stream is capable of supporting a higher level of dividends than a more variable earnings stream, having a favorable effect in the value of the firm's shares as overall riskiness of the firm is reduced. He states: "To the extent that the observed variability about a trend of reported earnings influences investor' subjective expectations for possible outcomes of future earnings and dividends, management might be able favorably to influence the value of the firm's shares by smoothing earnings."[39]

The second argument attributes to smoothing the ability to counter the cyclical nature of reported earnings and likely reduce the correlation of a firm's expected returns with returns on the market portfolio. He states: "To the degree that auto-normalization of earnings is successful, and that the reduced covariance of returns with the market is recognized by investors and incorporated into their evaluation process, smoothing will have added beneficial effects in share values."[40]

It results from the need felt by management to neutralize environmental uncertainty and dampen the wide fluctuations in the operating performance of the firm subject to an intermittent cycle of good and bad times. To do so, management may resort to organizational slack behavior,[41] budgetary slack behavior,[42] or risk-avoiding behavior.[43] Each of these behaviors necessitates decisions affecting the incurrence and/or location of discretionary expenses (costs), which result in income smoothing.

In addition to these behaviors intended to neutralize environmental uncertainty, it is also possible to identify organizational characterizations that differentiate among different firms in their extent of smoothing. For example, Kamin and Ronen[44] examined the effects of the separation of ownership and control on income smoothing, under the hypothesis that management-controlled firms are more likely to be engaged in smoothing as a manifestation of managerial discretion and budgetary slack. The results confirmed that income smoothing is higher among management-controlled firms with high barriers to entry.

Management was also assigned to circumvent news of the constraints of generally accepted accounting principles by attempting to smooth income numbers so as to convey their expectations of future cash flows, enhancing in the process the apparent reliability of prediction based on the observed smoothed series of numbers.[45] Three constraints are presumed to lead managers to smooth:

1. the competitive market mechanisms, which reduce the options available to management;

2. the management compensation scheme, which is linked directly to the firm's performance; and

3. the threat of management displacement.

This smoothing is not limited to high management and external accounting, it is also presumed to be used by lower level management and internal accounting in the form of organizational slack and slack budgeting.[46]

More recently the terminology changed from "income smoothing" to "earnings management." Earnings management is shown to be motivated by management's desire to increase annual corporate income[47,48] and to influence proxy contests[49] and the likelihood of foreign trade regulation.[50]

The Dimensions of Smoothing

The dimensions of smoothing are basically the means used to accomplish the smoothing of income numbers. Dascher and Malcolm distinguished between real smoothing and artificial smoothing as follows: "Real smoothing refers to the actual transaction that is undertaken or not undertaken on the basis of its smoothing effect on income, whereas artificial smoothing refers to accounting procedures which are implemented to shift costs and/or revenues from one period to another."[51]

Both types of smoothing may be indistinguishable. For example, the amount of reported expenses may be lower or higher than previous periods because of either deliberate actions on the level of the expenses (real smoothing) or the reporting methods (artificial smoothing). For both types, an operational test proposed is to fit a:

curve to a stream of income calculated two ways,

a) excluding a possible manipulative variable and

b) including it

If the variations of the observations around the curve are smaller in the latter case, income smoothing has been the consequence of transaction in the account.[52]

Artificial smoothing was also considered by Copeland and defined as follows: "Income smoothing involves the repetitive selection of accounting measurement or reporting rules in a particular pattern, the effect of which is to report the stream of income with a smaller variation from trend than would otherwise have appeared.''[53]

Besides real and artificial smoothing, other dimensions of smoothing were considered in the literature. A popular classification adds a third smoothing dimension, namely, classificatory smoothing. Barnea et al. distinguished between three smoothing dimensions, as follows:

1. Smoothing through events' occurrence and/or recognition: Management can time actual transactions so that their effects on reported income would tend to dampen its variations over time. Mostly, the planned timing of events' occurrences (e.g., research and development) would be a function of the accounting rules governing the accounting recognition of the events.

2. Smoothing through allocation over time: Given the occurrence and the recognition of an event, management has more discretionary control over the determination over the periods to be affected by the events' quantification.

3. Smoothing through classification (hence classificatory smoothing): When income statement statistics other than net income (net of all revenues and expenses) are the object of smoothing, management can classify intraincome statement items to reduce variations over time in that statistic.[54]

Basically real smoothing corresponded to the smoothing through events' occurrence and/or recognition, whereas artificial smoothing corresponded to the smoothing through the allocation over time. Earnings management continues on income smoothing by focusing on management's use of discretionary accruals.

Positive Theory of Accounting

The call for a positive approach to accounting came when M. C. Jensen charged that ''research in accounting has been (with one or two notable exceptions) unscientific . . . because the focus of this research has been overwhelming nominative and definitional.''[55] Jensen then called for ''the development of a positive theory of accounting which will explain why accounting is what it is, why accountants do what they do, and what effects these phenomena have on people and resource utilization.''[56] The basic message, later to become known as ''the Rochester School of Accounting,'' is that most accounting theories are unscientific because they are normative and should be replaced by positive theories that explain actual accounting practices in terms of management's voluntary choice of accounting procedures and how the regulated standards have changed over time.

The major thrust of the positive approach to accounting is to explain and predict management's choice of standards by analyzing the costs and benefits of particular financial disclosures in relation to various individuals and to the allocation of resources within the economy. The positive theory is based on the propositions that managers, shareholders, and regulators/politicians are rational and that they attempt to maximize their utility, which is directly related to their compensation and, hence, to their wealth. The choice of an accounting policy by any of these groups rests on a comparison of the relative costs and benefits of alternative accounting procedures in such a way as to maximize their utility. For example, it is hypothesized that management considers the effects of the reported accounting of numbers on tax regulation, political costs, management compensation, information production costs, and restrictions found in bond-indenture provisions. Similar hypotheses may be related to standard setters, academicians, auditors, and others. In fact, the central ideal of the positive approach is to develop hypotheses about factors that influence the world of accounting practices and to test the validity of these hypotheses empirically.

1. To enhance the reliability of prediction based on the observed smoothed series of accounting numbers along a trend considered best or normal by management.
2. To reduce the uncertainty resulting from the fluctuations of income numbers in general and the reduction of systematic risk in particular by reducing the covariance of the firm's returns with the market returns.

Unlike the income-smoothing hypothesis, positive theories in accounting assume that the stock price depends on cash flows rather than on reported earnings. Furthermore, given an efficient market, two firms with identical cash-flow distributions are valued the same way despite the use of different accounting procedures. The central problem in positive theories is to determine how accounting procedures affect cash flows and, therefore, management's utility functions to obtain an insight into the factors that influence a manager's choice of accounting procedures. Resolution of the problem is guided by the following theoretical assumptions:

1. The *agency theory* may have originated with the emphasis on voluntary contracts that arise among various organizational parties as the efficient solution to these conflicts of interest. The theory evolves to a view of the firm as a "nexus of contracts" with the statement by M. C. Jensen and W. H. Meckling that firms are "legal fictions which serve as a nexus for a set of contracting relationships among individuals."[57] Fama expanded this "nexus of contracts" view to include both capital markets and markets for managerial labor.[58]

2. Given this "nexus of contracts" perspective of the firm, the *contracting cost theory* views the role of accounting information as the monitoring and enforcing of these contracts to reduce the agency costs of certain conflicts of interest. One possible conflict may be the conflict of interest between bondholders and stockholders of firms with debts outstanding; in such instances, decisions favorable to stockholders are not necessarily in the best interests of bondholders. This may require that lending agreements define the measurement rules to calculate accounting numbers for the purposes of restrictive covenants. Other possible agreements that may require the use of accounting numbers from audited financial statements to monitor the covenants of the agreements include management-compensation contracts and corporate by-laws. Thus the contracting cost theory assumes that accounting methods are selected as part of the wealth-maximizing process.

Both propositions imply that management is selecting the choice of the optimal accounting procedure for a given purpose.[59] The central problem of the positive approach rests in determining what factors are likely to affect the optimum choice, guided by the assumption of agency and contrasting cost theories.[60]

METHODS

Methods in Income Smoothing Research

The test was used also by Kamin and Ronen[61] and Belkaoui and Picur[62] and consists of observing the behavior of these smoothing variables: (1) operating expenses (OPEX) not included in cost of sales; (2) ordinary expenses (OREX); and (3) operating expenses plus ordinary expenses (OPEX + OREX), vis-à-vis the behavior of two objects of smoothing: (a) operating income (OP) and (b) ordinary income (OR).

It is assumed that management knows the future streams of inflows and outflows and their time distinction and has determined what should be the normal trend of OP and OR. We use the following methods to determine their normal trend model and a market trend model.

The Time Trend

Two models are used. First, the series of smoothed variables, OP and OR, and of smoothing variables OPEX, OREX, and OPEX + OREX were detrended in a time regression over a maximum span of 20 years, 1958 to 1977, as

$$Y = A_{ij} + B_{ijt} + E_{ijt} = 1, 2, 3, 4, 5, \quad t = 1958, \ldots, 1977, \qquad (1)$$

where

$i = 1$ for OP,

$i = 2$ for OR,

$i = 3$ for OPEX, $i = 4$ for OREX,

$i = 5$ for OPEX + OREX

$Y_{ijt} =$ observed OP, OR, OPEX, OREX, and OPEX + OREX for firm j in year t.

Second, the first differences in OPEX, OREX, and OPEX + OREX were detrended in a time regression as

$$Y_{ijt} = \delta'_{ij} + \gamma'_{ijt} = 1, 2, 3 \quad t = 1958, \ldots, 1977, \qquad (2)$$

where

$i = 1$ for OPEX, 2 for OREX, and 3 for OPEX + OREX.

The Market Trend

The first differences in OP, OR, OPEX, OREX, and OPEX + OREX were regressed on a macro index of first differences measured, respectively, as the mean observed first differences of OP, OR, OPEX, OREX, and OPEX + OREX as

$$Y = A'_{ij} + B'_{ij}M_{ij} + E'_{ijt} = 1, 2, 3, 4, 5 \quad t = 1958, \ldots, 1977, \qquad (3)$$

where

$i = 1$ for OP, 2 for OR, 3 for OPEX, 4 for OREX, and 5 for OPEX + OREX,

M_{ij} = Sample mean index of OP, OR, OPEX, OREX, and OPEX + OREX,

where

$$M_{ij} = \frac{1}{N} \sum_{i=1}^{N} Y,$$

where N is the sample size.

Methods in Positive Theory Research

Three assumptions characterize the positive agency paradigm in developing positive theories of financial accounting, namely, (1) *survival of the efficient,* in that surviving accounting principles will be efficient: (2) *capital-market efficiency,* in that the market will not be misled by cosmetic accounting changes; and (3) *nonzero agency costs,* in that accounting members can affect cash flows, in particular via debt contracts, management-compensation flows, and political regulation costs.[63] Given these assumptions of survival of the efficient, capital-market efficiency, and nonzero agency costs, three hypotheses have been used in testable form as follows:

1. Ceteris paribus, the greater a firm's debt-equity ratio, the more likely the firm's equilibrium accountancy procedures will shift expected reported earnings from later periods to earlier periods (the bond-covenant hypothesis).

2. Ceteris paribus, the larger the firm (the greater the political costs), the more likely the equilibrium accounting procedures will defer expected reported earnings from the current periods to later periods (the political-costs hypothesis).

3. Ceteris paribus, firms with bonus plans are more likely to have accounting procedures which shift expected reported earnings from later periods to earlier periods (the bonus-plan hypothesis).[64]

The methodology that follows for the three hypotheses is an investigation of the relationship between a dependent variable indicating an accounting or managerial choice and accounting variables depicting one or all of the three hypotheses.

Methods in Earnings Management Research

Earnings management research focuses on the managerial use of discretionary accruals.[65] McNichols and Wilson's[66] accrual-based tests for earnings management were based on the following linear framework:

$$DA_t = \alpha + \beta PART_t \sum_{k=1}^{K} \gamma_k X_{kt} + \varepsilon_t,$$

where

DA = discretionary accruals (typically deflated by lagged total assets),

PART = a dummy variable pertaining the data set into two groups for which earnings management predictions are specified by the researcher,

X_k = (for $k = 1, \ldots, K$) other relevant variables influencing discretionary accruals, and

ε = an error term that is independently and identically normally distributed.

PART is set equal to one in five years where earnings management is hypothesized, and equal to zero where it is not. The null hypothesis of no earnings management is tested by applying a t-test to the null hypothesis that $b_i = 0$. Because DA is not observable, it is replaced by a proxy (DAP), where

$$DAP_t = DA_t + V_t$$

where

V_t = error.

Therefore the correct model is

$$DAP_t = \alpha + \beta PART_t + \sum_{k=1}^{K} \gamma_k X_{kt} + V_t + E_t,$$

or

$$DAP_t = \alpha + \beta PART_t + \mu_t + E_t.$$

Healy used the following model for nondiscretionary accruals (NDA):[67]

$$NDA_t = \frac{\sum_t TA_t}{T}$$

where

NDA = estimated nondiscretionary accruals,

TA = total accruals scaled by lagged total assets,

$t = 1, 2, \ldots, T$ is a year subscript for years included in the estimation period, and

τ = a year subscript indicating a year in the event period.

DeAngelo noted the following for nondiscretionary accruals:[68]

$$NDA_t = TA_{t-1}.$$

The Jones model for nondiscretionary accruals in the event years follows[69]

$$NDA_t = \alpha_1 (1/A_{t-1}) + \alpha_2 (\Delta REV_t) + \alpha_3 (PPE_t),$$

where

ΔREV_t = revenues in year τ less revenues in year $\tau - 1$ scaled by total assets at $\tau - 1$,

PPE_τ = gross property plant and equipment in year τ scaled by total assets at $\tau - 1$,

$A_{\tau-1}$ = total assets at $\tau - 1$, and

$\alpha_1, \alpha_2, \alpha_3$ = firm-specific parameters.

where parameters α_1, α_2, and α_3 are estimated using the following model:

$$TA_t = \alpha_1 (1/A_{t-1}) + \alpha_2(\Delta REV_t) + \alpha_3 (PPE_t) + V_t.$$

A modified Jones model used by Dechron and Sloan.[70] follows:

$$NDA_\tau = (\alpha_1(1/A_{\tau-1}) + \alpha_2(\Delta REV_\tau - \Delta REC_\tau) + \alpha_3(PPE_\tau),$$

where

ΔREC_τ = net receivables in year τ less net receivables in year $\tau - 1$ scaled by total assets at $\tau - 1$.

The industry model used by Dechow and Sloan[71] follows:

$$NDA_\tau = v_1 + v_2 \text{ median}_1 (TA_\tau),$$

where

median$_1$ (TA_τ) = the median value of total accruals scaled by lagged assets for all nonsample firms in the same two-digit Standard Industry Classification (SIC) code.

$$TA_t = (\Delta CA_t - \Delta CL_t - \Delta Cash_t + \Delta STD_t - Dep_t)/(A_{+1}),$$

where

ΔCA = change in current assets,

ΔCL = change in current liabilities,

$\Delta Cash$ = change in cash and cash equivalents,

ΔSTD = change in debt included in current liabilities,

Dep = depreciation and amortization expense, and

A = total assets.

EVALUATION OF THE POSITIVE APPROACH

The optimism about the few findings of the positive paradigm is not widely shared. A summary of the papers reviewing positive theory is presented in Exhibit 2.1. A few of the criticisms follow.

First, "crude," "unsophisticated," or "naive" proxy variables have been used, which casts doubt on the findings of the positive theories of financial accounting. The use of these proxies is due to the lack of better theories. There is consequently a call for developing richer theories. Zimmerman, for example, stated:

There is a symbiotic relationship between theory development and empirical testing. The construction of proxy variables requires a theory, no matter how crude or articulated. The test results then allow the theory to be refined which in turn often suggests "better" (i.e., less aggregated) proxy variables. Calling for "better specified," "less ad hoc" proxy variables is equivalent to calling for "better" more developed theories because it is the theories that provide the guidance for selection of the proxy variables. The use of "crude," highly aggregate proxy variables does not necessarily imply lax research design but often a paucity of theory. Better theories are, of course, always desirable."[72]

Exhibit 2.1
Summary of the Papers Reviewing Watts and Zimmerman (1978 and 1979)

Authors	Number of References		Topic	Major Criticisms
	WZ (1978)	WZ (1979)		
Ball and Foster (1982)	13	1	Review of Empirical Accounting Research	• Firm size and bonus plans can proxy for omitted variables • Weak theoretical underpinning for size-political cost construct • Holdout sample not used
Tinker et al. (1982)	1	4	Positive versus normative theories	• Positive theories are value-laden and mask a conservative bias • Ignores underlying class struggles
Christenson (1983)	6	9	Methodology of Positive Accounting	• Logical Positivism is an obsolete methodological approach • Approach is a "sociology of accounting" instead of accounting theory • Tests introduce *ad hoc* arguments to excuse the exceptions to the theory • Inappropriate methods are used for constructing explanatory theories
Holthausen and Leftwich (1983)	7	0	Review of "Economic Consequences Literature"	Interpretation of results limited because: • Incomplete political and contracting theories • Specification problems in left-hand-side and right-hand-side variables
Lowe et al. (1983)	0	12	WZ (1979)	• Economic framework is unjustified • Positive approach open to dispute • Nature of proof is unscientific • Contrary evidence presented

56

Study				Criticisms
McKee et al. (1984)	4	0	Replication of WZ (1978)	• Results do not hold in a new sample • Holdout sample not used • Foreknowledge of sample proportions biases parameter estimates
Whittington (1987)	0	7	Review of WZ (1986)	• Presentation of arguments and evidence is unbalanced • Extreme methodological stance • Positive theories are value-laden • Approach is a "sociology of accounting" instead of accounting theory
Hines (1988)	4	0	Christenson (1983) and Methodology	• Popper is not a practical evaluative guideline for empirical accounting research

Source: R. L. Watts, and J. L. Zimmerman, "Positive Accounting Theory: A Ten Year Perspective," *The Accounting Review* (January 1990): 141–42. Reprinted with permission.

Second, the main limitation to a development of richer positive theories of accounting is due to the lack of well-specified theories of the firm, of capital structure, and of the political process. Watts and Zimmerman elaborated on this crucial limitation as follows:

The lack of a well-developed positive accounting theory results from the lack of rich economic theories of the firm (including the contracting process) and the political process. A richer contracting theory that explained variations in debt contracts and compensation plans across firms and industries would explain the use and nonuse of accounting-based covenants and variations in the accepted accounting procedures. A richer political process theory would enable researchers to use more refined political cost measures than size in studies explaining cross-sectional variations in accounting procedure choice or the stock price effects of accounting standards.[73]

Third, to the preceding limitation, Watts and Zimmerman acknowledged two more limitations:

1. specification of the cross-sectional models and
2. collinearity among the contracting variables.[74]

Fourth, the most striking criticism of the positive approach was based on four points:

1. The Rochester School's assertion that the kind of "positive" research they are undertaking is a prerequisite for normative accounting theory is based on a confusion of phenomenal domains at the different levels (accounting entities versus accountants) and is mistaken.

2. The concept of "positive theory" is drawn from an obsolete philosophy of science and is, in any case, a misnomer, because the theories of empirical science make no positive statement of "what is."

3. Although a theory can be used merely for prediction even if it is known to be false, an explanatory theory of the type sought by the Rochester School, or one that is to be used to test normative proposals, ought not to be known to be false. The method of analysis, which reasons backward from the phenomena to the premises that are acceptable on the basis of independent evidence, is the appropriate method for constructing explanatory theories.

4. Contrary to the empirical method of subjecting theories to severe attempts to falsify them, the Rochester School introduces ad hoc arguments to excuse the failure of their theories.[75]

Another criticism is based on the argument that positive or empirical theories are also normative and value laden because they usually mask a conservative ideology in their accounting-policy implications.[76]

CONCLUSIONS

The anthropological/inductive paradigm better known as the positive approach in accounting serves to provide a theory of accounting that can be derived from the particular individual instances that occur in practice. It is a theory based on deriving a general explanation from an examination of particular cases. It is experiencing a period of primacy as an accounting field of inquiry and may be expected to continue to be popular.

NOTES

1. Henry Rand Hatfield, *Accounting* (New York: D. Appleton & Company, 1927); S. Gilman, *Accounting Concepts of Profit* (New York: The Ronald Press, 1939); W. A. Paton, and A. C. Littleton, *An Introduction to Corporate Accounting Standards,* Monograph No. 3 (Sarasota, FL: American Accounting Association, 1953); Yuji Ijiri, *Theory of Accounting Measurement,* Studies in Accounting Research, No. 10 (Sarasota, FL: American Accounting Association, 1975).

2. Ijiri, *Theory of Accounting Measurement,* 37.

3. A. C. Littleton, *Structure of Accounting Theory,* Monograph No. 5 (Sarasota, FL: American Accounting Association, 1953), 185.

4. Ibid., 31.

5. M. J. Gordon, "Postulates, Principles, and Research in Accounting," *The Accounting Review* (April 1964): 251–63; R. L. Watts, and J. L. Zimmerman, "Towards a Positive Theory of the Determination of Accounting Standards," *The Accounting Review* (January 1978): 112–34.

6. Gordon, "Postulates, Principles, and Research in Accounting," op. cit., 261–62.

7. Watts and Zimmerman, "Towards a Positive Theory of the Determination of Accounting Standards," 14.

8. Ibid.

9. Ijiri, *Theory of Accounting Measurement,* 28.

10. Gerald A. Feltham, "The Value of Information," *Accounting Review* (October 1968): 684–96; Robert H. Crandall, "Information Economics and Its Implications for the Further Development of Accounting Theory," *Accounting Review* (July 1969): 457–66; Gerald A. Feltham and Joel S. Demski, "The Use of Models in Information Evaluation," *Accounting Review* (July 1969): 475–66.

11. Feltham and Demski, "The Use of Models in Information Evaluation," 626.

12. Feltham, "The Value of Information," 684–91.

13. R. B. Wilson, "The Theory of Syndicates," *Econometrica* (January 1968): 119–32; J. S. Demski, and R. J. Swieringa, "A Cooperative Formulation of the Audit Choice

Problem," *Accounting Review* (July 1974): 506–13; J. Demski, "Uncertainty and Evaluation Based on Controllable Performance," *Journal of Accounting Research* (Autumn 1976): 230–45.

14. Stanley Baiman, "Agency Research in Managerial Accounting: A Survey," *Journal of Accounting Literature* (Spring 1982): 159.

15. J. Demski, and Gerald A. Feltham, *Cost Determination: A Conceptual Approach* (Ames: Iowa State University Press, 1977).

16. Baiman, "Agency Research in Managerial Accounting," 159–60.

17. J. Marschak, and R. Radner, *Economic Theory of Games,* Aroles Foundation Monograph No. 22 (New Haven, CT: Yale University Press, 1972).

18. Baiman, "Agency Research in Managerial Accounting."

19. M. Loeb, "Coordination and Information Incentive Problems in the Multidivisional Firm" (Ph.D. diss., Graduate School of Management, Northwestern University, May 1975); T. Groves, "Information Incentives and the Internationalization of Production Externalities," in *Theory and Measurement of Economic Externalities,* S. Liu, ed. (New York: Academic Press, 1975); T. Groves and M. Loeb, "Incentives in Divisionalized Firms," *Management Science* (March 1979): 221–30.

20. M. C. Jensen, "Organizational Theory and Methodology," *Accounting Review* (April 1983): 334–35.

21. R. J. Coase, "The Nature of the Firm," *Economica* 4 (November 1937): 386–405.

22. M. C. Jensen, and J.W.H. Meckling, "Theory of the Firm: Managerial Behavior, Agency Costs and Ownership Structure," *Journal of Financial Economics* (October 1976): 305–60.

23. E. F. Fama, "Agency Problems and the Theory of the Firm," *Journal of Political Economy* 2 (1980): 288–307.

24. Jensen and Meckling, "Theory of the Firm," 308.

25. Fama, "Agency Problems and the Theory of the Firm," 289.

26. Baiman, "Agency Research in Managerial Accounting," 162.

27. K. J. Arrow, *Limits of Organization* (New York: Norton, 1974), 35–36.

28. Baiman, "Agency Research in Managerial Accounting," 163.

29. Ibid., 165–72.

30. S. R. Heyworth, "Smoothing Periodic Income," *The Accounting Review* (January 1953): 32.

31. R. J. Monsen, and A. Downs, "A Theory of Large Managerial Firms," *The Journal of Political Economy* (June 1965): 221–36.

32. M. J. Gordon, "Postulates, Principles, and Research in Accounting," *The Accounting Review* (April 1964): 251–63.

33. Ibid., 261–62.

34. Carl R. Beidelman, "Income Smoothing: The Role of Management," *The Accounting Review* (October 1973): 653.

35. Heyworth, "Smoothing Periodic Income," 34.

36. Gordon, "Postulates, Principles, and Research in Accounting," 251–63.

37. Ibid.

38. Beidelman, "Income Smoothing: The Role of Management," 658–67.

39. Ibid., 654.

40. Ibid.

41. R. N. Cyert, and J. G. March, *A Behavior Theory of the Firm* (Englewood Cliffs, NJ: Prentice-Hall, 1967).

42. M. Schiff, and A. Y. Levin, "Where Traditional Budgeting Fails," *Financial Executive* (May 1968): 57–62.

43. J. D. Thompson, *Organizational in Action* (New York: McGraw-Hill, 1967).

44. J. Y. Kamin, and J. Ronen, "The Smoothing of Income Numbers: Some Empirical Evidence in Systematic Differences Among Management-Controlled and Owner-Controlled Firms," *Accounting, Organizations and Society* 3, no. 2 (1978): 141–53.

45. A. Barnea, J. Ronen, and S. Sadan, "Classificatory Smoothing of Income with Extraordinary Items," *The Accounting Review* (January 1976): 110–12.

46. Ahmed Belkaoui, *Behavioral Accounting* (Westport, CT: Greenwood Press, 1989).

47. P. Healy, "The Effects of Bonus Schemes on Accounting Decisions," *Journal of Accounting and Economics* (April 1985): 85–107.

48. M. McNichols, and G. Wilson, "Evidence of Earnings Management from the Provision for Bad Debts," *Journal of Accounting Research* 26 (Supplement 1988): 1–31.

49. L. DeAngelo, "Managerial Competition, Information Costs, and Corporate Governance. The Use of Accounting Performance Measures in Proxy Contests," *Journal of Accounting and Economics* (January 1988): 3–36.

50. J. Jones, "The Effect of Foreign Trade Regulation on Accounting Choices and Production and Investment Decisions," working paper, Ann Arbor, the University of Michigan, 1988.

51. Paul E. Dascher and Robert E. Malcolm, "A Note on Income Smoothing in the Chemical Industry," *Journal of Accounting Research* (Autumn 1970): 253–54.

52. M. J. Gordon, "Discussions of the Effects of Alternative Accounting Rules for Nonsubsidiary Investments," *Empirical Research in Accounting: Selected Studies, 1966,* supplement to Vol. 4, *Journal of Accounting Research* (1966): 223.

53. R. M. Copeland, "Income Smoothing, Empirical Research in Accounting: Selected Studies," *Journal of Accounting Research* 6 (Supplement 1981): 101.

54. Barnea, Ronen, and Sadam, "Classificatory Smoothing of Income with Extraordinary Items," 111.

55. M. C. Jensen, "Reflections on the State of Accounting Research and the Regulation of Accounting," in *Stanford Lectures in Accounting* (Stanford, CA: Stanford University, 1976), 11.

56. Ibid., 13.

57. Jensen and Meckling, "Theory of the Firm," 31.

58. Fama, "Agency Problems and the Theory of the Firm," 288–307.

59. Jerold L. Zimmerman, "Research on Positive Theories of Financial Accounting," in *Accounting Research Convocation,* John O. Mason, Jr., ed. (Birmingham, AL: School of Accountancy, The University of Alabama, November 1982), 19–20.

60. Ibid., 22.

61. Kamin and Ronen, "The Smoothing of Income Numbers," 141–53.

62. Ahmed Belkaoui, and Ronald D. Picur, "The Smoothing of Income Numbers: Some Empirical Evidence on Systematic Differences Between Core and Periphery Industrial Sectors," *The Journal of Business Finance and Accounting* (Winter 1984): 527–46.

63. Zimmerman, "Research on Positive Theories of Financial Accounting."

64. Ibid.

65. A good survey of the methods used is provided in P. M. Dechow, R. G. Sloan, and A. P. Sweeney, "Detecting Earnings Management," *The Accounting Review* (April 1995): 193–296.

66. McNichols and Wilson, "Evidence of Earnings Management from the Provisions for Bad Debts," 1–31.

67. Healey, "The Effect of Bonus Schemes on Accounting Decisions," 85–107.

68. L. DeAngelo, "Accounting Numbers as Market Vibration Substitutes: A Study of Management Buyouts of Public Stockholders," *The Accounting Review* 61 (1986): 400–20.

69. J. Jones, "Earnings Management During Import Relief Investigations," *Journal of Accounting Research* 25 (1991): 193–228.

70. P. M. Dechow, and R. G. Sloan, "Executive Incentives and the Horizon Problem: An Empirical Investigation," *Journal of Accounting and Economics* 18 (1994): 3–42.

71. Ibid.

72. Zimmerman, "Research on Positive Theories of Financial Accounting," 24.

73. R. L. Watts, and J. L. Zimmerman, *Positive Accounting Theory* (Englewood Cliffs, NJ: Prentice-Hall), 357.

74. Ibid.

75. C. Christenson, "The Methodology of Positive Accounting," *Accounting Review* (January 1983): 19–20.

76. A. M. Tinker, B. D. Merino, and M. D. Neimark, "The Normative Origins of Positive Theories: Ideology and Accounting Thought," *Accounting, Organizations and Society* 2 (May 1982): 167–200.

REFERENCES

Ball, R., and G. Foster. "Corporate Financial Reporting: A Methodological Review of Empirical Research." *Journal of Accounting Research* (Supplement 1982): 161–234.

Christenson, C. "The Methodology of Positive Accounting." *The Accounting Review* (January 1983): 1–22.

Dechow, P. M., R. G. Sloan, and A. P. Sweeney. "Detecting Earnings Management." *The Accounting Review* (April 1995): 193–226.

Hines, R. D. "Popper's Methodology of Falsificationism and Accounting Research." *The Accounting Review* (October 1988): 657–62.

Holthausen, R. W., and R. W. Leftwich. "The Economic Consequences of Accounting Choice: Implications of Costly Contracting and Monitoring." *Journal of Accounting and Economics* (August 1990): 77–117.

Lowe, E. A., A. G. Puxty, and R. C. Laughlin, "Simple Theories for Complex Processes: Accounting Policy and the Market for Myopia." *Journal of Accounting and Public Policy* (Spring 1983): 19–42.

McKee, A. J., Jr., T. B. Bell, and J. R. Boatsman. "Management Preferences over Accounting Standards: A Replication and Additional Tests." *The Accounting Review* (October 1984): 647–59.

Schipper, K. "Commentary on Earnings Management." *Accounting Horizons* 3 (1989): 91–102.

Tinker, T. A., B. D. Merino, and M. D. Neimark. "The Normative Origins of Positive Theories: Ideology and Accounting Thought." *Accounting Organizations and Society* 2 (May 1982): 167–200.

Watts, R. L., and J. L. Zimmerman. "Towards a Positive Theory of the Determination of Accounting Standards." *The Accounting Review* (January 1978): 112–34.

Watts, R. L., and J. L. Zimmerman. "The Demand and Supply of Accounting Theories: The Market for Excuses." *The Accounting Review* (April 1979): 273–305.

Watts, R. L., and J. L. Zimmerman. "Positive Accounting Theory: A Ten Year Perspective." *The Accounting Review* (January 1990): 131–156.

Whittington, G. "Positive Accounting: A Review Article." *Accounting and Business Research* (Autumn 1987): 327–36.

3 The True Income/Deductive Paradigm

INTRODUCTION

The second accounting paradigm, examined in this chapter, is the true income/deductive paradigm. In what follows this paradigm is examined in terms of exemplars, the image of the subject matter, theories, and methods. The methods are also illustrated by a factorial example.

EXEMPLARS

Studies that qualify as exemplars of the *true income/deductive paradigm* are the works of Paton and Canning.[1] Others to note are Alexander, Edwards, Bell, MacNeal, Moonitz, Sprouse, and Sweeney. These authors share a concern for a normative-deductive approach to the construction of an accounting theory and, with the exception of Alexander, a belief that, ideally, income measured using a single valuation base would meet the needs of all users. These researchers are also in complete agreement that current price information is more useful than conventional historical-cost information is to users in making economic decisions. Paton, for example, refutes the propriety theory of accounts view by restating the theory of accounting in a way that is consistent with the conditions and needs of the business enterprise as a distinct entity or personality. According to Paton, accounting plays a significant and relevant role in the firm and in society:

If the tendencies of the economic process as evidenced in market prices are to be reflected rationally in the decisions of business managers, efficient machinery for the recording and interpreting of such statistics must be available; and sound accounting scheme represents an essential part of such a mechanism. . . . To put the matter in very general terms, accounting, insofar as it contributes to render effective the control of the price system in its direction of economic activity, contributes to general productive efficiency and has a clear-cut social significance, a value to the industrial community as a whole.[2]

Paton's theory of the accounting system consists of a logical discussion and justification of the accounting structure in terms of the fundamental classes of accounts; the proprietorship and liabilities; the property and equity accounts; the types of transactions; the expense, revenue, and supplementary accounts; the account classification; the periodic analysis; and the concepts of debit and credit. Paton states:

The liberal view that, ideally, all bona fide value changes in either direction, from whatever cause, should be reflected in the accounts has been adopted without argument. To show that all possible types of situations and transactions can be handled in a rational manner in accordance with the principles enunciated is a chief reason for this attitude.[3]

IMAGE OF THE SUBJECT MATTER

To those who adopt the true income/deductive paradigm, the basic subject matter is

1. the construction of an accounting theory on the basis of logical and normative reasoning and conceptual rigor, and
2. a concept of ideal income based on some other method than the historical-cost method.

MacNeal argues for an ideal-income concept as follows: "There is one correct definition of profits in an accounting sense. A 'profit' is an increase in net wealth. A 'loss' is decrease in net wealth. This is an economist's definition. It is terse, obvious, and mathematically demonstrable."[4] Sidney S. Alexander, who also argues for an ideal income concept, states: "We must find out whether economic income is an ideal from which accounting income differs only to the degree that the ideal is practically unattainable, or whether economic income is appropriate even if it could conveniently be measured."[5]

THEORIES

Theories in the deductive paradigm aim at providing a definition and justification of their brand of ideal or true income. The differences between these theories derive from their different interpretation of the concept of income. It is therefore appropriate to proceed first with an explanation of the concept of income.

The Concept of Income

The concept of income was first examined by economists before being investigated by accountants. Definitions of the concept of income by four economists had the greatest influence.

1. Adam Smith defined income as an increase in wealth.[6] Therefore a measurement of wealth preceded the measurement of income.

2. Irving Fisher defined income as a series of events that corresponds to different states: the enjoyment of psychic income, the real income, and the money income.[7] They are best defined as follows:

    a. *Psychic income* is the actual personal consumption of funds and services that produces a psychic enjoyment and satisfaction of wants.

    b. *Real income* is an expression of events that give rise to psychic enjoyments.

    c. *Money income* represents all the money received and intended to be used for consumption to meet the cost of living.

3. E. Lindhal defined income as *interest,* resulting from the continuous appreciation of capital goods over time.[8] The interest is self-allocated between *consumption* and *saving*. What resulted is the generally accepted definition of economic income as consumption plus saving. In other words,

$$Y^e = C + (k_t - K_{t-1}),$$

where

Y_e = economic income,

C = consumption,

K_t = capital as of period t,

K_{t-1} = capital as of period $t - 1$.

4. J. R. Hicks used the preceding concepts to provide the following accepted definition of economic income:

> The purpose of income calculation in practical affairs is to give people an indication of the amount which they can consume without impoverishing themselves. Following out this idea it would seem that we ought to define a man's income as the maximum value he can consume during a week, and still enjoy to be as well off at the end of the week as he was at the beginning.[9]

Hicks's definition became the standard definition used by accountants for the definition of the concept of income. It was translated by Alexander into a concept of corporate income for a year: "the amount the corporation can distribute to the owners of equity in the corporation and be as well off at the end of the year as at the beginning."[10] Therefore earnings is the increase in wealth from all sources. It is the amount that can be distributed while maintaining capital intact. The interpretation of the term "as well-off" or "welloffness" in Hicks's and Alexanders' definitions is that of capital maintenance.

Concepts of Capital Maintenance

Capital maintenance is the level that divides return of capital or cost recovery from return on capital or earnings. Which capital is maintained is interpreted as either *invested financial capital* or *invested physical capital*. Either can be expressed in financial or money terms or in dollars of constant purchasing power. In other words, the concepts of capital maintenance or cost recovery are

1. Financial capital maintenance
   —measured in terms of money and known as *money maintenance*
   —measured in units of the same purchasing power and known as *general purchasing power money maintenance*
2. Physical capital maintenance
   —measured in terms of money and known as *productive capacity maintained*
   —measured in terms of units of the same purchasing power and known as *general purchasing power productive capacity maintenance*

They may be defined as follows:

1. The first concept implies that the financial capital invested or reinvested by the owners is maintained. Income is equal to the change in net assets adjusted

for capital transactions expressed in terms of dollars. Conventional accounting, as it relies on historical cost for the valuations of assets and liabilities, conforms to the money maintenance concept.

2. The second concept implies that the purchasing power of the financial capital invested or reinvested by the owners is maintained. Income is equal to the change in net assets adjusted for capital transactions expressed in units of the same purchasing power. General price-level-adjusted, historical cost financial statements conform to the general purchasing power money maintenance concept.

3. The third concept implies that the physical productive capacity of the firm is maintained. It is used in current value accounting where assets and liabilities are disclosed at their current values. Current values can be computed on the basis of

   a. the *capitalization method,* where the capitalized value or present value of an asset, group of assets, or total assets is the net amount of the discounted expected cash flows pertaining to the asset, group of assets, or total assets during their useful lives;

   b. the *current exit price or replacement cost,* where the replacement cost is the amount of cash or other consideration that would be needed to obtain an equivalent, identical or new asset; and

   c. the *current exhibit price or net realizable value,* where the value is the amount of cash for which an asset might be sold or a liability might be refinanced.

4. The fourth concept of capital maintenance implies the maintenance of the physical productive capacity of the firm measured in units of the same purchasing power. General purchasing power productive capacity maintenance is the concept of capital maintenance used in general price-level-adjusted current value accounting.

METHODS

Income Determination Models

The difference between the alternative income determination models arise from the different attribute to be measured and the units of measure to be used.

The attribute of assets and liabilities, referring to what is being measured, include historical cost, replacement cost, net realizable value, and present or capitalized value. These attributes can be measured in terms of either (1) units of money or (2) units of general purchasing power.

The choice of one of the attributes and one of the units of measures leads to the following income determination models:

1. *Historical cost accounting* measures historical cost in units of money.
2. *Replacement cost accounting* measures replacement cost in units of money.
3. *Net realizable value accounting* measures net realizable value in units of money.
4. *Present value accounting* measures present value in units of money.
5. *General price level accounting* measures historical cost in units of purchasing power.
6. *General price level replacement cost accounting* measures replacement cost in units of purchasing power
7. *General price level net realizable value accounting* measures net realizable value in units of purchasing power.
8. *General price level present value accounting* measures present value in units of purchasing power.

Evaluation Criteria

The income determination models presented are based on whether they avoid timing errors and measuring unit errors and are evaluated in terms of interpretability and relevance.[11]

1. Timing errors result when changes in value occur in a given period but are accounted for and reported in another period.
2. Measuring unit errors occur when financial statements are not expressed in units of general purchasing power.
3. Interpretability implies understandability in terms of both meaning and use. The interpretation of the accounting models, by definition, will be one of the following:
   a. If the accounting model measures any of the attributes in units of money, its results are expressed in the *number of dollars* (NOD) or, as Chambers refers to it, the *number of odd dollars* (NOOD).[12]
   b. If the accounting model measures historical cost in units of general purchasing power, its results still are expressed in NOD.
   c. If the accounting model measures current values in units of general purchasing power, its results are expressed in the *command of goods* (COG) or, as Chambers refers to it, the *command of goods in general* (COGG).[13]
4. Relevance implies usefulness of the end results.

Illustrative Example

A simplified example is used to illustrate the main differences between the main asset valuation and income determination models. For example, let's assume that the Qochinski company was formed January 1, 1993, to distribute a new product called "Anna." Its capital is composed of $8,000 equity and $8,000 liabilities carrying interest of 10%. On January 1, the company purchased 100 units of Anna at $40 per unit. On June 1, the company sold 500 units at $60 per unit. Changes in general and specific price levels for 19×3 are as follows:

	January 1	June 1	December 31
Replacement cost	$40	$44	$52
Net realizable value		$60	$70
General price level income	100	120	144

In what follows, this example is used to illustrate asset valuation and income determination models.

Historical Cost Accounting

Historical cost accounting, or conventional accounting, rests on the adoption of strict principles for both asset valuation and income determination. These principles include the use of historical costs as the elements of financial statements, the assumption of a stable monetary unit, the matching principle, and the realization principle.

What results from the adoption of these principles is that historical cost income or accounting income becomes the difference between realized revenues and their corresponding historical costs. The financial statements resulting from the use of historical cost accounting are shown in Exhibits 3.1 and 3.2. Exhibit 3.1 shows accounting income to be equal to $9,200. To the Qochinski company, this $9,200 figure represents an acceptable basis for the determination of taxes and dividends and the evaluation of performance. For general taxation purposes worldwide, accounting income is an acceptable measure because it is objective, verifiable, practical, and easy to understand. It is, however, a known and empirical fact that accounting income includes both timing and measuring unit errors that are reflected in the $9,200 figure. First, accounting income contains timing errors because it includes operating income and

Exhibit 3.1
Qochinski Company Income Statements for the Year Ending
December 31, 19X3

	HISTORICAL COST	REPLACEMENT COST		NET REALIZABLE VALUE
REVENUES	$30,000[a]	$30,000		$44,000[b]
COST OF GOODS SOLD	20,000[c]	22,000[d]	32,400[e]	
GROSS MARGIN	$10,000	8,000		$11,600
INTEREST(10%)	800	800		800
OPERATING INCOME	$9,200	7,200		$10,800
REALIZED HOLDING GAINS & LOSSES	(INCLUDED ABOVE)	2,000[f]		2,000
UNREALIZED HOLDING GAINS & LOSSES	(NOT APPLICABLE)	2,400[g]		2,400
GENERAL PRICE-LEVEL GAINS & LOSSES	(NOT APPLICABLE)	(NOT APPLICABLE)		(NOT APPLICABLE
NET INCOME	$9,200	$11,600		$15,200

a. $500 \times \$60 = \$30,000$
b. $\$30,000 + (200 \times \$70) = \$44,000$
c. $500 \times \$40 = \$20,000$
d. $500 \times \$44 = \$22,000$
e. $\$22,000 + 200 (\$52) = \$32,400$
f. $500 (\$44 - \$40) = \$2,000$
g. $200 (\$52 - \$40) = \$2,400$

holding gains and losses that are recognized in the current period and that occurred in a previous period, and it omits the operating profit and holding gains and losses that occurred in the current period but that are recognizable in future periods. Second, the accounting income contains measuring-unit errors because it does not take into account changes in the general price level that would have resulted in amounts expressed in units of general purchasing power, and it does not take into account changes in the specific price level, because it relies on historical cost (rather than replacement cost or net realizable value) as the attribute of the elements of financial statements.

Then how should we evaluate historical cost financial statements?

Exhibit 3.2
Qochinski Company Balance Sheets for the Year Ending
December 31, 19X3

	HISTORICAL COST	REPLACEMENT COST	NET REALIZABLE VALUE
ASSETS			
CASH	$17,200[a]	$17,200	$17,200
INVENTORY	8,000	10,400	14,000[d]
TOTAL ASSETS	$25,200	$27,600	$31,200
EQUITIES			
BONDS (10%)	$8,000	$8,000	$8,000
CAPITAL	8,000	8,000	8,000
RETAINED EARNINGS			
REALIZED	9,200	9,200	9,200
UNREALIZED	NOT APPLICABLE	2,400	6,000[e]
TOTAL EQUITIES	$25,200	$24,600	$31,200

a. ($8,000 + 8000 − 28,000 + 30,000 − 800) = $17,200
b. (200 × $52) = $10,400
c. $7,200 + 2,000 = $9,200
d. 200 × $10 = $14,000
e. Unrealized Operating Gain $3,600 + Unrealized Holding Gain $2,400

First, they are interpretable. Historical cost financial statement are based on the concept of money maintenance, and the attribute being expressed in the number of dollars. The balance sheet reports the stock in NOD as of December 31, 19×3, and the income statement reports the change in NOD during the year.

Second, historical cost financial statements are not relevant because the command of good is not measured. A measure of COG reflects changes in both the specific price level and the general price level, and as such, represents the ability to buy the amount of goods necessary for capital maintenance.

In summary, historical cost financial statements contain timing errors, contain measuring-unit errors, are interpretable, and are not relevant.

Replacement Cost Accounting

Replacement cost accounting, as a particular case of current-entry price-based accounting, is characterized primarily by the use of replacement cost as the attribute of the elements of financial statements, the assumption of a stable monetary unit, the realization principle, the dichotomization of operating income and holding gains and losses, and the dichotomization of realized and unrealized holding gains and losses.

Accordingly, replacement cost net income is equal to the sum of replacement cost operating income and holding gains and losses. Replacement cost operating income is equal to the difference between realized revenues and their corresponding replacement costs. From Exhibit 3.1, the Qochinski company's replacement cost net income of $11,600 is composed of (1) replacement cost operating income of $7,200, (2) realized holding gains and losses of $2,000, (3) and unrealized holding gains and losses of $2,400.

What do these figures represent for Qochinski? The replacement cost operating income of $7,200 represents the "distributable" income, or the maximum amount of dividends that the firm can pay while still maintaining its productive capacity. The realized holding gains and losses of $2,000 are an indicator of the efficiency of holding resources up to the point of sale. The realized holding gains and losses are an indicator of the efficiency of holding resources after the point of sale and may act as a predictor of future operating and holding performances.

In addition to these practical advantages, replacement cost net income contains timing errors only on operating profit. It does, however, contain measuring-unit errors. First the replacement cost net income contains timing errors because (1) it omits the operating profit that occurred in the current period but that is realizable in future periods, (2) it includes the operating profit that is recognized in the current period but that occurred in previous periods, and (3) it includes holding gains and losses in the same period in which they occur. Second, the replacement cost net income contains measuring-unit errors because (1) it does not take into account changes in the general price level that would have resulted in the amount expressed in units of general purchasing power and (2) it does take into account changes in the specific price level, because it relies on replacement cost as the attribute of the elements of financial statements. We can evaluate replacement cost financial statements as follows. First, they are interpretable. Replacement cost financial statements are based on the concept of productive-capacity maintenance, and the attribute being expressed is the number of dollars in the income statement. The asset figures, however, are interpretable as measures of the command of goods. The asset figures shown in Exhibit 3.2 are expressed in terms of the purchase power of the dollar at the end of the year. They reflect changes in both the specific price level and the general price level and therefore represent the COG required for capital maintenance. Second, because COG is the relevant attribute, the replacement cost net income is not relevant, even though the asset figures are relevant.

In summary, replacement cost financial statements contain timing errors in operating profit, contain measuring-unit errors, are interpretable as NOD for income statement figures and as COG for asset figures, and provide relevant measures of COG only for asset figures.

Net Realizable Value Accounting

Net realizable value accounting, as a particular case of current-exit price-based accounting, is characterized primarily by the use of net realizable value as the attribute of the elements of financial statements, the assumption of a stable monetary unit, the abandonment of the realization principle, and the dichotomization of operating income and holding gains and losses.

Accordingly, net realizable value net income is equal to the sum of net realizable value operating income and holding gains and losses. Net realizable value operating income is equal to the operating income on sales and the net operating income on inventory. Operating income on sales is equal to the difference between realized revenues and the corresponding replacement costs of the items sold. In Exhibit 3.1, the Qochinski company's net realizable value net income of $15,200 is composed of (1) net realizable value operating income of $10,800, (2) realized holding gains and losses of $2,000, and (3) unrealized holding gains and losses of $2,400.

Note that the net realizable value operating income of $10,800 is composed of operating income on inventory. Thus, in Exhibit 3.2, unrealized retained earnings equal the sum of unrealized holding gains and losses of $3,600 and operating income on inventory of $2,400.

What do these figures represent for Qochinski? They are similar to the figures obtained with replacement cost accounting except for the operating income in inventory, which results from the abandonment of the realization principle and the recognition of revenues at the time of production and at the time of sale. Net realizable value net income is an indicator of the ability of the firm to liquidate and to adapt to new economic situations.

To these practical advantages, we can add that net realizable value net income contains no timing errors, but it does not contain measuring-unit errors. First, the net realizable value net income does not contain any timing errors because (1) it reports all operating profit and holding gains and losses in the same period in which they occur and (2) it excludes all operating and holding gains and losses that occurred in previous periods. Second, the net realizable value net income contains measuring-unit errors because (1) it does not take into account changes in the general price level (if it had, it would have resulted in amounts expressed in units of general price level) and (2) it relies on net realizable value as the attribute of the elements of financial statements.

We can evaluate net realizable value financial statements as follows. First, they are interpretable. Net realizable value financial statements are based on the concept of productive-capacity maintenance, the attribute being measured is expressed in NOD on the income statement and in COG on the balance sheet. Unlike replacement cost accounting, under net realizable value accounting asset figures are expressed as measures of COG in the output market rather than in the input market.

Second, because COG is the relevant attribute, net realizable value income is not relevant, although the asset figures are relevant.

In summary, net realizable value financial statements contain no timing errors; contain measuring unit errors, interpretable as NOD for net income and as COG for asset figures; and provide relevant measures of COG only for asset figures.

General Price-Level-Adjusted, Historical Cost Accounting

General price-level-adjusted, historical cost accounting is characterized primarily by the use of historic cost as the attribute of the elements of financial statements, the use of general purchasing power as the unit of measure, the matching principle, and the realization principle.

Accordingly, general price-level-adjusted, historical cost income is the difference between realized revenues and their corresponding historical costs, both expressed in units of general purchasing power. The corresponding financial statements are presented in Exhibits 3.3 and 3.4. In Exhibit 3.3 general price-level-adjusted, historical cost income is equal to $9,200. Included in the $9,200 historical cost income figure is a $2,800 general price level gain, computed as shown in Exhibit 3.5. Again, what

Exhibit 3.3

Qochinski Company General Price Level Income Statements for the Year Ending December 31, 19X3

	HISTORICAL COST	REPLACEMENT COST		NET REALIZABLE VALUE
REVENUES	$36,000[a]	36,000		50,000[g]
COST OF GOODS SOLD ·	28,800[b]	26,400[d]	36,800[f]	
GROSS MARGIN	$7,200	$9,600		$13,200
INTEREST(10%)	800	800		800
OPERATING INCOME	$6,400	$8,800		$12,400
REAL REALIZED HOLDING GAINS AND LOSSES	INCLUDED ABOVE	(2,400)[e]	(2,400)	
REAL REALIZABLE HOLDING GAINS AND LOSSES	NOT APPLICABLE	(1,120)[f]	(1,120)	
GENERAL PRICE LEVEL GAINS AND LOSSES	2,800[c]	2,800		2,800
NET INCOME	9,200	8,080		11,680

a. $30,000 × 144/120 = $36,000
b. $20,000 × 144/100 = $28,800
c. See Exhibit 3.5
d. $22,000 × 144/120 = $26,400
e. 500 [($44 × 144/120) − ($40 × 144/100)] = $(2,400)
f. 200 [$52 − ($40 × 144/100)] = ($1,120)
g. $36,000 + (200 × $70) = $50,000
h. $26,400 + ($52 × 200) = $36,800

does the $9,200 figure represent to the Qochinski? It represents accounting income expressed in dollars that have the purchasing power of dollars at the end of 19X3. In addition to the practical advantages listed for accounting income, general price-level-adjusted, historical cost income is expressed in units of general purchasing power. For these reasons, the use of such an accounting model may constitute a less radical change for those used to historical cost income than any current-value accounting model.

Despite these practical advantages, the general price-level-adjusted, historical cost income of $9,200 contains the same timing errors that historical cost income contains.

Exhibit 3.4
**Qochinski Company General Price Level Balance Sheets for the Year
Ending December 31, 19X3**

	HISTORICAL COST	REPLACEMENT COST		NET REALIZABLE VALUE	
ASSETS					
CASH	$17,200	$17,200		$17,200	
INVENTORY	11,520[a]	10,400		14,000	
TOTAL ASSETS	$28,720	$27,600		$31,200	
EQUITIES					
BONDS (10%)	$8,000	$8,000		$8,000	
CAPITAL	11,520[b]		11,520		11,520
RETAINED EARNINGS					
REALIZED	6,400	6,400		6,400	
UNREALIZED	NOT APPLICABLE	(1120)		2,480[c]	
GENERAL PRICE LEVEL GAINS AND LOSSES	2,800	2,800		2,800	
TOTAL EQUITIES	$28,720	$27,600		$31,200	

a. $8,000 × 144/100 = $11,520
b. $8,000 × 144/100 = $11,520
c. Unrealized operating gains of $3,600 plus unrealized holding gains of ($1,120)

However, general price-level-adjusted, historical cost income contains no measuring-unit errors, because it takes into account changes in the general price level. It does not, however, take into account changes in the specific price level, because it relies on historical rather than replacement cost or net realizable value as the attribute of the elements of financial statements.

How should we evaluate the general price-level-adjusted, historical cost financial statements presented in Exhibits 3.3 and 3.4? First, they are interpretable. General price-level-adjusted, historical cost financial statements are based on the concept of purchasing power money maintenance. The attribute being measured is NOD in some cases and COG in other cases. Hence, general price-level-adjusted, historical cost income and all balance sheet figures, with the exception of cash (and monetary

Exhibit 3.5
**Qochinski Company General Price Level Gain or Loss for the Year
Ending December 31, 19X3**

	UNADJUSTED AMOUNT	CONVERSION FACTOR	ADJUSTED AMOUNT
NET MONETARY ASSETS ON JAN 1, 19x3	$8,000	144/100	$11,500
ADD:MONETARY RECEIPTS IN 1993(SALES)	$30,000	144/120	$36,000
NET MONETARY RECEIPTS	$38,000		$47,520
LESS MONETARY PAYMENTS			
1. PURCHASES	$28,000	144/100	$40,320
2. INTEREST	800	144/144	800
TOTAL MONETARY PAYMENTS	$28,800		$41,120
COMPUTED NET MONETARY ASSETS DECEMBER 31, 19x3			$6,400
ACTUAL NET MONETARY ASSETS DECEMBER 31, 19x3	$9,200		$9,200
GENERAL PRICE LEVEL			$2,800

assets and liabilities), can be interpreted as NOD measures. Only the cash figures (and monetary assets and liabilities) can be interpreted as COG measures. Second, only the cash figures (and monetary assets and liabilities) are relevant, because they are expressed as COG measures.

In summary, general price-level-adjusted, replacement cost financial statements contain timing errors, contain no measuring-unit errors, are interpretable, and provide relevant measures of COG only for cash figures (and monetary assets and liabilities).

General Price-Level-Adjusted, Replacement Cost Accounting

General price-level-adjusted, replacement cost accounting is characterized primarily by the use of replacement cost as the attribute of the elements of financial statements, the use of general purchasing power as the unit measure, the realization principle, the dichotomization of operating income and real realized holding gains and losses, and the dichotomization of real realized and real unrealized holding gains and losses. Accordingly, general price-level adjusted, replacement cost income is equal to the difference between realized revenues and their corresponding replacement costs, both expressed in units of general purchasing power. Similarly, general price-level-adjusted, replacement cost financial statements eliminate "fictitious holding gains and losses" to arrive at "real holding gains and losses." Fictitious holding gains and losses represent the general price level restatement that is required to maintain the general purchasing power on nonmonetary items. We can see from Exhibit 3.3 that general price-level-adjusted, replacement cost income is equal to $8,080. Included in the $8,080 income figure is a ($2,800) general price-level gain, computed as shown in Exhibit 3.5. The $8,080 figure represents the Qochinski replacement cost net income, expressed in units of general purchasing power, at the end of 19×3. Such a measure of income has all the advantages of replacement cost accounting income and the added advantage of being expressed in units of general purchasing power. For these reasons, general price-level-adjusted, replacement cost accounting constitutes a net improvement over replacement cost accounting, because this accounting model not only adopts replacement cost as the attribute of the elements of financial statements but also employs general purchasing power as the unit of measure. Despite these improvements, however, general price-level-adjusted, replacement cost income contains the same timing errors that replacement cost income contains. Second, general price-level-adjusted, replacement cost income contains no measuring-unit errors, because it takes into account changes in the general price level. In addition, this measure of income takes into account changes in the specific price level, because it adopts replacement cost as the attribute of the elements of financial statements.

How should we evaluate the general price-level-adjusted, replacement cost financial statements presented in Exhibits 3.3 and 3.4? First, they are interpretable. General price-level-adjusted, replacement cost financial statements are based on the concept of purchasing power, productive-capacity maintenance. The figures on both the income statement and the balance sheet are expressed as COG measures. Second, general price-level-adjusted, replacement cost financial statements are relevant, because they are expressed as COG measures. Note, however, that COG is in the input market, rather than the output market.

In summary, general price-level-adjusted, replacement cost financial statements contain timing errors, contain no measuring-unit errors, are interpretable, and provide relevant measures of COG in the input market.

General Price-Level-Adjusted, Net Realizable Value Accounting

General price-level-adjusted, net realizable value accounting is characterized primarily by the use of net realizable value as the attribute the elements of financial statements, the use of general purchasing power as the unit of measure, the abandonment of the realization principle, the dichotomization of operating income and real holding gains and losses, and the dichotomization of real realized and real unrealized gains and losses.

Accordingly, general price-level-adjusted, net realizable value net income is equal to the sum of net realizable value operating income and holding gains and losses, both expressed in units of general purchasing power. The general price-level-adjusted, net realizable value operating income is equal to the sum of operating income arising from sale and operating income on inventory, both expressed in units of general purchasing power. From Exhibits 3.3 and 3.4 there is (1) general price-level-adjusted net realizable value operating income of $12,400, (2) real realized holding losses of $2,400, (3) real unrealized holding losses of $1,120, and (4) general price-level gains of $2,800.

In addition to the advantages of net realizable value net income, general price-level-adjusted net realizable value net income is expressed in units of general purchasing power. For these reasons, general price-level-adjusted, net realizable value accounting represents an overall improvement on net realizable value accounting, because it not only adopts net realizable value as an attribute of the elements of financial statements but also employs general purchasing power as the unit of measure.

Thus, general price-level-adjusted, net realizable value income involves no timing errors (as explained in the discussion of net realizable value accounting) and no measuring-unit errors, because it is expressed in units of general purchasing power.

How should we evaluate the general price-level-adjusted, net realizable value financial statements presented in Exhibits 3.3 and 3.4? First, they are interpretable. General price-level-adjusted, net realizable value financial statements are based on the concept of purchasing power, productive-capacity maintenance. The figures in both the income statement and the balance sheet are expressed as COG measures. Second, these

Exhibit 3.6
Error-Type Analysis

ACCOUNTING MODEL	NET INCOME	NET VALUE ADDED	TIMING OPERATING PROFIT	ERROR HOLDING GAINS	MEASURING UNIT ERRORS
1. HISTORICAL COST ACCOUNTING	$2,200	$2,500	YES	YES	YES
2. REPLACEMENT COST ACCOUNTING	$2,500	$2,800	YES	ELIMINATED	YES
3. NET REALIZABLE VALUE ACCOUNTING	$2,900	$3,200	ELIMINATED	ELIMINATED	ELIMINATED
4. GENERAL PRICE LEVEL ADJUSTED, HISTORICAL COST ACCOUNTING	$1,080	$1,380	YES	YES	ELIMINATED
5. GENERAL PRICE LEVEL ADJUSTED, REPLACEMENT COST ACCOUNTING	$820	$1,120	YES	ELIMINATED	ELIMINATED
6. GENERAL PRICE LEVEL ADJUSTED, NET REALIZABLE VALUE ACCOUNTING	$1,220	$1,520	ELIMINATED	ELIMINATED	ELIMINATED

financial statements are relevant, because they are expressed as COG measures. Note, however, that COG is in the output market, rather than the input market.

In summary, general price-level-adjusted, net realizable value financial statements contain no timing errors, contain no measuring-unit errors, are interpretable, and provide relevant measures of COG in the output market. Such statements, therefore, meet all of the criteria established for the comparison and evaluation of the alternative accounting models, as shown in Exhibit 3.6.

A Taxonomy of Price Change Models

The difference between price change models rests on the differences in their implicit and explicit specification of (1) a valuation model or a measured attribute for assets and liabilities and (2) a capital maintenance concept. Various studies have provided a taxonomy of price change models based on a useful algebraic approach.[14,15,16,17] Professor Chasteen's approach is used here to illustrate the different price change models.[18] He based his analysis on the following assumptions and price change data. The twelve price change models, based on an attribute measured/capital maintenance concept, were:

1. historical cost/nominal dollars (HC/N$) model,
2. historical cost/constant dollars (HC/C$) model,
3. historical cost/constant dollars model à la Ijiri,
4. historical cost/constant dollars model using the one-line adjustment,
5. current cost/nominal dollars (CC/N$) model,
6. current cost/constant dollars (CC/C$) model,
7. current cost/physical capital (CC/PC) model,
8. current cost/physical capital model that incorporates purchasing power gains and losses on monetary items based on specific price changes,
9. current cost/physical capital model that incorporates both specific price changes adjustment as in the previous model and a "gearing" adjustment,
10. current exit value/nominal dollars (EV/N$),
11. current exit value/constant dollars (EV/C$) à la Sterling,
12. current exit value/constant dollars à la Chambers.

The algebraic formulation of each model is as follows:

1. A firm begins operations at a time $t = 0$ with monetary assets of M, non-monetary assets acquired at a price of N, and monetary liabilities of L. Thus, at $t = 0$ the firm's financial position is given by $M + N = L + R$, where R equals equity and $R > 0$.
2. No transactions occur from $t = 0$ to $t = 1$.
3. During the time interval from $t = 0$ to $t = 1$, the following price changes occur:

	At $t = 0$	At $t = 1$
General price index	1	$1 + p$
Current cost of nonmonetary assets	N	$N(1 + s_1)$
Current exit value of nonmonetary assets	N	$N(1 + s_2)$

where p is the proportional change in the general level of prices (divide by 100), s_1 is the proportional change in the asset's current cost (divide by 100), and s_2 is the proportional change in the asset's current exit value (divide by 100).

4. For simplicity, assume that p, s_1, and $s_2 > 0$ and that p, s_1, and s_2 are not necessarily equal.

The twelve models that follow represent some of the models that can be used and/or adapted by any country to deal with accounting for inflation.

1. The historical cost/nominal dollars model is represented as follows:

$$M + N = \quad L \quad + \quad R.$$
$$(t=1 \text{ capital}) \tag{1}$$

Both inventory and equity security can be reported at $n(1 + s_2)$ or $N(1 + s_2)$ if s_1 and s_2 were negative.

2. The historical cost/constant dollar model is represented as follows:

$$M + N (1 + p = L + R (1 + P) - p(M-L).$$
$$(t = 1 \text{ capital}) \quad \text{(income loss)} \tag{2}$$

3. The historical cost/constant dollars model based on the Ijiri's interpretation[19] is represented as follows:

$$M + N (1 + p) = L + \quad R(1 + p) \quad + \quad Np - Rp.$$
$$(t = 1 \text{ capital}) \quad \text{(income loss)} \tag{3}$$

4. The historical cost/constant dollars model based on the one-line adjustment[20,21,22] is represented as follows:

$$M + N = L + \quad R(1 + p) \quad - \quad RP.$$
$$(t = 1 \text{ capital}) \quad \text{(loss)} \tag{4}$$

5. The current cost/nominal dollars model[23,24] is represented as follows:

$$M + N(1 + s_1) = \quad L + R \quad + \quad Ns_1,$$
$$(t = 1 \text{ capital}) \quad \text{(income)} \tag{5}$$

allowing the disaggregation of the firm's replacement or current cost income into two elements: (a) the current operating profit (revenues less the current costs of earning the revenues) and (b) holding gains (Ns_1).

6. The current cost/constant dollars model is represented as follows:

$$M + N(1 + s_1) = L + \quad R(1 + p) \quad + N(s_1 - p) - p(M - L),$$
$$(t = 1 \text{ capital}) \quad \text{(income loss)} \tag{6}$$

where $N(s_1 - p)$ is the holding gain or loss resulting from the specific price level changes, and $p(m - L)$ is the purchasing power gain or loss resulting from the general price level changes.

7. The current cost/physical capital model is represented as follows:

$$M + N(1 + s_1) = L + \quad (R + Ns_1),$$
$$(t = 1 \text{ capital}) \tag{7}$$

where unlike the current cost/nominal dollars model, the holding gains are considered a capital maintenance adjustment rather than an element of income.

8. The current cost/physical capital model that incorporates purchasing power gains and losses on monetary items based on specific price changes[25] is represented as follows:

$$M + N(1 + s_1) = L + \quad (R + Rs_1) \quad - \quad s_1(M - L).$$
$$(t = 1 \text{ capital}) \quad (\text{income/loss}) \tag{8}$$

9. The current cost/physical capital model that incorporates both a specific price change adjustment and a "gearing" adjustment[26] is represented as follows:

$$M + N(1+s_1) = L + \left(R + Ns_1 \frac{R}{L+R} + Ms_1 \frac{R}{L+R} \right) +$$
$$(t = 1 \text{ capital})$$

$$\left(Ns_1 \frac{L}{L+R} - Ms_1 \frac{R}{L+R} \right),$$
$$(\text{income}) \tag{9}$$

where the gearing adjustment is calculated by allocating the holding gain (specific price increase) on nonmonetary assets between income and capital as follows:

Income portion $\dfrac{L}{L + R} (Ns_1)$

Capital maintenance portion $= \dfrac{R}{L + R} (Ns_1).$

10. The current exit value/nominal dollars is represented as follows:

$$M + N(1 + s_2) = \quad L + R \quad + \quad Ns_2.$$
$$(t = 1 \text{ capital}) \quad (\text{income}) \tag{10}$$

11. The current exit value/constant dollars model à la Sterling[27,28] is represented as follows:

$$M + N(1 + s_2) = L + \quad R(1 + p) \quad + N(s_2 - p) - p(M - L),$$
$$(t = 1 \text{ capital}) \qquad (\text{income}) \qquad\qquad (11)$$

where the nonmonetary assets are valued at exit prices instead of replacement costs.

12. The current exit value/constant dollars à la Chambers[29] is represented as follows:

$$M + N(1 + s_2 = L + \quad R(1 + p) \quad + N(s_2 - Rp).$$
$$(t = 1 \text{ capital}) \qquad (\text{income}) \qquad\qquad (12)$$

CRITIQUE OF THE TRUE INCOME/DEDUCTIVE PARADIGM

The deductive paradigm in accounting attempted to provide a normative theory of income determination and asset valuation through deductive reasoning rather than empirical and evidential analysis. The search was for what "should be" done rather than for "what is" in the normative approach did not proceed uncritizied. Various attempts were made to discredit its relevance. The criticism took at least two avenues: (a) the falsity of desirability and (b) the market for excuses.

The Falsity of Desirability

The falsity of desirability was the argument used to justify the need for researchers to examine the "what should be" question.[30,31] To make this point, Gonedes and Dopuch presented the two critical underfindings of the arguments that rely upon capital market efficiency in dealing with creative accounting procedures as follows:

A.1. Capital market efficiency, taken by itself, provides sufficient justification for using prices of (or rates of return on) firms' ownership shares in assessing the *desirability* of alternative accounting procedures or regulations.

A.2. Capital market efficiency, taken by itself, provides sufficient justification for using prices of (or rates of return on) firms' ownership shares in assessing the *effects* of alternative accounting procedures and regulations.[32]

Then they proceeded to conclude that assertion A.1 is logically false, whereas assertion A.2 is formed to have logical validity. In other words, desirability is logically false, whereas it is still possible to evaluate the effects of accounting procedures and techniques. This criteria of the normative approach and of the quest for "desirable" techniques may have been politically motivated. As stated by Tinker and Puxty:

Attempts to their manate the normative guests for assurance to "ought" and "should" questions were particularly opportune. They occurred at a time when practicing accountants were under attack for their role in a number of takeover and merger scandals. Positive accountancy offered them academic sanctuary from this barrage of public criticism by contending that, given the theoretical impossibility of distinguishing between good and bad accounting practices, the accounting industry could not be held reliable for the financial debackles in the late 1960's and early 1970's.[33]

The Market for Excuses

The deductive paradigm has also been criticized as an attempt by some authors to justify their preconceived notions. For example, Zeff reaches the following conclusions:

A study of the U.S. experience clearly shows that the academic literature has remarkably little impact on the writings of practioners and upon the accounting policies of the American Institute and SEC. Too often, accounting theory is involved more as a tactic to buttress one's preconceived notions, rather than as a genuine arbiter of contending views.[34]

This argument of accounting theory as a justification tool was also pursued by Watts and Zimmerman's suggestion that accounting theories prescribing specific accounting procedures are used by individuals seeking specific wealth transfers, compatible with a self-interest argument.[35] There is therefore a demand and supplies of theories or "excuses" that meet the interests of specific interest groups. No normative theory can explain the accounting standards because

1. Accounting standards are justified using the theory (excuse) of the vested interest groups which is benefited by the standard;
2. Vested interest groups use different theories (excuses) for difference issues; and
3. Different vested interest groups prevail or different issues.[36]

This raises the question of the general usefulness of self-interest-based normative theories in justifying accounting standards. Watts and Zimmerman conclude that justification is very possible in many cases. They share that "while a self-interest theory can explain accounting standards, such a theory will not be used to justify accounting standards because self-interest theories are politically unpalatable. As a consequence, *not only is there no generally accepted accounting theory to justify accounting standards there will never be one.*[37]

Logically, fallacies were detected in the manner "the market for excuses" was developed. They are as follows:

Fallacy number 1: Argument from Ignorance

Researchers commit this fallacy whenever they attempt to place the burden of disproof on the reader, and then argue that the reader's inability to disprove the assertion is itself proof of the assertion. . . .

Fallacy number 2: Post Hoc Ergo Ropter Hoc

This fallacy is based on the false assumption that because two events stand in temporal succession they are therefore related. . . .

Fallacy number 3: Confusion of Condition and Cause

The fallacy arises whenever a researcher confuses conditions and cause or regards them as identical.

Fallacy number 4: Fallacy of the Declarative Question

The fallacy consists of the use of a declarative statement about what will be found in past events.[38]

CONCLUSIONS

The true income/deductive paradigm focuses on the development of theory based on logical reasoning and on a concept of true and ideal income to be constructed in a way that is relevant for external and internal reporting. The contributions to this paradigm rely on specific environmental assumptions to derive their theory or to justify their idea of true income. What results is a plethora of alternative asset valuation and income determination models, each with its own arsenal of arguments and rationalizations. The paradigm that seems to regain some vigor in a period of inflation is generally not a very popular one in academic research. The loss of primacy seems to be permanent.

NOTES

1. W. A. Paton, *Accounting Theory* (New York: The Ronald Press, 1922); J. B. Canning, *The Economics of Accountancy* (New York: The Ronald Press, 1929).

2. Paton, *Accounting Theory,* 8.

3. Ibid., 5–8.

4. Kenneth MacNeal, *Truth of Accounting* (Philadelphia: University of Pennsylvania Press, 1939), 295.

5. Sidney S. Alexander, "Income Measurement in a Dynamic Economy," in *Five Monographs on Business Income* (New York: Study Group on Business Income, American Institute of Certified Public Accountants, 1950), 159.

6. Adam Smith, *An Inquiry into the Nature and Causes of the Wealth of Nations* (London: George Routledge, 1890).

7. Irving Fisher, *The Nature of Capital and Income* (New York: Macmillan, 1912), 38.

8. E. Lindhal, *Die Gerechtigkeit der Besteuerung* (London, 1919), Translated in R. A. Musgrave, and A. Peacock, *Classics in the Theory of Public Finance* (New York: Macmillan, 1958)

9. J. R. Hicks, *Value and Capital* (Oxford: The Clarendon Press, 1946).

10. Alexander, "Income Measurement in a Dynamic Economy," 15.

11. Robert R. Sterling, "Relevant Financial Reporting in an Age of Price Changes," *Journal of Accounting* (February 1975): 42–51; S. Basu and J. R. Hanna, *Inflation Accounting: Alternatives, Implementation Issues, and Some Empirical Evidence* (Hamilton, Ontario: The Society of Management Accountants of Canada, 1977).

12. R. J. Chambers, "NOD, COG, and PuPu: See How Inflation Teases," *Journal of Accountancy* (September 1975): 61.

13. Ibid.

14. Y. Ijiri, "The Price Level Restatement and its Dual Interpretation," *The Accounting Review* (April 1967): 227–43.

15. R. J. Chambers, "The Use and Misuse of a Notation: The History of an Idea," *Abacus* (December 1978): 122–44.

16. A. Barton, *An Analysis of Business Income Concepts,* ICRA Occasional Paper No. 7, (London: University of Lancaster; International Center for Research in Accounting, 1975), 50.

17. Lanny Chasteen, "A Taxonomy of Price Change Models," *The Accounting Review* (July 1984): 515–23.

18. Ibid.

19. Ijiri, "The Price Level Restatement and Its Dual Interpretation," 227–43.

20. Chambers, "The Use and Misuse of a Notation: A History of an Idea."

21. P. Grady, "Purchasing Power Accounting," *Price Waterhouse Review* (Fall 1975): 3–5.

22. S. Agrawal, and K. Rosenweig, "One Line Adjustment Methods of Accounting for the Effects of Inflation," *Collected Abstracts of the AAA Annual Meeting* (Sarasota, FL: American Accounting Association, 1982), 29.

23. E. Edwards, and P. W. Bell, *The Theory and Measurement of Business Income* (Berkeley: University of California Press, 1961).

24. R. A. Samuelson, "Should Replacement-Cost Changes Be Included in Income?" *The Accounting Review* (April 1980): 254–68.

25. R. Gynther, *Accounting for Price Level Changes* (Oxford: Pergamon Press, 66).

26. "Statement of Standard Accounting Practice No 16: Current Cost Accounting," *Accountancy* (April 1980): 99–100.

27. R. R. Sterling, *Theory of the Measurement of Enterprise Income* (Lawrence: University of Kansas Press, 1970).

28. Sterling, "Relevant Financial Reporting in an Age of Price Changes," 42–51.

29. R. J. Chambers, "NOD, COG and PuPu: See How Inflation Teases," *Journal of Accountancy* (September 1975): 56–62.

30. Nicholas Dopuch, "Empirical vs Non-Empirical Research: Balancing Theory and Practice," in *1979 Accounting Research Convention,* Jonathan Davies, ed. (Tuscaloosa: University of Alabama Press, 1980): 67–83.

31. Carl Nelson, "A Priori Research in Accounting," in *Accounting Research 1960– 70: A Critical Evaluation,* N. Dopuch and L. Revsine, eds. (Urbana: University of Illinois, 1973).

32. N. Gonedes, and N. Dopuch, "Capital Market Equilibrium, Information Production, and Selecting Accounting Techniques: Theoretical Framework and Review of Empirical Work," *Studies on Financial Accounting Objectives,* supplement to the *Journal of Accounting Research* (1974): 50.

33. Tony Tinker, and Tony Puxty, *Policing Accounting Knowledge: The Market for Excuses Affair* (Princeton, NJ: Markus Wiener Pub., 1995), 6–7.

34. Stephen A. Zeff, "Comments on Accounting Principles—How They Are Developed," in *Institutional Issues in Public Accounting,* Robert R. Sterling, ed. (Lawrence, KS: Scholars Books Co., 1974), 177.

35. Ross L. Watts and Jerold L. Zimmerman, "The Demand for and the Supply of Accounting Theories: The Market for Excuses," *The Accounting Review* (April 1979): 273–306.

36. Ibid.

37. Ibid.

38. Germaine Boer, and Ross Moseley, "Some Comments on Logical Reasoning and the Market for Excuses," in *Policing Accounting Knowledge: The Market for Excuses Affair,* Tony Tinker and Tony Pustay, eds. (Princeton, NJ: Marcus Wiener Pub., 1995), 92–97.

REFERENCES

Basu, S., and J. R. Hanna. *Inflation Accounting: Alternatives, Implementation Issues, and Some Empirical Evidence.* Hamilton, Ontario: The Society of Management Accountants of Canada, 1977.

Canning, J. B. *The Economics of Accountancy.* New York: The Ronald Press, 1929.

Chambers, R. J. *Accounting, Evaluation, and Economic Behavior.* Englewood Cliffs, NJ: Prentice-Hall, 1966.

Chambers, R. J. "NOD, COG, and PuPu: See How Inflation Teases." *Journal of Accountancy* (September 1975): 56–62.

Edwards, E. O., and P. W. Bell. *The Theory and Measurement of Business Income.* Berkeley: University of California Press, 1961.

Gynther, R. S. "Capital Maintenance, Price Changes, and Profit Determination." *The Accounting Review* (October 1970): 712–30.

Hanna, J. R. *Accounting-Income Models: An Application and Evaluation. Special Study No. 8.* Toronto: The Society of Management Accountants of Canada, July 1974.

Kerr, Jean St. G. "Three Concepts of Business Income." In *An Income Approach to Accounting Theory* edited by S. Davidson et al., 40–48. Englewood Cliffs, NJ: Prentice-Hall, 1964.

Louderback, J. G. "Projectability as a Criterion for Income Determination Methods." *The Accounting Review* (April 1971): 298–305.

Macneal, Kenneth. *Truth of Accounting.* Philadelphia: University of Pennsylvania Press, 1939.

Moonitz, Maurice. *Accounting Research Study No. 1, The Basic Postulates of Accounting.* New York: American Institute of Certified Public Accountants, 1961.

Parker, P. W., and P. M. D. Gibbs. "Accounting for Inflation: Recent Proposals and Their Effects." *Journal of the Institute of Actuaries* (December 1974): 1–10.

Paton, W. A. *Accounting Theory.* New York: The Ronald Press, 1922.

Revsine, L., and J. J. Weygandt. "Accounting for Inflation: The Controversy." *Journal of Accountancy* (October 1974): 72–78.

Rosen, L. S. *Current-Value Accounting and Price-Level Restatements.* Toronto: Canadian Institute of Chartered Accountants, 1972.

Rosenfield, Paul. "Accounting for Inflation: A Field Test." *Journal of Accountancy* (June 1969): 45–50.

Rosenfield, Paul. "The Confusion between General Price-Level Restatement and Current-Value Accounting." *Journal of Accountancy* (October 1972): 63–68.

Rosenfield, Paul. "CPP Accounting: Relevance and Interpret." *Journal of Accountancy* (August 1975): 42–51.

Sprouse, R. T., and Maurice Moonitz. *Accounting Research Study No. 3, A Tentative Set of Broad Accounting Principles for Business Enterprises.* New York: American Institute of Certified Public Accountants, 1962.

Sterling, Robert R. *Theory of Measurement of Enterprise Income.* Lawrence: University Press of Kansas, 1970.

Sterling, Robert R. "Relevant Financial Reporting in an Age of Price Changes." *Journal of Accountancy* (February 1975): 42–51.

Sweeney, Henry W. *Stabilized Accounting.* New York: Harper, 1936.

Watts, Ron L., and Jerold L. Zimmerman. "The Demand for and the Supply of Accounting, Theories: The Market for Excuses." *The Accounting Review* (April 1979): 273–306.

Wolk, H. I. "An Illustration of Four Price-Level Approaches to Income Measurement." In J. Don Edwards (ed.), *Accounting Education: Problems and Prospects* edited by Don Edwards, 415–23. Sarasota, FL: American Accounting Association, 1974.

4 The Decision Usefulness/ Decision Model Paradigm

INTRODUCTION

The decision usefulness/decision model paradigm focuses on the determination and testing of decision models that can be used to explain and/or predict diverse economic events of importance to users of accounting information. It is also known as the predictive approach. One general objective of accounting is to provide information that can be used to explain and predict economic events. In the perspective of the predictive approach to the formulation of an accounting theory, alternative accounting measurements should be evaluated on the basis of their ability to explain and/or predict economic or business events. In general, the predictive value criterion is a probability relationship between economic events of interest to the decision maker and relevant prediction variables derived in part from accounting information. Its application to various economic events has been successful and shows promise in providing a strong paradigm.

EXEMPLARS

Chambers was one of the first to point to the decision usefulness/ decision model paradigm:

It is therefore a corollary of the assumption of rational management that there shall be an information-providing system; such a system is required both as a basis for decisions and as a basis for reviewing the consequences of decisions. . . .A formal information-providing system would conform with two general propositons. The first is a condition of all logical discourse. The system should be logically consistent; no rule or process can be permitted that is contrary to any other rule or process. . . . The second propositon arises from the use of accounting statements as a basis for making decisions of practical consequence. The information yielded by any such system should be relevant to the kinds of decision making of which it is expected to facilitate.[1]

Chambers does not pursue this view of the decision usefulness/decision model paradigm. He prefers to base an accounting theory on the usefulness of "current cash equivalents," rather than on the decision models of specific user groups. Similarly, May[2] offers a list of uses of financial accounts without explicitly employing the decision model approach to the formulation of an accounting theory. According to May, financial accounts are used as

1. a report of stewardship,

2. a basis of fiscal policy,

3. a criterion of the legality of dividends,

4. a guide to wise dividend activity,

5. a basis for the granting of credit,

6. information for prospective investors,

7. a guide to the value of investments already made,

8. an aid to governmental supervision,

9. a basis for price or rate regulation, and

10. a basis for taxation.

In fact, the works of Beaver, Kennelly, and Voss and of Sterling[3] can be considered true exemplars of the decision usefulness/decision model paradigm. Beaver, Kennelly, and Voss examine the origin of the predictive-ability criterion, its relationship to the facilitation of decision making, and the potential difficulties associated with its implementation. According to the predictive-ability criterion, alternative methods of accounting measurement are evaluated in terms of their ability to predict economic events: "The measure with the greatest predictive power with respect to a given event is considered to be the 'best' method for that particular purpose.''[4]

The predictive-ability criterion is presented as a purposive criterion in the sense that accounting data ought to be evaluated in terms of their purpose or use, which is generally accepted in accounting to be the facilitation of decision making. The predictive-ability criterion is assumed to be relevant, even when applied in conjunction with a low specification of the decision model:

Because prediction is an inherent part of the decision process, knowledge of the predictive ability of alternative measures is a prerequisite to the use of the decision-making criterion. At the same time, it permits tentative conclusions regarding alternative measurements, subject to subsequent confirmation when the decision models eventually become specified. The use of predictive ability as a purposive criterion is more than merely consistent with accounting's decision-making orientation. It can provide a body of research that will bring accounting closer to its goal of evaluation in terms of decision-making criterion.[5]

Sterling develops criteria to be used in evaluating the various measures of wealth and income. Given the conflicting viewpoints about the objectives of accounting reports, Sterling chooses usefulness as the overriding criterion of a measurement method, emphasizing its importance over such requirements as objectivity and verifiability.[6]

Due to the diversity of decision makers and the inherent economic and physical impossibility of providing all of the information that users want, Sterling opts for usefulness as the relevant criterion of decision models. ''The basis for selection that I prefer is to supply information for rational decision models. The modifier 'rational' is defined to mean those decision models that are most likely to allow decision makers to achieve their goals.''[7]

In summary, an accounting system should be designed to provide relevant information to rational decision models. The accounting system cannot supply all the information desired by all decision makers and, therefore, we must decide to exclude some kind of information and to include other kinds. Restricting the decision models to rational ones permits the exclusion of a raft of data based on the whims of decision makers. It permits us to concentrate on those kinds that have been demonstrated to be effective in achieving the decision maker's goals.[8]

IMAGE OF THE SUBJECT MATTER

To those who adopt the decision usefulness/decision model paradigm, the basic subject matter is the usefulness of accounting information to decision models. Information relevant to a decision model or criterion is determined and then implemented by choosing the best accounting alternative. Usefulness to a decision model is equated with relevance to a decision model. For example, Sterling states: "If a property is specified by a decision model, then a measure of that property is relevant (to that decision model). If a property is not specified by a decision model, then a measure of that property is irrelevant (to that decision model)."[9]

The paradigm utilizes the criterion of predictive ability in which the choice among different accounting options depends on the ability of a particular method to predict events that are of interest to users. More specifically, "the measure with the greatest predictive power with respect to a given event is considered to be the 'best' method for that particular purpose."[10]

The criterion of predictive ability follows from the emphasis on relevance as the primary criterion of financial reporting. Relevance connotes a concern with information about future events. Relevant data, therefore, are characterized by an ability to predict future events.

The criterion of predictive ability is also well accepted in the natural and physical sciences as a method of choosing among competing hypotheses. Beaver, Kennelly, and Voss,[11] by showing that alternative accounting measures have the properties of competing hypotheses, have rationalized the use of predictive ability in accounting. An obvious advantage of the predictive approach is that it enables us to evaluate alternative accounting measurements empirically and to make a clear choice on the basis of a discriminatory criterion.

Predictive ability is also a purposive criterion that can easily be related to one purpose of gathering accounting data—the facilitation of decision making. The accounting literature has always held that the accounting data must facilitate decision making. As soon as the facilitation of decision making is introduced, however, two problems arise. First, it is difficult to identify and define all the decision models employed by accounting information users, because most of the models are descriptive rather than normative. Second, even when the decision model is well defined, a criterion for the choice of relevant information is missing. Intended to resolve this second problem, the criterion of predictive ability enables us to determine which accounting measure produces the better decisions. Note here the fundamental distinction between prediction and decision. It is possible to predict without making a decision, but it is not possible to make a decision without a prediction.

It appears that the predictive method may suffer from a failure to identify and define the decision models of users and types of events that ought to be predicted. Even if a given theoretical structure were developed to identify items or events that ought to be predicted, the problem remains of specifying a theory that will link those events to the accounting measures in terms of an explanatory and predictive relationship.

THEORIES

Time-Series Analysis

Time-series analysis is a structural methodological approach by which temporal statistical dependencies in a data set can be examined.[12] Past values of a single data set are used to give clues regarding future realizations of the same data set. Time-series analysis research focuses mainly on (1) time-series properties of reported earnings and (2) prediction issues in time-series analysis. Each is examined next.

Time-Series Properties of Reported Earnings

Knowledge of the properties of reported earnings can enhance their information content, predictive ability, and feedback value. The application of statistical procedures to the study of the time-series properties of accounting variables stems from the thesis that accounting variables can best be described as random variables. The research has examined both the behavior of reported earnings and models that describe quarterly earnings:[13]

1. With respect to the *annual earnings series,* findings present a *moving average process,* a *submartingale,* or one of two processes: *martingale* or *moving average regressive.* What results is a continuous debate over which time-series model(s) should be applied to observed accounting numbers. Fortunately, a new line of research may provide some closure on the debate. It consists of first modeling the observed time series, and then using the method to test the fit of the derived models.[14,15] In any case, this type of research would be of more use and more interest to policy makers if it were applied to determine the effect of accounting policy changes on probabilistic models of earnings behavior.[16]

2. With respect to the *quarterly earnings series,* findings seem to show that the quarterly earnings process is not totally random in character. It appears to follow an *autoregressive process* characterized by seasonal and quarter-to-quarter components.[17,18]

Predicting Future Accounting Earnings

The reported earning number is an aggregate number in two dimensions: one dimension is temporal in that annual earnings are an aggregate of four individual quarterly earnings; one dimension is compositional in that annual earnings are an aggregate of time-equivalent subseries, such as sales and cost of goods sold.[19] Accounting time-series-based research has considered the predictive ability of past annual earnings, past quarterly earnings, and earnings components:

1. With respect to the use of *past annual earnings* to predict future earnings, studies show that sophisticated autoregressive (or moving average) processes developed using Box and Jenkins' procedures do not appear to forecast significantly better than the random walk model.[20,21]

2. With respect to the use of *past quarterly earnings* to predict future earnings, studies show a better predictive ability of the models of quarterly earnings compared with annual models and more comprehensive Box and Jenkins' "individually identified" model.[22]

3. With respect to the use of *earnings components* to predict future earnings, evidence is in favor of good forecasting ability of disaggregated sales and earnings data[23] but this is not demonstrated for models based on components such as interest expense, depreciation expense, and operating income before depreciation.[24] More work needs to be done before closure can be reached on the subject.

Distress Prediction

The most relevant applications of the predictive approach are attempts made to seek empirically validated characteristics that distinguish financially distressed from nondistressed firms. Both univariate and multivariate models have been used to help an auditor determine when a firm is approaching default. Scott provides the following brief overview of the process:

Most bankruptcy-prediction models are derived using a paired-sample technique. Part of the sample contains data from firms that eventually failed; the other part contains contemporaneous data from firms that did not fail. A number of plausible and traditional financial ratios are calculated from financial statements that were published before failure. Next, the researcher searches for a formula based either on a single ratio or a combination of ratios, that best discriminates between firms that eventually failed and firms that remained solvent. A careful researcher also tests the resulting formula both on the original sample and a holdout sample that was not used to derive the formula.[25]

In Beaver's univariate study,[26] which tested a set of accounting ratios to predict corporate failure, the most noticeable result was the superior predictive ability of cash flow to total debt ratios, followed by net income to total assets. Among the multivariate studies, Altman's use of a multiple discriminant analysis for the prediction of corporate failure resulted in a discriminant model that contained five variables: (1) working capital/total assets (liquidity), (2) retained earnings/total assets (age of firm and cumulative profitability), (3) earnings before interest and taxes/total assets (profitability), (4) market value of equity/book value of debt (financial structure), and (5) sales/total assets (capital turnover). The known discriminant analysis model, by E. I. Altman, is as follows:

$$Z_i = 1.2x_1 + 1.4x_2 + 3.3x_3 + 0.6x_4 + 1.0x_5,$$

where

$x_1 =$ (current assets − current liabilities)/total assets,

$x_2 =$ retained earnings/total assets,

$x_3 =$ earnings before interest and taxes/total assets,

$x_4 =$ market value of preferred and common equity/book value liabilities, and

$x_5 =$ sales/total assets.[27]

The discriminant rule used is that any firm with a Z score below 1.8 is considered to be a prime candidate for bankruptcy and a Z score above 2.99 is a safe candidate. Because some firms do not have publicly traded securities, Altman's reestimation of the model, with x_{4i} as the book value of preferred and common equity/book value of total liabilities, was as follows:[28]

$$Z_1 = 0.717x_1 + 0.847x_2 + 3.10x_3 + 0.420x_4 + 0.998x_5.$$

The prediction rule was that any company with a Z score below 1.20 was a candidate for bankruptcy and with a Z score above 2.90 was a safe candiate.

The success of these models led Altman and associates to develop a commercial model: THE ZETA CREDIT RISK.[29] It is reported to include the following seven variables:

1. size as total assets;
2. profitability as earnings before interest and taxes/total assets;
3. debt service as earnings before interest and taxes/total interest payments;
4. liquidity as current ratio;
5. cumulative profitability as retained earnings/total assets;
6. market capitalization as five-year coverage of market value of common equity/five-year average of market value of total capital (includes preferred stock, long-term debt, and capitalized leases); and
7. earnings stability as a normalized measure of the standard error of estimate around a ten-year trend in the overall profitability table

Because it is a commercial product, the coefficients of each variable have not been disclosed. However, the promotional literature provided the ZETA Services includes the following description:

ZETA is a risk evaluation model developed by ZETA Services Inc. For the development of ZETA, risk was defined as the inability of a company to meet its obligations. The ZETA SCORE tells a user how much a company resembles firms that have recently filed bankruptcy petitions. We are not interested in bankruptcy per se but we feel that it is an unequivocal credit standard. Prior to bankruptcy, companies have a strong tendency to pass common and preferred dividends, go into technical defaults and engage in forced of assets, all to the detriment of securities values. The ZETA model does not forecast failure or nonfailure and ZETA Service Inc. did not design it to do so. Rather, it compares a company's operations and financial characteristics to those of over 50 firms which have already failed. The test sample [used to develop the model] was composed of 53 industrial corporations which filed for bankruptcy or were taken over by their banks. No banks, finance companies, real estate companies or railroads were included. All firms were required to have at least $20 million in reported assets in the two years prior to bankruptcy. These firms were paired with other randomly selected, nonbankrupt firms in similar industries. The ZETA SCORE is a result of a linear combination of all seven variables (weighted by the discriminant analysis technique) plus a constant. Zero was the dividing line between nonfailing (positive scores) and failing firms (negatives scores).

In addition to the Z-score model and the ZETA model, we should also cite the gambler's ruin model.[30,31] The question remains how useful these models are internationally. The Z-score model was applied successfully to Japanese bankruptcy cases, with a "Japanese cut-off score" of 1.0, lower than Altman's score of 1.8. In addition, C. J. Ko developed a unique Z-score model of the following form:[32]

$$Z_j = 0.868x_1 + 0.198x_2 - 0.048x_3 + 0.436x_4 + 0.115x_5,$$

where

x_1 = earnings before interest and taxes/sales,

x_2 = inventory turnover two years prior/inventory turnover three years prior,

x_3 = standard error of net income (four years),

x_4 = working capital/total debt,

x_5 = market value of equity/total debt, and

Z_j = Z score for the Japanese model.

The model yielded an 82.9 percent correct classification rate.

The Altman Z-score model with modifications on x_2 and x_4 were used in the Brazilian context.[33] Calculations for x_2 are

$$X_2 = \frac{\text{total equity} - \text{capital contributed by shareholders}}{\text{total assets}},$$

and x_4 was computed as book value of equity divided by total liabilities. Two equations are derived with one excluding x_1 and one excluding x_2. They are as follows:

$$Z_1 = 1.44 + 4.03x_2 + 2.25x_3 + 0.14x_4 + 0.425x_5,$$

and

$$Z_2 = -1.84 - 0.51x_1 + 6.23x_3 + 0.71x_4 + 0.56x_5.$$

The vertical cutoff score was chosen to be zero, with any firm with a score lower than zero defined as a potentially bankrupt firm. The failure prediction models were provided by A. D. Castagna and Z. P. Mato-besy,[34] for Australia, and R. M. Kinglit[35] and E. I. Altman[36] and M.T.R. Lavallee, for Canada and France. Altman and Lavallee's model was as follows:

$$Z_c = -1.626 + 0.234x_1 - 0.531x_2 + 1.002x_3 + 0.972x_4 + 0.612x_5,$$

where

Z_c = Canadian Z score,

x_1 = sales/total assets,

x_2 = total debt/total assets,

x_3 = current assets/current liabilities,

x_4 = net profits after tax/total debt, and

x_5 = rate of growth-rate of asset growth.

Two prediction models are used for the case of the Netherlands. J. B. Bilderbeek's five-ratio model is as follows:

$$Z_{nb} = 0.45 - 5.03x_1 - 1.57x_2 - 4.55x_3 + 0.17x_4 + 0.15x_5,$$

where

Z_{nb} = Z score for the Netherlands,

x_1 = retained earnings/total assets,

x_2 = added value/total assets,

x_3 = accounts payable/sales,

x_4 = sales/total assets, and

x_5 = net profit/equity.[37]

The model yielded a 70 to 80 percent accuracy score for one year before bankruptcy and remained stable during a five-year period preceding bankruptcy.

The Van Fredrikslust model is as follows:

$$Z_{nf} = 0.5293 + 0.4488x_1 + 0.2863x_2,$$

where

Z_{nf} = Z score for the Netherlands,

x_1 = liquidity ratio for internal coverage, and

x_2 = profitability ratio as rate of return on equity.[38]

The prediction of bankruptcy in France included attempts by Altman and associates,[39] P. O. Bontemps,[40] Yves Collongues,[41] and F. R. Mader.[42,43] The usefulness of these models are best summarized as follows: "The application of statistical credit scoring techniques in the French environment appears to be problematic but the potential remains. One problem usually is the quality of the data and the representativeness of it. But this is a problem in all countries and is not unique to France."[44]

P. F. Weibel used cluster analysis to arrive at six ratios that best predict bankruptcy in the Swiss case.[45] G. T. Wenrich's factor analysis[46,47,48] and K. B. Beerman's discriminant analysis[49] were used in the German case. Other German efforts include the one by G. L. Gebhardt.[50]

These models cover selected developed countries and omit completely most of the Asian countries and all of the developing world. It is clear that a lot remains to be done in the area of business failure models internationally.

The major limitation of the research on distress prediction arises from the absence of an articulated economic theory of financial distress. Witness the following statement made by Ohlson:

This paper presents some empirical results of a study predicting corporate failure as evidenced by the event of bankruptcy. . . . One might ask a basic and possibly embarrassing question: Why forecast bankruptcy? This is a difficult question, and no answer or justification is given here. . . . Most of the analysis should simply be viewed as descriptive statistics—which may, to some extent, include estimated prediction error-rates—and no "theories" of bankruptcy or usefulness of financial ratios are tested.[51]

Despite the absence of an economic theory of distress, the discriminant-analysis-based models can be very helpful in a variety of practical decision contexts. For example, "(i) they can process information quicker and at a lower cost than do individual loan officers and bank examiners, (ii) they can process information in a more consistent manner, and (iii) they can facilitate decisions about loss function being made at more senior levels of management."[52]

Various limitations are associated with research on corporate distress prediction.[53] The first limitation arises from the absence of a general economic theory of financial distress that can be used to specify the variables to be included in the models.

A second limitation relates to the different definition of the event of interest. All of the studies examined observable events, such as legal bankruptcy, loan default, and omission of preferred dividend rather than financial distress per se. Finally, the results of the superior predictive ability of some accounting ratios may not be generalized to permit the formulation of an accounting theory based on consistent predictors of corporate failure.

Prediction of Bond Premiums and Bond Ratings

The following four factors are assumed to create bond risks and consequently to affect the yields to maturity of bonds:

1. *Default risk:* the inability of a firm to meet part of or all bond interest and principal payments.

2. *Marketability risk:* the possibility having to dispose of the bonds at a loss.

3. *Purchasing-power risk:* the loss incurred by bondholders due to changes in the general price level.

4. *Interest-rate risk:* the effect of unexpected changes in the interest rates on the market value of bonds.

Fisher examined the power of a four-factor model to explain differences in the risk premiums of industrial corporate bonds.[54] The following four variables are included in the model:

1. earnings variability, measured as the coefficient of variation on after-tax earnings of the most recent nine years;

2. solvency or reliability in meeting obligations, measured as the length of time since the latest of the following events occurred: the firm emerged from bankruptcy, or a compromise was made in which creditors settled for less than 100 percent of their claims;

3. capital structure, measured by the market value of the firm's equity/par value of its debt; and

4. total value of the market value of the firm's bonds.

The first three variables represent different proxies for default risk; the fourth variable represents a proxy for marketable risk. The four variables account for 75 percent of the variation in the risk premiums on bonds.

Firms resort to financial leverage through debt financing as a way of financing growth more readily and more efficiently. For firms to be able to accomplish this financing task readily and efficiently, their bond issues need to have the attractive investment features of profitability, stability, and liquidity, to name only a few. Above all, the investors need to assume that the issuers will be able to fulfill their obligations. Fortunately, the market provides the investor one way of judging the quality of a bond through the unbiased opinions of informed and experienced professionals working for the bond-rating agencies. These professionals rate bonds by assigning to them known bond ratings designed essentially to rank the issues in order of the probability of default, that is, the inability to meet interest obligations, sinking-fund payments, or repayments of principal. This is reflected in the wording used by the agencies to describe what a rating represents: "Ratings are designed exclusively for the purpose of grading bonds according to investment qualities"[55] and "A Standard & Poor's corporate or municipal debt rating is a current assessment of the credit worthiness of obligor with respect to a specific obligation."[56]

The functions of these ratings have been to provide a superior low-cost source of information on the ability of firms to make timely repayments of principle and interest. The implications are as follows. First, they are intended to be an indicator of the probability of default or loss of market value that may be experienced by firms facing degrees of financial difficulties. Second, they have been found to be good predictors of default and of the magnitude of the losses at default. Third, the bond ratings were found to be consistent with the systematic risk of securities.

The bond ratings issued by the three ratings agencies in the United States (Fitch Investors' Service, Moody's Investors Service, and Standard & Poor's Corporation) are judgments about the investment quality of long-term obligations. Each rating is an aggregation of default probability. Despite the claims by these agencies that their ratings cannot be empirically explained and predicted, various studies have attempted to develop models to predict the rating categories assigned to industrial bonds,[57] electric utility bonds,[58] and general-obligation municipal bonds.[59]

All of these studies tried in the first stage to develop a bond-ratings model from an experimental sample of bond ratings based on a selected list of accounting and financial variables, using either regression, dichotomous probability function, or multiple discriminant or multivariate probit analysis. In the second stage, the obtained model was applied to a holdout sample to test the predictive ability of the model. Despite the general success of such models, some unresolved problems may limit their usefulness.

1. With one exception, these models suffer from the lack of an explicit and testable statement of what a bond rating represents and the absence of an economic rationale for the variables included.

2. None of these models account for possible differences in the accounting treatments used by individual companies.

3. The studies among the regression models treat the dependent variable as if it were on an interval scale. In other words, the assumption is that the risk differential between an AAA and an AA bond is the same as the risk differential between a BB bond and a B bond.

4. With one exception, all the studies confused ex ante predictive power with ex post discrimination. When a given discriminant model is developed on the basis of a sample A_1 and tested on a time coincident sample A_2, the authors claim predictive success but actually demonstrate only ex post discriminant success. Testing on A_2 implies only that the inference about the importance of the independent variables in the discriminant function is warranted. Prediction requires intertemporal validation. Ex ante prediction means using the discriminant model developed based on the basis of A_2 from time dimension t_1 on a sample B from time dimension $t + 1$.[60]

Various recent bond-rating models have shown the importance of profit-based measures as well as other measures of financial fitness in the explanation and prediction of bond ratings. For example, Belkaoui developed a discriminant-analysis-based bond-rating model based on the following variables:

x_1 = total assets;

x_2 = total debt;

x_3 = long-term debt/total invested capital;

x_4 = short-term debt/total invested capital;

x_5 = current assets/current liabilities;

x_6 = fixed charge coverage ratio;

x_7 = five-year cash flow divided by a five-year sum of (1) capital expenditure, (2) change in inventories during most recent five years, and (3) common dividends;

x_8 = stock price/common equity per share; and

x_9 = subordination (0–1 dummy variable), 1 if the bond being rated is subordinated.[61]

Six discriminant functions are proposed to explain or predict bond ratings, including the following for an AAA rating:

$$Z = -31.6004 + 0.000737x_1 + 0.000119x_2 + 0.44234x_3 + 0.62823x_4 \\ + 7.26898x_5 + 0.68425x_6 + 0.06102x_7 + 0.01802x_8 + 10.26302x_9.$$

For an AA rating:

$$Z = -26.0425 + 0.000431x_1 - 0.000174x_2 + 0.49299x_3 + 0.67906x_4 \\ + 6.80279x_5 + 0.54641x_6 + 0.06600x_7 + 0.01687x_8 + 9.7664x_9.$$

For an A rating:

$$Z = -26.1304 + 0.00269x_1 - 0.000149x_2 + 0.58069x_3 + 0.60516x_4 \\ + 7.83642x_5 + 0.48850x_6 + 0.06777x_7 + 0.00809x_8 + 8.18782x_9.$$

For a BBB rating:

$$Z = -29.3824 + 0.000250x_1 - 0.000233x_2 + 0.71530x_4 + 0.79864x_4 \\ + 8.5763x_5 + 0.50766x_6 + 0.0711x_7 + 0.00235x_8 + 4.27079x_9.$$

For a BB rating:

$$Z = -31.3397 + 0.000265x_1 - 0.000295x_2 + 0.76589x_3 + 0.80544x_4 \\ + 9.15411x_5 + 0.48010x_6 + 0.05952x_7 + 0.00705x_8 + 1.69732x_9.$$

For a B rating:

$$Z = -34.8229 + 0.000242x_1 - 0.000357x_2 + 0.85499x_3 + 0.84459x_4 \\ + 9.24043x_5 + 0.49208x_6 + 0.06970x_7 + 0.00099x_8 - 1.73660x_9.$$

The classification method consists simply of using the discriminant functions on new data as follows. For each firm that needs to be classified into a bond-rating category, compute the classification score for each rating category from the discriminant function coefficients (multiply the data by the coefficients and add the constant term). The firm is then classified into the group for which the classification score is the highest.

Corporate Restructuring Behavior

The prominence of takeovers all over the world has prompted several studies. R. N. Marris's study of managerial capitalism showed that the companies acquired are those that are undervalued by the market.[62] Similarly, Michael Gort supported a related hypothesis that the level of takeover activity varies with the degree of share undervaluation in the market.[63] This type of analysis relies heavily on a meaningful share price valuation model. More explicitly, the parameters measuring the relationship between the market prices of shares and relevant factors should be reasonably constant. M. D. Bonford found that the market will sometimes attach different weights to those factors.[64] Similarly, J. T. Tzoannos and J. M. Samuels, in experimenting with a number of valuation models, found that the variables, whether explaining earning yield or dividend yield, were not significant.[65] Thus the type of analysis based on share valuation might lack external validity.

Because of the difficulties of appraising the "true" value of a share, most of the other studies have attempted to identify the financial characteristics of the acquired firms. Accordingly, R. J. Chambers examined the undervaluation of net assets as a result of conservative accounting policies.[66] The undervaluation of net assets was seen as a key factor for predicting takeovers. These findings were later contested by R. A. Taussig and S. L. Hayes based on the absence of a control group in the Chambers study.[67] They rejected the hypothesis of a statistically significant relationship between understated asset values and the possibility of a takeover. Both studies were univariate, however, and considered only voluntary mergers. The first limitation with regard to the univariate nature of the analysis was corrected by J. S. Vance.[68] The second limitation was first corrected by various studies that considered companies acquired through voluntary mergers in England and the United States.[69,70,71]

In fact, the corporate restructuring internationally also included mergers, consolidations, divestitures, going private transactions, leverage buyouts (LBOs), and spinoffs, aimed at either (a) maximizing the market value of equities held by existing shareholders or (b) maximizing the welfare of existing management.[72,73] The modes of takeovers, however, are most often the subject of empirical analysis. The analyses taking place in the U.S. context include several studies.[74,75,76,77,78]

Palepu's multivariate logit model was based on the following eleven variables:

x_1 = average excess security return per day over the prior four years,

x_2 = average market adjusted security return per day over the prior four years,

x_3 = 0/1 dummy variable with 1 for low growth/high liquidity/low leverage combinations and 0 for all other combinations and high growth/low liquidity/high leverage combinations and 0 for all other combinations,

x_4 = average annual sales growth rate over the prior three years,

x_5 = ratio of net liquid assets to total assets averaged over the prior three years,

x_6 = ratio of long-term debt to total equity averaged over the prior three years,

x_7 = 0/1 dummy variable with 1 if there is at least one acquisition in a firm's four-digit SIC industry in the prior year,

x_8 = net book assets of firm ($ millions),

x_9 = ratio of firm's market price to book value of common equity in the prior year,

x_{10} = ratio of firm's market price to book value of common equity in the prior year, and

x_{11} = ratio of firm's market price to earnings at end of the prior fiscal year.

A likelihood of 9.93 percent to 12.45 percent was obtained. The Meeks study focused on the profitability of mergers of U.K. firms in the 1964–1972 period. The acquiring firms were examined using a standardized profitability measure E, called "the profitability of the amalgamation (standardized for industry and year) less three-year average premerger profitability of the amalgamation (similarly standardized)."[79] An average decline was reported, leading the author to title the study *Disappointing Marriage: A Study of the Gains from Mergers.*

Studies of mergers in Belgium, the Federal Republic of Germany, France, the Netherlands, Sweden, the United Kingdom, and the United States show little improvement in profitability as measured by accounting profitability measures. As concluded by D. C. Mueller:

No consistent pattern of either improved or deteriorated profitability can be claimed across the seven countries. Mergers would appear to result in a slight improvement here, a slight worsening of performance there. If a generalization is to be drawn, it would have to be that mergers have hit modest effects, up or down, on the profitability of the merging firms in the three to five years following merger. An economic efficiency gain from the merger would appear too small.[80]

In the context of the United Kingdom, Paul Barnes estimated the following discriminant function:

$$Z = -1.91218 - 1.61605x_1 + 4.99448x_2 + 1.11363x_3 - 0.70484x_4 - 0.11345x_5,$$

where

x_1 = quick assets/current liabilities,

x_2 = current assets/current liabilities,

x_3 = pretax profit margin,

x_4 = net profit margin, and

x_5 = return on shareholders' equity.

The model was able to predict accurately 74.3 percent of a holdout sample.[81]

Ahmed Belkaoui's study focused on predicting Canadian takeovers on the basis of linear combination of sixteen ratios:

x_1 = cash flow/net worth,

x_2 = cash flow/total assets,

x_3 = net income/net worth,

x_4 = net income/total assets,

x_5 = long term debt + preferred stock/total assets,

x_6 = current assets/total assets,

x_7 = cash/total assets,

x_8 = working capital/total assets,

x_9 = quick assets/total assets,

x_{10} = current assets/total liabilities,

x_{11} = quick assets/current liabilities,

x_{12} = cash/current liabilities,

x_{13} = current assets/sales,

x_{14} = quick assets/sales,

x_{15} = working capital/sales, and

x_{16} = cash/sales.[82]

Five discriminant functions were produced for each of the five years preceding the takeover of Canadian firms.

Corporate restructuring behavior includes such mechanisms as mergers, consolidations, acquisitions, divestitures, going private, leverage buyouts, and spinoffs. They are undertaken to either (a) maximize the market value of equities held by existing shareholders or (b) maximize the welfare of existing management. Research focused on the characteristics of acquired and nonacquired firms, and covered two areas (a) ex post classificatory analysis and (b) ex ante predictive analysis, using either univariate or multivariate models. All the studies point to the relevance of various accounting ratios in classifying or predicting takeovers. The limitations of these studies are similar to those advanced in the case of distress prediction.

Credit and Bank Lending Decisions

Trade and bank lending decisions constitute another example of economic events that may be explained and/or predicted based on accounting and other financial information.

Various organizations, such as Dun & Bradstreet, Inc.; the National Credit Office; the National Association of Credit Management; Robert Morris Associates; and various industry trade associations, engage in some form of trade-credit analysis. From the perspective of the predictive approach, the research consists of replicating or predicting the credit evaluation or change therein based on accounting and other financial information. For example, Ewert evaluates, with some success, the extent to which financial ratios can be used to differentiate good from bad accounts, where bad accounts are either placed in collection or written off as uncollectable.[83] On the other hand, Backer and Gosman have had less success in predicting the firms that would be likely to be downgraded by Dun & Bradstreet on the basis of financial ratios.[84]

The bank lending decision has also been the subject of empirical and predictive research. Three areas of research can be identified.

The first area deals with efforts to simulate aspects of a bank's investment and lending processes. The investment decision is the subject of simulation analysis by Clarkson[85] and Cohen, Gilmore, and Singer.[86] The results imply that financial information plays a major role in the decision.

The second area deals with prediction of the loan classification decision. With minor success, Orgler uses a multiple regression model to replicate the Federal Deposit Insurance Corporation's classification of bank loans into "criticized" and "uncriticized" categories.[87] However, Dietrich and Kaplan have been more successful in using a statistical "logit" model to explain and predict four classes of loans from "current/in good standing" to "doubtful."[88]

The third area deals with the estimation and prediction of commercial bank financial distress. Studies have examined the feasibility of predicting bank financial distress based on accounting data. Sinkey has been able to predict a large proportion of failures based on a model that includes two variables: (a) operating expenses to operating income and (b) investments to assets.[89] Similarly, Pettaway and Sinkey have continued the same line of research using both market- and accounting-based screening models.[90] The accounting screen has been found to provide valuable lead time that regulators can use to carry out their statutory responsibilities more effectively.

Forecasting Financial Statement Information

Because security analysts and most forecasting agencies focus on the U.S. environment, management accountants and financial managers of multinational corporations (MNCs) may have to rely on their own efforts to forecast other companies' earnings and to provide forecasts of their own earnings. Their choice of techniques may be mechanical or non-mechanical and univariate or multivariate. Mechanical univaritate forecasting approaches include moving average models and Box-Jenkins univariate models. Mechanical multivariate forecasting models include regression models, Box-Jenkins transfer function models, and econometric models. Finally, nonmechanical models include univariate models such as visual curve extrapolation and multivariate models such as security analyst approaches. These forecasts can be evaluated in terms of either dispersion or bias. Dispersion of forecast errors is generally measured by the mean square error (MSE) as follows:

$$MSE = 1/n \ (ax_{it} - fx_{it})^2,$$

where

ax_{it} = actual value of the variable in period t for firm i,

fx_{it} = forecasted value of the variable in period t for firm i, and

n = number of forecasts examined.

Bias is measured by the expected value of the error (EVE):

$$EVE = 1/n(ax_{it} - fx_{it}).$$

Earnings forecasts are becoming increasingly popular and important to an efficient functioning of capital markets. These forecasts are assumed to be particularly useful to users of accounting information. Earnings forecasts may be provided by analysts, management, or statistical models. The relevance of these forecasts rests to a great extent on their reasonable accuracy; the investors in particular and the capital markets in general would have no confidence in inaccurate earnings forecasts, and consequently would not utilize them. An important question centers then on the predictive accuracy of each type of forecasts. Accordingly, various studies have examined the research question, "Are forecasts of earnings by analysts or management superior to statistical models?"

At this stage of the research, there seems to be a disagreement as to whether earnings forecasts made by analysts and/or management are more accurate than forecasts based on a statistical analysis of the pattern in historical annual earnings and quarterly earnings time-series models. In addition, industry variables seem to "make a difference" in the ability to forecast a firm's earnings. It is too early to have closure on the subject. Various issues remain unanswered, and the research to date suffers from various limitations. Abdel-Khalik and Thompson identify the following unanswered issues: "the relevance of forecasted data, the value of non-accounting information in forecasting, the randomness of earnings time series, the cost of alternative forecasting procedures, and the respective motives of management and security analysts in making forecasts."[91]

Similarly, Griffin identifies the following caveats of the research:

First, the results are typically based on an "average" firm or a firm at the median position in a cross section. Such average results may have application in specific contexts. Second, analysis by industry, size, risk, and other possible explanatory variables has received only scant attention so far in developing statistical models. Third, most studies use rather naive models and thus do not recognize recent research on the properties of accounting earnings. This suggests that they are potentially biased in favor of the superiority of the published forecasts.

Finally, the finding that managers and analysts have about the same degree of forecasting success is probably not unreasonable given the present institutional setting. Company investor-relations programs and analysts' period meetings with management suggest that, insofar as the earnings forecast is concerned, the overlap of information accessible to management and analysts is consider-able.[92]

METHODS

Advocates of the decision usefulness/decision model paradigm or predictive approach tend to rely on statistical techniques to determine the predictive ability of selected items of information. The general approach has been to use the discriminant analysis to classify into one of several a priori groupings dependent on a firm's individual financial characteristics. To avoid the limitations of the studies surveyed, the following methodology should be used: First, the prediction model, based on either the discriminant analysis, probit, or regression models, should include items of information derived from a theoretical model of the economic event.

Second, to avoid confusion between tests of validation or classification efficiency and tests of predicition the following steps are required:[93] The first step is the fit a discriminant function over a sample of firms A_1 from data collected in t_1. This is the analysis sample.

The second step is to use the linear discriminant function obtained in the first step to classify firms of a time-coincident holdout or validation sample A_2. This sample A_2 of firms with data collected in t_1 is the validation sample. In most studies, this step has been confused with prediction. Ex post discrimination may provide a useful foundation for explanation of the past, but it does not provide sufficient evidence for concluding that the future can be predicted. Assuming careful ex post discrimination, the explanatory significance of the financial variables (independent variables) is investigated using both samples A_1 and A_2 from t_1 data. That is, the samples are recombined to form an estimating sample, and a new linear discriminant model from the total t_1 sample is estimated. This merely involves a reestimation of the coefficients and not a search for variables.

The next step is to used the discriminant model, obtained as just explained, to classify sample B observations from another year t_2. As stated correctly: "Prediction thus requires intertemporal validation whereas explanation requires only cross validation."[94]

Both cross validation (the second step) and intertemporal validation (the preceding paragraph) will yield a classification matrix showing the hit rate for the model. The success of the predictions will be measured by the hit rate, that is, the percentage of industrial bonds correctly classified.

CONCLUSIONS

The decision usefulness/decision models paradigm focuses on the production of accounting-data-based models that have both expanatory and predictive powers in the context of important economic events. The paradigm has been successful in terms of the interest it created and the number of predictive models proposed in the contexts of bankruptcy, takeovers, bond ratings, time-series analyses, and credit and bank lending decisions. The lack of good economic theories supporting these models continues, however, to plague the paradigm.

NOTES

1. R. J. Chambers, "Blueprint for a Theory of Accounting," *Accounting Research* (January 1955): 21–22.

2. G. O. May, *Financial Accounting* (New York: Macmillan, 1943), 19.

3. W. H. Beaver, J. W. Kennelly, and W. M. Voss, "Predictive Ability for the Evaluation of Accounting Data," *The Accounting Review* (October 1968): 675–83; R. R. Sterling, "Decision-Oriented Financial Accounting," *Accounting and Business Research* (Summer 1972): 198–208.

4. Beaver, Kennelly, and Voss, "Predictive Ability for the Evaluation of Accounting Data," 675.

5. Ibid., 680.

6. Sterling, "Decision-Oriented Financial Accounting," 198.

7. Ibid., 199.

8. Ibid., 201.

9. Ibid., 159.

10. Beaver, Kennelly, and Voss, "Predictive Ability as a Criterion for the Evaluation of Accounting Data," 675.

11. Ibid., 676.

12. Charles R. Nelson, *Applied Time Series Analysis for Managerial Forecasting* (New York: Holden-Day, 1973).

13. Surveys of the literature include A. R. Abdel-Khalik, "Three Generations of Research on Quarterly Reports: Some Thoughts on the Research Process," in *Perspectives on Research* R. D. Nair and T. H. Williams, eds. (Madison: University of Wisconsin, 1980); K. S. Lorek, R. Kee, and W. H. Van, "Time-Series Properties of Annual Earnings Data: The State of the Art," *Quarterly Review of Economics and Business* (Spring 1981): 97–113.

14. K. Cogger, "A Time-Series Analytic Approach to Aggregation Issues in Accounting Data," *Journal of Accounting Research* (Autumn 1981): 285–98.

15. B. C. Dharan, "Identification and Estimation Issues for a Causal Earnings Model," *Journal of Accounting Research* (Spring 1983): 18–41.

16. N. Dopuch, and R. L. Watts, "Using Time-Series Models to Assess the Significance of Accounting Changes," *Journal of Accounting Research* (Spring 1972): 180–94.

17. G. Foster, "Quarterly Accounting Data: Time-Series Properties and Predictive Ability Results," *The Accounting Review* (January 1977): 1–21.

18. P. A. Griffin, "The Time-Series Behavior of Quarterly Earnings: Preliminary Evidence," *Journal of Accounting Research* (Spring 1977): 18–41.

19. Ray Ball, and George Foster, "Corporate Financial Reporting: A Methodological Review of Empirical Research," *Studieson Current Research Methodologies in Accounting: A Critical Evaluation, Journal of Accounting Research* 20 (Supplement 1982): 209.

20. R. L. Watts, and R. W. Leftwich, "The Time-Series of Annual Accounting Earnings," *Journal of Accounting Research* (Autumn 1977): 253–71.

21. W. S. Albrecht, L. L. Lookabill, and J. C. McKeown, "The Time-Series Properties of Annual Accounting Earnings," *Journal of Accounting Research* (Autumn 1977): 226–44.

22. W. A. Collins, and W. S. Hopwood, "A Multivariate Analysis of Annual Earnings Forecasts Generated from Quarterly Forecasts of Financial Analysts and Univariate Time-Series Models," *Journal of Accounting Research* (Autumn 1980): 390–406.

23. D. W. Collins, "Predicting Earnings with Subentity Data: Some Further Evidence," *Journal of Accounting Research* (Spring 1976): 163–77.

24. J. G. Manegold, "Time-Series Properties of Earnings: A Comparison of Extrapolative and Components Models," *Journal of Accounting Research* (Autumn 1981): 360–73.

25. J. Scott, "The Probability of Bankruptcy: A Comparison of Empirical Predictions and Theoretical Models," *Journal of Banking and Finance* (September 1981): 320.

26. W. H. Beaver, "Financial Ratios as Predictors of Failure," Empirical Research in Accounting, *Journal of Accounting Research* (Supplements 1966): 71–111.

27. E. I. Altman, "Financial Ratios, Discriminant Analysis, and the Prediction of Corporate Bankruptcy," *Journal of Finance* (September 1968): 589–609.

28. E. I. Altman, *Corporate Financial Distress* (New York: Wiley, 1983).

29. E. I. Altman, R. G. Halderman, and P. Narayanan, "Zeta Analysis: A New Model to Identify Bankruptcy Risk of Corporations," *Journal of Banking and Finance* (June 1977): 29–54.

30. J. W. Wilcox, "A Prediction of Business Failure Using Accounting Data," *Empirical Research in Accounting: Selected Studies,* supplement to *Journal of Accounting Research* (March 1973): 163–79.

31. J. Vinso, "A Determination of the Risk of Ruin," *Journal of Financial and Quantitative Analysis* (March 1979): 77–100.

32. C. J. Ko, "A Delienation of Corporate Appraisal Models and Classification of Bankruptcy Firms in Japan" (Masters Thesis, New York University, 1982).

33. E. I. Altman, T. Baidya, and L. M. Ribero-Dias, "Assessing Potential Financial Problems of Firms in Brazil," *Journal of International Business Studies* (Fall 1979): 9–24.

34. A. D. Castagna, and Z. P. Matobesey, "The Prediction of Corporate Failure: Testing the Australian Experience," *Australian Journal of Management* (June 1981): 42–52.

35. R. M. Kinglit, "The Determinant of Failure in Canadian Firms" (paper presented at ASA Meetings of Canada, Saskatoon, Saskatchewan, May 28–30, 1980).

36. E. I. Altman, M. Margarine, M. Schlosser, and P. Vernimmen, "Statistical Credit Analysis in the Textile Industry: A French Experience," *Journal of Financial and Quantitative Analysis* (March 1974): 25–34.

37. J. Bilderbeek, *Finaciele Ratio Analyse* (Leiden: Strenfert-Kroese, 1977).

38. Altman, Margarine, Schlosser, and Vernimmen, "Statistical Credit Analysis in the Textile Industry: A French Experience," 67–80.

39. Ibid.

40. P. O. Bontemps, *La Notation du Risque de Credit* (Paris: Credit National, 1981).

41. Yves Collongues, "Ratios Financiers et Previsions des Faillites des Petites et Moyennes Entreprises," *Revue Banque* (March 1977): 16–25.

42. F. Mader, "Les Ratios et L'Analyse du Risque," *Analyse Financiere* 2 (1975): 18–32.

43. F. Mader, "Un Echantillon d'Entreprises en Difficulte," *Journee des Centrales de Bilan* (January 1979).

44. E. I. Altman, "The Success of Business Failure Prediction Models: An International Survey," *Journal of Banking and Finance* 8 (1984): 94.

45. Ibid.

46. G. Weinrich, *Prediction of Credit Worthiness, Direction of Credit Operations by Risk Classes* (Wiesbaden, Germany: 1978).

47. P. F. Wiebel, *The Value of Criteria to Judge Credit Worthiness in the Lending of Banks* (Bern/Stuttgart: 1973).

48. Ibid.

49. K. Beerman, *Possible Ways to Predict Capital Losses with Annual Financial Statements* (Dusseldorf: 1976).

50. G. Gebhardt, "Insolvency Prediction Based on Annual Financial Statements According to Company Law—An Assessment of the Reform of Annual Statements by the Law of 1965 from the View of External Addresses," in *Bochumer Beitrage Zur Unternchmungs and Unternelmerns-Forschung,* Vol. 22, H. Besters et al., eds. (Wiesbaden: 1980).

51. J. A. Ohlson, "Financial Ratios and Probabilistic Prediction of Bankruptcy," *Journal of Accounting Research* (Spring 1980): 109–31.

52. Ball and Foster, "Corporate Financial Reporting: A Methodological Review of Empirical Research," 218.

53. Frederick L. Jones, "Current Techniques in Bankruptcy Predictions," *Journal of Accounting Literature* 6 (1987): 131–64.

54. L. Fisher, "Determinants of Risk Premium on Corporate Bonds," *Journal of Political Economy* (June 1959): 217–37.

55. Moody's Investor Service, *Moody's Bond Record* (New York: Moody's Investor Service, 1984).

56. Standard & Poor's, *Credit Overview: Corporate and International Ratings* (New York: Standard & Poor's, 1984).

57. J. O. Horrigan, "The Determination of Long-Term Credit Standing with Financial Ratios," *Empirical Research in Accounting: Selected Studies,* supplement to vol. 4 *Journal of Accounting Research* (1966): 44–62; G. E. Pinches, and K. A. Mingo, "A Multivariate Analysis of Industrial Bond Ratings," *Journal of Finance* (March 1973): 1–18;

A. Belkaoui, "Industrial Bond Ratings: A Discriminant Analysis Approach," *Financial Management* (Autumn 1980): 44–51; A. Belkaoui, *Industrial Bonds and the Rating Process* (Westport, CT: Greenwood Press, 1984).

58. E. I. Altman, and S. Katz, "Statistical Bond-Rating Classification Using Financial and Accounting Data," in *Proceedings of the Conference on Topical Research in Accounting*, M. Schiff and G. H. Sorter, eds. (New York: New York University Press, 1976), 205–39.

59. J. J. Horton, "Statistical Classification of Municipal Bonds," *Journal of Bank Research* (Autumn 1970): 29–40.

60. Belkaoui, *Industrial Bonds and the Rating Process*.

61. Ibid.

62. R. N. Marris, *The Economic Theory of Managerial Capitalism* (New York: Macmillan, 1964).

63. Michael Gort, "An Economic Disturbance Theory of Mergers," *Quarterly Journal of Economics* (November 1969): 624–43.

64. M. D. Bonford, "Changes in the Evaluation of Equities," *The Investment Analyst* (December 1968): 62–75.

65. J. T. Tzoannos, and J. M. Samuels, "Mergers and Takeovers: The Financial Characteristics of Companies Involved," *Journal of Business Finance* (July 1972): 5–16.

66. R. J. Chambers, "Finance Information and the Securities Market," *Abacus* (September 1965): 4–30.

67. R. A. Taussig, and S. L. Hayes III, "Cash Takeovers and Accounting Valuation," *The Accounting Review* (January 1968): 68–72.

68. J. S. Vance, "Is Your Company a Takeover Target?" *Harvard Business Review* (May–June 1969): 93–102.

69. R. J. Monroe, and M. A. Sinkowitz, "Investment Characteristics of Conglomerate Targets: A Discriminant Analysis," *Southern Journal of Business* (November 1971): 59–81.

70. A. Single, "Takeovers, Economic Natural Selection, and the Theory of the Firm: Evidence from the Post-War United Kingdom Experience," *The Economic Journal* (September 1975): 497–515.

71. D. L. Stevens, "Financial Characteristics of Merged Firms: A Multivariate Analysis," *Journal of Financial and Quantitative Analysis* (March 1973): 149–58.

72. J. K. Baker, T. O. Miller, and B. J. Ramsberger, "A Typology of Merger Motives," *Akron Business and Economic Review* (Winter 1981): 24–25.

73. K. Schipper, and A. Smith, "Effects of Recontracting on Shareholder Wealth: The Case of Voluntary Spin-Offs," *Journal of Financial Economics* (December 1983): 437–67.

74. R. P. Boisjoly, and T. M. Corsi, "A Profile of Motor Carrier Acquisitions, 1976 to 1978," *Akron Business and Economic Review* (Summer 1982): 30–35.

75. R. S. Harris, J. F. Stewart, D. K. Guilkey, and W. T. Carleton, "Characteristics of Acquired Firms: Fixed and Random Coefficients Probits Analyses," *Southern Economic Journal* (July 1982): 164–184.

76. W. P. Rege, "Accounting Ratios to Locate Takeovers Targets," *Journal of Business Finance and Accounting* (Autumn 1984): 302–11.

77. J. K. Dietrich, and E. Sorensen, "An Application of Logit Analysis to Prediction of Merger Targets," *Journal of Business Research* (September 1984): 393–402.

78. K. Palepu, "Predicting Takeover Targets: A Methodological and Empirical Analysis," *Journal of Accounting and Economics* (March 1986): 3–35.

79. G. Meeks, *Disappointing Marriage: A Study of the Gains from Mergers* (Cambridge: Cambridge University Press, 1977).

80. D. C. Mueller, "A Cross-National Comparison of the Results," in *The Determinants and Effects of Mergers,* D. C. Mueller, ed. (Cambridge, MA: Oegeschlager, Gann & Hain, 1980).

81. Paul Barnes, "The Prediction of Takeover Targets in the U.K. by Means of Multiple Discriminant Analysis," *Journal of Business Finance and Accounting* (Spring 1990): 73–84.

82. Ahmed Belkaoui, "Financial Ratios as Predictors of Canadian Takeovers," *Journal of Business Finance and Accounting* 5 (Spring 1978): 93–101.

83. D. C. Ewert, *Trade Credit Management: Selection of Accounts Receivable Using a Statistical Model,* Research Monograph, No. 79 (Atlanta: Georgia State University, 1980).

84. Morton Backer, and M. L. Gosman, *Financial Reporting and Business Liquidity* (New York: National Association of Accountants, 1987).

85. G.P.E. Clarkson, *Portfolio Selection: A Simulation of Trust Investment* (Englewood Cliffs, NJ: Prentice-Hall, 1962).

86. K. J. Cohen, T. C. Gilmore, and F. A. Singer, "Bank Procedures for Analyzing Business Loan Applications," in *Analytical Methods in Banking,* K. J. Cohen, and F. S. Hammer, eds. (Homewood, IL: Richard D. Irwin, 1966).

87. Yuie E. Orgler, "A Credit-Scoring Model for Commercial Loans," *Journal of Money, Credit and Banking* 2 (November 1970): 435–45.

88. J. R. Dietrich, and Robert S. Caplan, "Empirical Analysis of Commercial Loan Classification Decisions," *The Accounting Review* (January 1982): 18–38.

89. J. F. Sinkey, Jr., "A Multivariate Statistical Analysis of the Characteristics of Problem Banks," *Journal of Finance* (March 1975): 21–36.

90. R. H. Pettaway, and J. F. Sinkey, Jr., "Establishing On-Site Bank Examination Priorities: An Early-Warning System Using Accounting and Market Information," *Journal of Finance* (March 1980): 137–50.

91. A. R. Abdel-Khalik, and R. B. Thompson, "Research on Earnings Forecasts: The State of the Art," *The Accounting Journal* (Winter 1977–78): 192.

92. P. A. Griffin, *Usefulness to Investors and Creditors of Information Provided by Financial Reporting: A Review of Empirical Accounting Research,* Research Report (Stamford, CT: Financial Accounting Standards Board, 1982), 83.

93. This procedure was suggested in O. Maurice Joy and John O. Tollefson, "On the Financial Applications of Discriminant Analysis," *Journal of Financial and Quantitative Analysis* (December 1975): 726–27.

94. Ibid., 727.

REFERENCES

Abdel-Khalik, A. R. "Three Generations of Research on Quarterly Reports: Some Thoughts on the Research Process." In *Perspectives on Research* edited by R. D. Nair, and T. H. William. Madison: University of Wisconsin Press, 1980: 61–82.

Ashton, R. H. "The Predictive Ability Criterion and User-Prediction Models." *The Accounting Review* (October 1974): 719–32.

Beaver, W. H., J. W. Kennelly, and W. M. Voss. "Predictive Ability as a Criterion for the Evaluation of Accounting Data." *The Accounting Review* (October 1968): 675–83.

Belkaoui, A. "The Entropy Law, Information Decomposition Measures, and Corporate Takeover." *Journal of Business Finance and Accounting* (Autumn 1976): 41–52.

Belkaoui, A. "Financial Ratios as Predictors of Canadian Takeovers." *Journal of Business Finance and Accounting* 5 (Spring 1978): 93–107.

Belkaoui, A. "Industrial Bond Ratings: A Discriminant Analysis Approach." *Financial Management* (Autumn 1980): 44–51.

Belkaoui, A. *Industrial Bonds and the Rating Process.* Westport, CT: Greenwood Press, 1984.

Lorek, K. S., R. Kee, and W. H. Van. "Time-Series Projection of Annual Earnings Data: The State of the Art." *Quarterly Review of Economics and Business* (Spring 1981): 97–113.

5 The Decision Usefulness/ Decision Maker/Aggregate Market Behavior Paradigm

INTRODUCTION

The decision usefulness/decision market/aggregate market behavior paradigm, better known as the market paradigm, attempts to assess the usefulness of accounting information to decision makers by an evaluation of the market behavior following the release of the information. The market paradigm focuses on market valuation as a guide to the assessment of the effect of accounting information and its decision usefulness.

EXEMPLARS

The exemplars of the decision usefulness/decision maker/aggregate market behavior paradigm are the works of Gonedes and of Gonedes and Dopuch.[1] In this pioneering paper, Gonedes extends the interest in decision usefulness from the individual user response to the aggregate market response. Arguing that market reactions (for example, anticipatory price reactions) to accounting numbers should govern the evaluation of the informational content of these numbers and of the procedures used to produce these numbers, Gonedes develops the aggregate market paradigm, which implies that accounting produces numbers that have informational content dictated by market reactions. To the counterarguments

1. that the procedures used to produce the numbers may induce market inefficiencies, and

2. that recipients may be conditioned to react to accounting numbers in a particular manner.

Gonedes argues that if both cases were true, the opportunity for those
who possess this knowledge to earn an abnormal profit would provide a
basis for the demise of the market paradigm within the context of an
efficient capital market. In their award-winning paper, Gonedes and Dopuch provide a theoretical framework for assessing the desirability and/
or effects of alternative accounting procedures. Their approach relies on
the use of prices of (rates of returns on) firms' ownership shares.
Gonedes and Dopuch conclude that the price-domain analysis is sufficient for assessing the effects of alternative accounting procedures or
regulations, but insufficient for assessing the desirability of alternative
accounting or regulations. This conclusion is based primarily on one case
of market failure in which information of a public good nature cannot
be excluded from nonpurchasers (the free-rider problem). In such a case,
the prices of firms' ownership shares cannot be used to assess the desirability of alternative accounting procedures or regulations.

Other market failure possibilities are the issue of adverse selection[2]
and the effect of information on the completeness of markets and efficient risk-sharing arrangements.[3] Gonedes and Dopuch also note that
some criticisms of work based on capital market efficiency, including
the works of Abdel-Khalik and of May and Sundem,[4] treat remarks on
assessing effects as if they were remarks on assessing desirability.

A contemporary work by Beaver[5] can also be viewed as an exemplar
of the decision usefulness/decision maker/aggregate market behavior paradigm. Beaver raises the issue of the importance of this relationship
between accounting data and security behavior. He argues that it is in-
conceivable that optimal information systems for investors can be selected without a knowledge of how accounting data are impounded in
prices, because the prices determine wealth and wealth affects the mul-
tiperiod investment decisions of individuals.

IMAGE OF THE SUBJECT MATTER

To those who adopt the decision usefulness/decision model/aggregate
market behavior paradigm, the basic subject matter is the aggregate mar-

ket response to accounting variables. These authors agree that, in general, the decision usefulness of accounting variables can be derived from aggregate market behavior, or as presented by Gonedes and Dopuch, only the effects of alternative accounting procedures or speculations can be assessed from aggregate market behavior. Basically, the selection of the accounting information system is determined by aggregate market behavior.

THEORIES

The relationship between aggregate market behavior and accounting variables is based on the theory of market efficiency, the capital asset pricing model, the arbitrage pricing theory, and the equilibrium theory of option pricing.

The Efficient Market Model

It is generally assumed that the securities market is efficient. A perfectly efficient market is in continuous equilibrium, so that the intrinsic values of securities vibrate randomly and market prices always equal underlying intrinsic values at every instant in time. "Intrinsic value" is generally regarded as what the price ought to be and what price would be, given by other individuals who possessed the same information and competence as the person making the estimate.[6]

Various definitions of market efficiency need to be examined. One definition, suggests Fama, is that in an efficient market, prices "fully reflect" the information available and, by implication, prices react instantaneously and without bias to new information.[7] A mathematical formulation of this definition, called the expected-return model or the fair-game model, is also suggested by Fama:

$$Z_{j,t+1} = r_{j,t+1} - E(r_{jt+1} + q_t),$$
$$E(Z_{j,t+1}q_t) = 0,$$

where

$r_{j,t+1}$ = the realized return on security j in period $t + 1$ (where "return" is defined as percentage change in security price adjusted for dividends received),

$E(r_{jt+1}q_t)$ = the expected return on security j in period $t + 1$, conditioned on the value of q_t,

q_t = the information set assumed to be fully reflected in prices in period t, and

Z_{jt+1} = abnormal return on security j in period $t + 1$.

In other words, the rate-of-return series (r_{jt+1}) is "a fair game" relative to the information series (q_t).

Fama's definition has been criticized for being tautological (in that it merely implies that the expected deviation of a realization from its expected value is zero), for not being empirically testable unless some equilibrium model of security returns is specified, for failing to give a clear meaning to the term "information set," and for requiring prices to exist in an imaginary "as if" economy and the information set to be available in that "as if" economy.[8]

The second definition is based on some form of a model derived from the theory of rational expectations whereby correct expectations are formed based on all the available information, including prices. A behavioral process is generated whereby more informed individuals reveal information to less informed individuals through their trading actions or exchange of information. As a result, the rational expectations model that is derived produces prices that do not fully reveal everything. Information is not free, and efficiency, in the strong sense, does not exist unless there is a decrease in the cost of information.

A third definition, proposed by Beaver, makes the distinction between market efficiency with respect to a signal (such as a particular type of accounting change) and with respect to an information system (such as all published accounting information).[9] Signal efficiency (or y-efficiency) and information system efficiency (or n-efficiency), respectively, are defined as follows:

y-efficiency: A securities market is efficient with respect to a signal y_t' if and only if the configuration of security prices $\{P_{jt}\}$ is the same as it would be in an otherwise identical economy (with an identical configuration of preferences and endowments), except that every individual receives y_t' as well as y_{jt}.

n-efficiency: A securities market is efficient with respect to n_t if y-efficiency holds for every signal y_t' from n_t'.[10]

The Efficient Market Hypothesis

By defining the information set q_t in three different ways, Fama distinguishes three levels of market efficiency: the weak, the semi-strong, and the strong forms.[11]

The Weak Form of the Efficient Market Hypothesis

The weak form of the efficient market hypothesis states that the equilibrium expected returns (prices) "fully reflect" the sequence of past returns (prices). In other words, historical price and volume data for securities contain no information that can be used to earn a profit superior to a simple "buy-and-hold" strategy. The weak form of the hypotheses began with the theory that price changes follow a true random walk (with an expected value of zero). This school of thought is challenged by "technical analysts" or "chartists" who believe that their rules, based on past information, can earn greater-than-normal profits. Filter rules, serial correlation, and run tests have tested the weak efficient market hypothesis. The results support the hypothesis, particularly for returns longer than a day.

The Semi-Strong Form of the Efficient Market Hypothesis

The semi-strong form of the efficient market hypothesis states that the equilibrium expected return (prices) "fully reflect" all publicly available information. In other words, no trading rule based on available information can be used to earn an excess return. The semi-strong form of the hypothesis is relevant to accounting because publicly available information includes financial statements. Tests of the semi-strong hypothesis have been concerned with the speed with which prices adjust to specific kinds of events. Some of the events examined have been stock splits, announcements of annual earnings, large secondary offerings of common stocks, new issues of stocks, announcements of changes in the discount rate, and stock dividends.

The results again support the efficient market hypothesis in so far as prices adjust rather quickly after the first public announcements of information. The list of events examined is not exhaustive, and further empirical research is warranted to prove this hypothesis, which is of extreme importance to accounting.

The Strong Form of the Efficient Market Hypothesis

The strong form of the efficient market hypothesis states that the equilibrium expected returns (prices) ''fully reflect'' all information (not just publicly available information). In other words, no trading rule based on any information, including inside information, can be used to earn an excess return.

Evidence on the strong form of the efficient market hypothesis is not conclusive.

The Capital-Asset Pricing Model

The efficient market hypothesis requires the use of ''expected returns'' and assumes that securities are properly priced. A theory is needed to specify the relationship between the expected returns and the prices of the individual stock in question. One such theory is the Sharpe,[12] Lintner,[13] and Mossin[14] capital-asset pricing model, which relates asset returns to asset risk as follows:

$$E(R_{it}) = R_{it} + \{E[E(R_{mt}) - R_{it}]\}B,$$

where

$E(R_{it})$ = the expected return of security i in period t,

R_{it} = the return on a riskless asset in period t,

$E(R_{mt})$ = the expected return on the market portfolio in period t, and

$\sigma(R_{it}R_{mt})$ = the covariance between R_{it} and R_{mt}.

$\sigma^2(R_{mt}) = (R_{it}R_{mt})$ = risk coefficient,

$B = \dfrac{\sigma(R_{it}R_{mt})}{\sigma^2(R_{mt})}$ = risk coefficient.

Given certain assumptions, the capital-asset pricing model asserts that there is a linear relationship between our individual security and its systematic risk.

The Arbitrary Pricing Theory (APT)

APT assumes that security returns are related to an unknown number of unknown factors. A multifactor model will be as follows:

$$r_i = a_i + b_{i1} \cdot F_1 + b_{i2}F_2 + \cdots + b_{ij}F_3 + e_i.$$

The securities will be priced as follows:

$$E(r_i) = R_f + Y_1 b_{i1} + Y_2 b_{i2} + \cdots + b_{ij}Y_j,$$

where

R_f = returns on riskless asset,

b_{ij} = sensitivity of security i to factor j, and

Y_j = security return premium (i.e., in excess of R_f) per unit of security to factor j.

That is to say, the security expected returns are linearly related to the securities of the pervasive factors, with a common intercept equal to the riskless rate of interest.[15] Various studies attempted to identify the factors. Chen, Roll, and Ross identified the following four factors:

1. growth rate in industrial production,
2. rate of inflation (both expected and unexpected),
3. spread between long-term and short-term interest rates, and
4. spread between low-grade and high-grade bonds.[16]

In addition to the last three factors, Berry, Burnmeister, and McElroy identified the two factors of the growth rate in aggregate sales in the economy and the rate of return on the Standard & Poor's (S&P) 500.[17] Finally, the Salomon Brothers used the following five factors in their fundamental factor model:

1. rate of inflation (both expected and unexpected),
2. growth rate in gross national product,
3. rate of interest,
4. rate of change in oil prices, and
5. rate of growth in defense spending.[18]

Equilibrium Theory of Option Pricing

Options give one party the right to buy (call option or put option) a specific number of shares of a specific company from the option writer at a specific price at any time up to and including a specific date. An equilibrium pricing of valuing (call) options was proposed by Black and Scholes[19] under the following formula:

$$V_c = N(d_1) P_s - \frac{E}{e^{RT}}N(d_2),$$

$$d_1 = \frac{\ln(P_s/E) + (R + 0.5\sigma^2)T}{\sigma\sqrt{T}}$$

$$d_2 = \frac{\ln(P_s/E) + (R - 0.5\sigma^2)T}{\sigma\sqrt{T}}$$

$$= d_1 - \sigma\sqrt{T}.$$

where

P_s = current market price of the underlying stock,

E = exercise price of the option,

R = continuously compounded risk-free rate of return expressed on an annual basis,

T = time remaining before expiration, expressed as a fraction of a year, and

σ = risk of the underlying common stock, measured by the standard deviation of the continuously compounded annual rate of return on the stock.

METHODS

The Market Model

The capital-asset pricing model does not lend itself to our easy test of the efficient market hypothesis. Instead, the Markovitz[20] and Sharpe[21] market model is used for this purpose. The model defines the stochastic process generating security price as

$$R_{it} = \alpha_i + B_i R_{mt} + U_{jt},$$

where

$$E(M_{it}) = 0,$$
$$\sigma(R_{mt}, M_{it}) = 0,$$
$$\sigma(M_{mt}, M_{it}) = 0,$$

R_{it} = the return of security i in period t,

α_i, B_i = the intercept and the slope of the linear relationship between R_{it} and R_{mt},

R_{mt} = the market factor in period t, and

M_{it} = the stochastic portion of the individualistic component of R_{it}.

The market model asserts that the return of each security is linearly related to the market return. More specifically, it states that the total return R_{it} can be separated into a systematic component $B_i R_{mt}$, which reflects the extent of common movement of the return of security i in conjunction with the average return on all securities in the market. The systematic risk B_i reflects the response of security i to economy-wide events reflected in the market factor, and M_{ij} reflects the response of the class of events having an impact on security i only. Thus, the isolation of the individualistic component of security i, or M_{it}, enables an evaluation of the effect of specific information items or measurements. The model has been used in most studies evaluating the relation between market return and accounting return. To estimate the parameters α and β researchers have generally relied on the ordinary least-squares approach (or the generalized least-squares approach), which assumes that the market model parameters are consistent during the event period. There is, however, evidence of changes in both parameters in response to various economic events. Some studies relied on Ibbotson's[22] returns across times and securities (RATS) procedure to account for the variables of the regression parameters. The method proceeds with the estimation of the pooled cross-sectional coverage beta for each event date. Other methods call for using the switching regression involved, the Kalman filter model,[23] and the random coefficient model,[24] and the Bayesian random coefficient model (BERAB).[25] For example, the Bayesian estimates for random X and B (BERAB) at time t are

$$\alpha_{Bt} = \alpha_0 + \frac{(R_t - \alpha_0 - \beta_0 R_{mt})(\sigma_u^2 + \sigma_{uv} R_{mt})}{(\sigma_\epsilon^2 + \sigma_u^2 + \sigma_v^2 R_{mt}^2 + 2\sigma_{uv} R_{mt})},$$

$$\beta_{Bt} = \beta_0 + \frac{R_t - \alpha_0 - \beta_0 R_{mt})(\sigma_v^2 R_{mt} + \sigma_{uv})}{\sigma_\epsilon^2 + \sigma_u^2 + \sigma_v^2 R_{mt}^2 + 2\sigma_{uv} R_{mt})}$$

A description of BERAB follows:

The Bayesian analysis suggests that the degree of belief we currently hold concerning any proposition depends on the information currently available to us. As the information about a proposition changes, our belief or probability is revised, representing learning behavior. In this scheme, the initial information based on previous observations is expressed as a prior probability distribution concerning the proposition, and new data is expressed as a likelihood function. Then the prior probability density and the likelihood function are combined by Bayes' theorem to yield a posterior probability density function. The posterior density combines both the sample and prior information. It characterizes the revision that has occurred because of the sample data and is the basis for subsequent decision-making.[26]

Beta Estimation

The estimation of systematic risk or beta is essentially needed for studies examining the market impact of accounting information, and the association of beta with accounting-based indicators. Because of the potential econometric problem of error in the market model estimates various necessary corrections have been proposed.

First, the generalized Scholes-Williams correction provides the following estimator:[27]

$$B_1 = (B_{i+1} + B^u{}_i + B^{-1}{}_i)/1 + 2P_1,$$

where

B^{+1}, B^0, B^{-1} = leading, contemporaneous, and lagged betas and

$\quad\quad P_1$ = first-order serial correlation of the index.

Cohen, Hawawini, Mayer, Schwartz, and Whitecomb[28] suggest a generalized form of this estimator:

$$\beta_i = \left(\sum_{+n=1}^{+N} \beta_i^{+n} + \beta_i^0 + \sum_{-n=1}^{-N} \beta_i^{-n} \right)/1 + \sum_{+n=1}^{+N} 2P_{+n}$$

where

$+ N$ = number of leads in the estimator and

$- N$ = number of lags in the estimator.

Second, Vasicek's Bayesian correction provides the following estimator:

$$B_i = (B_p/S^{2p} + B^B/S^{B2})/(1/S^{2p} + 1/S^{2B}),$$

where

B_p = best prior estimate,

S^{2p} = estimated variance of the estimate,

B_B = unweighted market average of betas, and

S^2_B = estimated variance of market betas.[29]

A typical application of these corrections is provided in Karpik and Belkaoui.[30]

Event Study Methodology

Event study methodology is used to study shareholders' wealth effects following the announcement of an event. For each security i, the market model is used to calculate excess returns (XR) for day t as follows:

$$XR_{it} = R_{it} - a_i + b_i R_{mt},$$

where R_{it} and R_{mt} are the rate of return on security i and the market rate of return on event day t. The coefficients of the regression are ordinary least-squares estimates of the intercept and slope of the market regression model. The average excess return (AXR) for the portfolio of n securities during day t is as follows:

$$AXR_t = (1/n) \sum_{i=1}^{n} XR_{it},$$

where n is the number of securities with excess returns during day t. Standardized excess returns (SAR$_i$'s) are computed as follows:

$$SAR_{it} = AXR_{it}/S_{it},$$

where

$S_{it} = (S_i^2 \{1 + (1/L) + [(R_{mt} - R_m)^2/(R_{mk} - R_m)^2]\})^{0.5}$,

S_i^2 = residual variance for security i from the market model regression,

L = number of observations during the estimation period,

R_{mt} = return on the market portfolio for day t,

R_m = average return of the market portfolio for the estimation period, and

R_{mk} = return on the market portfolio for the kth day of the estimation period.

The significance of AXRs is evaluated using a Z_t statistic as follows:

$$Z_t = \Sigma \; SAR_{it}/n^{0.5.}$$

The mean AXRs are then accumulated through time to give the cumulative abnormal returns (CARs), where the CARs for period t_1 to t_2 are

$$CARs \; (t_1, t_2) = \sum_{t1}^{t2} AXR_{it}.$$

Ohlson's Valuation Model

In Ohlson's model, the market value of the firm's equity is a linear and Stochastic function of the book value of equity, current earnings, current dividends, and a variable representing other value relevant factors.[31] It is stated as follows:

$$P_t = k(\phi x_t - d_t) + (1 - k)y_t + \alpha_2 v_t,$$

where

P_t = market value or price of the firm at date t,

$k = R_{fw}/(1 + R_f - w)$,

R_t = the risk-free interest rate,

w = persistence parameter for abnormal earnings (x^a): $x^a_{i+1} = wx^a_t + e_{1,t+1}$,

$\phi = (R_f + 1)/R_f$,

x_t = earnings for period $t - 1$ to t,

d_t = dividends paid at date t less new capital contributions for period $t - 1$ to t,

y_t = net book value at date t,

$\alpha_2 = (R_f + 1)/(R_f + 1 - w)(R_f + 1 - y)$,

v_t = a variable summarizing other information that influences the prediction of future expected abnormal earnings, and

y = persistence parameter for v_t: $v_{t+1} = yv_t + e_{2,t+1}$.

Price-Level Balance Sheet Valuation Models

These models focus on the relation between equity values and book values. In general, the reaction is stated as follows:

$$MVE = f(BVA),$$

where

MVE = market value of equity,
BVA = book value of assets.

For example, Barth used the example as follows:[32]

$$MVE = y_0 + y_1BVA + y_2BVL + y_3PA_i + y_4PL_i + v,$$

where BVA and BVL are the book values of total nonpension assets and liabilities, and PA_i and PL_i are the ith alternative measure of the pension asset or liability. Other examples are provided in Landsman[33] and Shelvin.[34]

Information Content of Earnings

The information content of earnings is generally tested by the relationships between security returns and unexpected earnings. It is inferred by the significance of the slope coefficient (b) and the explanatory power of a cross-sectional overtime estimated model of the following form:[35]

$$CAR_k = a + bUX_k + e_k,$$

where

CAR_{it} = cumulative abnormal return for security i over period t,
UX_{it} = unexpected earnings (preferably scaled), and
b = earnings response coefficient (ERC).

UX is measured either (a) using a random walk model as a proxy for the market earnings expectation as of the beginning of the year or (b) unexpected earnings using more sophisticated time-series models.

Models of the Relation Between Earnings and Return

Two models of the relation between earnings and returns have been used in research.[36]

The first model, model A, bases the returns and earnings association on a book valuation model. It is derived as follows: First, the price and book value as measures of the ''stock'' value of the shareholders' equity are related as follows:

$$P_{jt} = BV_{jt} + U_{jt}, \tag{1}$$

where P_{jt} is the price per share of firm j at time t and BV_{jt} is the book value per share of firm j at time t.

Second, the accounting earnings and security returns as measures of the ''flow'' value or changes in value of the shareholder's equity can be derived by taking first differences of the variables in equation (1) as follows:

$$\Delta P_{jt} = \Delta BV_{jt} + U_{jt}, \tag{2}$$

where

$$\Delta BV_{jt} = A_{jt} - d_{jt}, \tag{3}$$

A_{jt} = accounting earnings of firm j over the time period $t - 1$ to t, and

d_{jt} = the dividend of firm j over time period $t - 1$ to t.

Third, the relations between earnings and returns is obtained by substituting equation (3) into equation (2) and dividing by P_{jt-1} as follows:

$$R_{jt} = A_{jt}/P_{jt-1} + U_{jt}, \tag{4}$$

where

$$R_{jt} = (\Delta P_{jt} + d_{jt})/P_{jt-1}.$$

Equation (4) shows that if stock price and book value are related, then earnings divided by beginning-of-period price (earnings level divided by beginning-of-period price) allows to explain returns.

The second-model, model B, bases the returns and earnings association on an earnings valuation model. It is derived as follows: first, an earnings valuation model expresses price (including dividend) as a multiple of earnings as follows:

$$P_{jt} + d_{jt} = \sigma A_{jt} + V_{jt}.$$

Second, changes in both sides of the equation coupled with division by beginning-of-period price yields the second model as follows:

$$R_{jt} = \sigma(\Delta A_{jt}/P_{jt}) + V_{jt}.$$

EVALUATION OF MARKET-BASED RESEARCH IN ACCOUNTING[37]

Information Content Studies

These studies use the marginal information contribution of accounting signals to examine the determination of security-return behavior. The approach used is to examine whether the announcement of some event results in a change in the characteristics of the stock return distribution (i.e., mean or variance). The impetus was created by the famous Ball and Brown study[38] in which unexpected earning changes (with a form shown only by the sign of the change) were found to be correlated with residual stock returns. These results are consistent with the hypothesis that accounting information—especially earnings—convey information in the sense of leading to changes in equilibrium prices held with the following situations: (a) changes in the earnings-expectation models from a random-walk-generating process to more complex models, (b) examining both the magnitude and the sign of the unexpected earnings, (c) using a methodology focusing on another property of the return distribution—the variance of residual returns, (d) analyzing trading rather than price changes, and (e) examining the impact of some nonearnings financial variables.

Voluntary Differences and Changes in Accounting Techniques

These studies examine the impact of the differences and changes on investors. The issue is whether the market is "sophisticated enough" not to be "fooled" by cosmetic accounting differences or accounting changes. If the investors are not able to "see through" the veil of accounting practices, the phenomenon is labeled as a functional fixation or naive investor hypothesis. The functional fixation or naive investor hypothesis assumes that a sufficient number of investors are unable to perceive the cosmetic nature of certain accounting changes, or are "fixated" on the bottom figure of net income. The efficient market hypothesis stipulates instead that rational investors should see through the veil of accounting practices, packaging of information, and forms of disclosure. In addition, an extended functional fixation hypothesis assumes that when responding to accounting data, sometimes the price of a firm's stock is set by a sophisticated marginal investor, and sometimes it is set by an unsophisticated marginal investor.[39]

Research on the subject has distinguished between accounting differences or changes having cash flow consequences and those having no cash flow consequences.[40]

The Market Impact of Accounting Regulation

The interest in these studies is with the market effects of accounting regulation. Concerted research effects in this area have focused on line of business, oil and gas accounting, and replacement costs, to name only a few. The main evidence is that concerted and direct research effects in this area seem to create convergent results; for example, (a) mandated line-of-business information has affected investor assessment of the return distributions of multiproduct firms; (b) the Financial Accounting Standards Board (FASB) and the Securities and Exchange Commission (SEC) regulations on the "full cost"/"successful-effects" issue are associated with statistically significant stock price reactions of oil and gas stocks; and (c) price-adjusted estimates of earnings as well as replacement cost data did not generate any noticeable market reaction. One consequence of this research is the increased demand for these studies by policy makers, aware of the relevance of research to the consequences of their decisions. The research, however, has failed to answer fundamental questions.

The cynic is still tempted to say "so what?" to the many identified consequences of regulations. The key question still open can be stated as follows: How do we identify a successful or effective regulation? A corollary is: what market variables are potentially relevant and why? Formal theoretical analysis has the advantage of guiding research toward variables that bear directly on the impact of regulation. This is not to suggest that the identification of such variables would lead to a direct or easy resolution of policy issues—just that the variables researched would be more relevant.[41]

Impact on Related Disciplines

We will evaluate the research in terms of the implications of the evidence for financial reporting and in terms of the adequacy of the methodology used.

Implications of the Evidence for Financial Reporting

The findings identified earlier are not trival. They have important implication for corporate financial reporting and planning. For example, Copeland uses the empirical evidence on the effect of various accounting changes in efficient capital markets to suggest the following implications for corporate financial reporting and planning:

1. Relevant new information, which will affect the future cash flows of the firm, should be announced as soon as it becomes available, so that shareholders can use it without the (presumably greater) expense of discovering it from alternative resources.

2. The most important information is forward-looking. Old news is no news. Shareholders are interested in information that can be presented in the president's letter or in an unaudited section of the annual report—information such as how much new investment is planned; what is the expected rate of return; how long will the expected rate be favorable; how much new equity will be issued; what is the firm's target capital structure; what are its plans and policies with respect to repurchasing its own common stock; and what is its dividend policy.

3. It does not matter whether cash-flow effects are reported in the balance sheet, in the income statement, or in footnotes; the market can evaluate the news as long as it is publicly available, whatever form it may take.

4. The market reacts to the cash-flow impact of management decisions, not to the effect on reported earnings per share. Companies should never seek to increase earnings per share if cash flow will decline as a result.

5. The Securities and Exchange Commission should conduct a thorough cost-benefit analysis of all proposed changes in disclosure requirements. It can be aided in its efforts by academic studies, which, in some cases, have already demonstrated that certain types of disclosures are irrelevant.[42]

Above all, most of the evidence cited earlier seems to imply that capital markets are reasonably efficient handlers of accounting information and can be used to evaluate published numbers. This optimism is not, however, generally shared.

First, the efficient market hypothesis has been contested by Gonedes and Dopuch on the grounds that stock-price associations are not sufficient grounds on which to evaluate alternative information systems, and that social welfare considerations are needed.[43] More specifically,

Gonedes and Dopuch have identified two assertions used in the predictive approach for the evaluation of alternative accounting procedures.

1. Capital market efficiency, taken by itself, provides justification for using prices of (or rates of return on) firms' ownership shares in assessing the desirability of alternative accounting procedures or regulations.
2. Capital market efficiency, taken by itself, provides justification for using prices of (or rates of return on) firms' ownership shares in assessing the effects of alternative accounting procedures or regulations.[44]

Gonedes and Dopuch argue that the contemporary institutional setting allows a "free-rider" effect that makes the desirability, assertion 1, logically invalid, although they consider the effects, assertion 2, to be valid.

Second, the efficient market hypothesis and the empirical evidence supporting it are silent concerning the "optimal" amount of information. This point in particular is recognized in the SEC's Sommer Report (named for its chairman, Al Sommer, Jr.) as follows:

The efficient market hypothesis—which asserts that the current price of a security reflects all publicly available information—even if valid, does not negate the necessity of a mandatory disclosure system. This theory is concerned with how the market reacts to disclosed information and is silent as to the optimum amount of information required or whether that optimum should be achieved on a mandatory or voluntary basis; market forces alone are insufficient to cause all material information to be disclosed.[45]

Third, a qualifier has been omitted in all of the studies cited earlier. The qualifier is whether the firm's decision making is unchanged as a result of the accounting change, because market efficiency can be implied only if both no change in stock prices and the firm's decision making are observed. This point is emphasized as follows: "If the accounting change triggered a revision of the decision making process which would, if extrapolated, alter the anticipated performance of the entity, and if the stock price remained unchanged, then market inefficiency would be the conclusion."[46]

Fourth, finding what information is used and should be provided to investors may be difficult. Published numbers are not the only source of information in terms of content and quality, and the task may be too complex for regulators and researchers to solve.[47]

Fifth, most of the empirical research cited suffers from the absence of a theory "to predict who should be better or worse off by accounting policy changes and which changes, if any, might include changes in management behavior to offset the effect of an accounting policy change."[48]

Sixth, some major arguments exist against the use of the predictive approach with capital markets. For example, it has been argued that users individually or in aggregate react because they have been conditioned to react to accounting data, rather than because the data have any informational content. Accordingly, observations of users' reaction should not guide the formulation of an accounting theory. Sterling contends that:

If the response of receivers to accounting stimuli is to be taken as evidence that certain kinds of accounting practices are justified, then we must not overlook the possibility that those responses were conditioned. Accounting reports have been issued for a long time, and their issuance has been accompanied by a rather impressive ceremony performed by the managers and accountants who issue them. The receivers are likely to have gained the impression that they ought to react and have noted that others react, and thereby have become conditioned to react.[49]

It may also be argued that the recipients of accounting information react when they should not react or do not react the way they should.

Adequacy of the Methodology Used

Most of the empirical evidence on the information content of financial accounting numbers rests on research designs and methodological assumptions, which are frequently the subject of critical assessment.[50]

1. *Anomalous evidence regarding market efficiency:* There are a number of scattered pieces of anomalous evidence regarding market efficiency. Ball, who examined evidence showing that postannouncement, risk-adjusted abnormal returns are systematically nonzero in the period following earnings announcements, argues that the anomalous evidence is due to inadequacies in the two-parameter, capital-asset-pricing model used to adjust for risk differentials and to market inefficiencies.[51]

Watts, however, examined evidence on systematic abnormal returns after quarterly earnings announcements to determine whether they emanate from market inefficiencies or deficiencies in the asset-pricing model.[52] The results show the abnormal returns to be due to market inefficiencies, and not to asset-pricing model inefficiencies. As a result, some accounting studies were based on dependent variables other than the change in security price, or some variant such as yield, volatility, or security beta. An analysis of trading volume is recommended when the theory suggests that the disclosure change may cause a change in the level of consensus.

Other suggested dependent variables are change in the variance-covariance structure, when it is deemed that the disclosure changes affect the risk levels of firms, and the use of systematic risk. Newer methodologies have also been proposed; these include the use of option prices and the use of intraday stock prices.[53]

2. *Self-selection bias and omitted variables:* One objective of the research design in capital market studies is to determine whether the observed market reaction is due to the variables being examined and to ensure that the reaction is caused by the variable of interest, and not by some other variable. This is basically a control problem. Hence, most studies evaluating the impact of accounting changes have shown an earnings bias, meaning that the changes in reported earnings of the firms are negatively related to the income effect of the accounting change.[54] This creates a systematic self-selection bias, given that a systematic characteristic of all these firms also affects market performance. This self-selection bias is in fact the result of a failure to account for other omitted variables that have an impact on market reaction. The impact of omitted variables should be thoroughly addressed in capital-market studies.

3. *Confounding effects:* A confounding effect arises with the release of other unrelated and relevant informational items by some of the test firms during the time period of interest. This effect can pose a serious threat to the internal validity of the study. Five alternative approaches to controlling for unrelated information events have been proposed:

Alternative 1: retain all firms in the sample and partition the firms into various event combination categories.

Alternative 2: delete firms experiencing other events in the time period from the sample.

Alternative 3: retain all firms in the sample, but delete an ''appropriate'' time period for each announcement.

Alternative 4: retain all firms in the sample, explicitly estimate the capital-market efficiency of other events, and subtract this estimate from the observed return for the sample.

Alternative 5: retain all firms in the sample, and assume that the net position of other events is minimal.[55]

4. *The timing of capital-market impact:* The choice of the most appropriate time to investigate the market reaction to an event is crucial to the interpretation of the results of a study. Although the date of public disclosure is the most evident and popular, the problem remains that the reaction may be anticipated or delayed, depending on the nature of the accounting issue being investigated. For instance, Foster refers to the fact that a policy process occurs in conjunction with many accounting issues, during which the following information can be disseminated to the market:

information relating to the policy decision itself,

information relating to the information that firms will release in compliance with a specific decision, and

information relating to the actions that management will take in response to a specific decision.[56]

Given this complex situation, the researcher must determine which event or set of events is the relevant one to examine.

5. *The choice of a control group:* The most effective research design used in capital-market studies of accounting policy decision is the pretest/posttest control-group design, in which

Group A: $O_1 \times O_2$,
Group B: O_3, O_4,

where O_1 is the capital-market reaction observation at point i and is the experimental effect expressed as either (1) the announcement of a policy decision by a standard-setting body or (2) the firm's disclosure of the "mandated" informational items. Although laboratory experimentation dictates a random assignment of firms to O_2 and O_4 samples, capital-market studies rely on self-selection, given the impossibility of random assignment. A self-selection bias is created in that the differences between O_2 and O_4 may not be due to the impact of ξ but to differences between the samples. To alleviate the self-selection problem, Foster provided the following two tests as interval validity checks:

a firm profile analysis and

a nontreatment period, security-return analysis.[57]

CONCLUSIONS

The market paradigm with its focus on aggregate market behavior for the evaluation of accounting information is very popular in the accounting literature. Its reliance on the assumption of market efficiency and the multiplicity of methods that can be used has given it a certain level of primacy among all followers of the "Chicago" School of accounting empiricism.

NOTES

1. N. J. Gonedes, "Efficient Capital Markets and External Accounting," *The Accounting Review* (January 1972): 11–21; N. J. Gonedes and N. Dopuch, "Capital-Market Equilibrium, Information Production, and Selecting Accounting Techniques: Theoretical Framework and Review of Empirical Work," *Studies on Financial Accounting Objectives,* supplement to *Journal of Accounting Research* (1974): 48–125.

2. M. Spence, "Job-Market Signaling," *Quarterly Journal of Economics* (August 1973): 356–74.

3. Roy Radner, "Competitive Equilibrium Under Uncertainty," *Econometrica* (January 1968): 60–85; George A. Akerloff, "The Market for 'Lemons': Quality Uncertainty and the Market Mechanism," *Quarterly Journal of Economics* (August 1970): 488–500; Richard Kihlstrom, and M. Pauly, "The Role of Insurance in the Allocation of Risk," *American Economic Review* (May 1971): 100–30; Roy Radner, "Existence of Equilibrium of Plans, Prices, and Price Expectations in a Sequence of Markets," *Econometrica* (March 1972): 71–82.

4. A. R. Abdel-Khalik, "The Efficient Market Hypothesis and Accounting Data: A Point of View," *The Accounting Review* (October 1972): 791–93; Robert G. May, and Gary L. Sundem, "Cost of Information and Security Prices: Market Association Tests of Accounting Policy Decisions," *The Accounting Review* (January 1973): 80–90.

5. W. H. Beaver, "The Behavior of Security Prices and Its Implications for Accounting Research (Methods)," *Committee Reports,* supplement to *The Accounting Review* (1972): 407–37.

6. J. Lorie and M. Hamilton, *The Stock Market: Theories and Evidence* (Homewood, IL.: Richard D. Irwin, 1973).

7. E. F. Fama, "Efficient Capital Markets: A Review of Theory and Empirical Work," *Journal of Finance* (May 1970): 383–417.

8. R. E. Verrecchia, "Consensus Beliefs, Information Acquisition, and Market Information Efficiency," *The American Economic Review* (December 1980): 874–84.

9. W. H. Beaver, "Market Efficiency," *The Accounting Review* (January 1981): 28.

10. Ibid.

11. Fama, "Efficient Capital Markets: A Review of Theory and Empirical Work," 383.

12. W. F. Sharpe, "Capital-Asset Prices: A Theory of Market Equilibrium Under Conditions of Risk," *Journal of Finance* (September 1974): 425–47.

13. J. Lintner, "The Valuation of Risky Assets and the Selection of Risky Investment

in Stock Portfolios and Capital Budgets,'' *Review of Economics and Statistics* (February 1965): 13–37.

14. J. Mossin, ''Equilibrium in a Capital-Asset Market,'' *Economica* (October 1966): 768–83.

15. S. A. Ross, ''The Artibrage Theory of Capital Asset Pricing,'' *Journal of Economic Theory* (December 1976): 341–60.

16. Nai-Fu Chen, Richard Roll, and Stephen A. Ross, ''Economic Forces and the Stock Market,'' *Journal of Business* (July 1986): 383–403.

17. Michael A. Berry, Edwin Burmeister, and Majorie B. McElroy, ''Sorting Out Risks Using Known APT Factors,'' *Financial Analysts Journal* (March–April 1988): 29–42.

18. William F. Sharpe, Gordon J. Alexander, and Jeffrey V. Bailey, *Investments* (Englewood Cliffs, NJ: Prentice-Hall, 1995), 337.

19. F. Black, and M. Scholes, ''The Pricing of Options and Corporate Liabilities,'' *Journal of Political Economy* (May–June 1973): pp. 637–54.

20. J. Markovitz, ''Portfolio Selection,'' *Journal of Finance* (March 1952): 77–79.

21. W. F. Sharpe, ''A Simplified Model of Portfolio Analysis,'' *Management Science* (January 1963): 277–93.

22. R. G. Ibbotson, ''Price Performance of Common Stock New Issues,'' *Journal of Financial Economics* (September 1975): 235–72.

23. A. H. Sarris, ''Kalman Filter Models: A Bayesian Approach to Estimation of Time-Varying Regression Coefficient,'' *Annuals of the Economic and Social Measurement* (Fall 1973): 501–23.

24. S. N. Chen, and C. F. Lee, ''Bayesian and Mixed Estimators of Time Varying Betas,'' *Journal of Economics and Business* (December 1982): 291–301.

25. Byungjun Ahn, and Hyun Mo Sung, ''The Bayesian Random Coefficient Market Model in Event Studies: The Case of Earnings Announcements,'' *Journal of Business Finance and Accounting* (September 1995): 907–22.

26. Ibid., 910.

27. M. Scholes, and J. Williams, ''Estimating Betas from Nonsynchronous Data,'' *Journal of Financial Economics* (December 1977): 309–28.

28. K. Cohen, G. Hawawini, S. Mayer, R. Schwartz, and D. Whitcomb, ''Friction in the Trading Process and the Estimation of Systematic Risk,'' *Journal of Financial Economics* (August 1983): 263–70.

29. O. Vasicek, ''A Note on Using Cross-Sectional Information in Bayesian Estimation of Security Betas,'' *Journal of Finance* (December 1973): 1233–39.

30. P. Karpik, and A. Belkaoui, ''The Relative Relationship Between Systematic Risk and Value Added Variables,'' *Journal of International Financial Management and Accounting* (Autumn 1989): 259–76.

31. J. Ohlson, ''Earnings Book Values, and Dividend in Security Valuation,'' working paper, New York: Columbia University, 1991.

32. M. Barth, ''Relative Measurement Errors Among Alternative Revision Asset and Liability Measures,'' *The Accounting Review* (July 1991): 433–63.

33. W. Landsman, ''An Empirical Investigation of Pension Fund Property Rights,'' *The Accounting Review* (October 1986): 662–71.

34. T. Shelvin, ''The Valuation of R&D Firms with R&L Limited Partnerships,'' *The Accounting Review* (January 1991): 1–22.

35. D. W. Collins, and S. P. Kothan, "An Analysis of Intertemporal and Cross-Sectional Determinants of Earnings Response Coefficients," *Journal of Accounting and Economics* 11 (1989): 143–81.

36. P. D. Easton, and T. S. Harris, "Earnings as an Explanatory Variable for Returns," *Journal of Accounting Research* (Spring 1991): 19–36.

37. B. Lev, and J. A. Ohlson, "Market-Based Empirical Research in Accounting: A Review, Interpretation, and Extension," *Studies on Current Research Methodologies in Accounting: A Critical Evaluation,* supplement to *Journal of Accounting Research* (1982): 257.

38. R. J. Ball and P. Brown, "An Empirical Evaluation of Accounting Income Numbers," *Journal of Accounting Research* (Autumn 1968): 102–26.

39. John R. M. Hand, "A Test of the Extended Functional Fixation Hypothesis," *Accounting Review* (October 1990): 740–63.

40. S. Sunder, "Stock Price and Risk Related to Accounting Changes in Inventory Valuation," *The Accounting Review* (April 1975): 305–15.

41. Lev and Ohlson, "Market-Based Empirical Research in Accounting: A Review, Interpretation, and Extension," 283.

42. R. M. Copeland, "Efficient Capital Markets: Evidence and Implications for Financial Reporting," *Journal of Accounting, Auditing and Finance* (Winter 1981): 47.

43. N. J. Gonedes, and N. Dopuch, "Capital-Market Equilibrium Information, Production, and Selecting Accounting Techniques: Theoretical Framework and Review of Empirical Work," 48–129.

44. Ibid., 50.

45. *Report of the Advisory Committee on Corporate Disclosure to the Securities and Exchange Commission* (Washington, DC: U.S. Government Printing Office, November 1977), D-6.

46. W. R. Greer, Jr., and L. E. Morrissey, Jr., "Accounting Rule-Making in a World of Efficient Markets," *Journal of Accounting, Auditing and Finance* (Winter 1981): 56.

47. George J. Benston, *Investors' Use of Financial Accounting Statement Number: A Review of Evidence from Stock Market Research, Arthur Young Lecture No. 2* (Glasgow: University of Glasgow Press, 1981), 37.

48. P. Griffin, *Usefulness to Investors and Creditors of Information Provided by Financial Reporting: A Review of Empirical Accounting Research* (Stamford, CT: Financial Accounting Standards Board, 1982), 15.

49. Robert R. Sterling, "On Theory Construction and Verification," *The Accounting Review* (July 1970): 453.

50. Many of the methodological issues covered in this section are also discussed in A. R. Abdel-Khalik, and Bipin B. Ayjinka, *Empirical Research in Accounting: A Methodological Viewpoint* (Sarasota, FL: American Accounting Association, 1979); G. Foster, "Accounting Policy Decisions and Capital-Market Research," *Journal of Accounting and Economics* (March 1980): 29–62; W. Ricks, "Market Assessment of Alternative Accounting Methods: A Review of the Empirical Evidence," *Journal of Accounting Literature* (Spring 1982): 59–99.

51. R. Ball, "Anomalies in Relationships Between Securities' Yields and Yield-Surrogates," *Journal of Financial Economics* (June–September 1978): 103–26.

52. R. L. Watts, "Systematic 'Abnormal' Returns After Quarterly-Earnings Announcements," *Journal of Financial Economics* (June–September 1978): 127–50.

53. J. M. Patell, and M. A. Wolfson, "Anticipated Information Releases Reflected in Call-Option Prices," *Journal of Accounting and Economics* (August 1979): 117–40.

54. W. G. Bremster, "The Earnings and Characteristics of Firms Reporting Discretionary Accounting Changes," *The Accounting Review* (July 1975): 563–73.

55. G. Foster, "Accounting Policy Decisions and Capital-Market Research," 55–56.

56. Ibid., 39.

57. Ibid., 47–48.

REFERENCES

Ball, R. J., and P. Brown. "An Empirical Evaluation of Accounting Income Numbers." *Journal of Accounting Research* (Autumn 1968): 159–78.

Beaver, W. H. "The Behavior of Security Prices and Its Implications for Accounting Research (Methods)." *Committee Reports,* supplement to *The Accounting Review* (1972): 402–37.

Beaver, W. H. "Market Efficiency." *The Accounting Review* (January 1981): 563–71.

Belkaoui, A. "The Impact of the Disclosure of the Environmental Effects of Organizational Behavior on the Market." *Financial Management* (Winter 1976): 26–31.

Black, F., and N. Scholes. "The Pricing of Options and Corporate Liabilities." *Journal of Political Economy* (May/June 1973): 637–54.

Fama, E. F. "Efficient Capital Markets: A Review of Theory and Empirical Evidence." *Journal of Finance* (May 1970): 383–417.

Foster, G. "Accounting Policy Decisions and Capital-Market Research." *Journal of Accounting and Economics* (March 1980): 29–62.

Gonedes, N. J., and N. Dopuch. "Capital-Market Equilibrium Information, Production, and Selecting Accounting Techniques: Theoretical Framework and Review of Empirical Work." *Studies on Financial Accounting Objectives,* supplement to *Journal of Accounting Research* (1974): 48–129.

Karpik, P., and A. Belkaoui. "The Relative Relationship Between Systematic Risk and Value Added Variables." *Journal of International Financial Management and Accounting* (Autumn 1989): 259–76.

Lev, B., and James A. Ohlson. "Market-Based Empirical Research in Accounting: A Review, Interpretation and Extension." *Studies on Current Research Methodologies in Accounting: A Critical Evaluation,* supplement to *The Journal of Accounting Research* (1982): 249–322.

Ross, S. A. "The Arbitage Theory of Capital Asset Pricing." *Journal of Economic Theory* (December 1976): 341–60.

Sharpe, W. F. "Capital-Asset Prices: A Theory of Market Equilibrium Under Conditions of Risk." *Journal of Finance* (September 1974): 425–42.

6   The Decision Usefulness/ Decision Maker/Individual User Paradigm

INTRODUCTION

The decision usefulness/decision maker/individual user paradigm focus on the behavioral impact of accounting information on individual users acting as decision makers. It is generally referred to as the behavioral approach or behavioral accounting.[1] It is a fact that most traditional approaches to the construction of an accounting theory have failed to take into consideration user behavior in particular, and behavioral assumptions in general. In 1960, Devine made the following critical remark:

Let us now turn to . . . the psychological reactions of those who consume accounting output or are caught in its threads of control. On balance, it seems fair to conclude that accountants seem to have waded through their relationships to the intricate psychological network of human activity with a heavy-handed crudity that is beyond belief. Some degree of crudity may be excused in a new discipline, but failure to recognize that much of what passes as accounting theory is hopelessly entwined with unsupported behavior assumptions is unforgivable.[2]

The behavioral approach to the formulation of accounting theory emphasizes the relevance to decision making of the information being communicated (communication decision orientation) and the individual and group behavior caused by the communication of the information (decision-maker orientation). Accounting is assumed to be action oriented; its purpose is to influence action (behavior) directly through the information content of the message conveyed and indirectly through the behavior of accountants. Because accounting is considered to be a behavioral process,[3] the behavioral approach to the formulation of an accounting theory applies behavioral science to accounting. The American Accounting Association's Committee on Behavioral Science Content of the Accounting Curriculum provides the following view of the objective of behavioral science, which may also apply to behavioral accounting:

The objective of behavioral science is to understand, explain, and predict human behavior—that is, to establish generalizations about human behavior that are supported by empirical evidence collected in an impersonal way by procedures that are completely open to review and replication and capable of verification by other interested scholars. Behavioral science thus represents the systematic observation of man's behavior for the purpose of experimentally confirming specific hypotheses by reference to observable changes in behavior.[4]

The behavioral approach to the formulation of an accounting theory is concerned with human behavior as it is relates to accounting information and problems. In this context, the choice of an accounting technique must be evaluated with reference to the objectives and behavior of the users of financial information.

Although relatively new, the behavioral approach has generated an enthusiasm and a new impetus in accounting research that focuses on the behavioral structure within which accountants function. A new multidisciplinary area in the field of accounting has been conveniently labeled behavioral accounting. The basic objective of behavioral accounting is to explain and predict human behavior in all possible accounting contexts. Research studies in behavioral accounting have relied on experimental, field, or correlational techniques. Most studies have made little attempt to formulate a theoretical framework that would support the problems or hypotheses to be tested. Instead, the studies generally have focused on the behavioral effects of accounting information or on the problems of human information processing. The results of these kinds of studies may provide an understanding of the behavioral environment of accounting that can serve as a guide in formulating an accounting theory. We will examine each group of studies and then evaluate the behavioral accounting approach.

EXEMPLARS

The works of Birnberg and Nath, of Bruns, and of Hofstedt and Kinard[5] can be considered exemplars of the decision usefulness/decision user paradigm. Bruns proposes hypotheses that relate the user of accounting information, the relevance of accounting information to decision making, the decision maker's conception of accounting, and other available information to the effect of accounting information on decisions. These hypotheses are also developed in a model that identifies and relates some factors that may determine when decisions are affected by accounting systems and information. Hofstedt and Kinard argue in favor of behavioral accounting research that stems from the realization that an accounting system can be designed to influence behavior. They define behavioral accounting research as the study of how accounting functions and reports influence the behavior of accountants and nonaccountants. These authors show that such an endeavor is a proper area of inquiry worthy of research, and they propose a research strategy.

Birnberg and Nath investigate the implications of behavioral science for managerial accounting and present examples of how behavioral science can be used to perceive the accounting process and to develop testable hypotheses about it. The principal rationale for this endeavor is that the implementation of accounting techniques depends on human responses and on interactions of the individual or group with the accounting system.

IMAGE OF THE SUBJECT MATTER

To those who adopt the decision usefulness/decision maker/individual user paradigm the basic subject matter is the individual user response to accounting variables. Advocates of this paradigm argue that, in general, the decision usefulness of accounting is viewed as a behavioral process. The American Accounting Association's Committee on the Behavioral Science Content of the Accounting Curriculum hypothesizes that "the very process of accumulating information, as well as the behavior of those who do the accumulating, will affect the behavior of others."[6] Consequently, the objective of behavioral accounting research is to understand, explain, and predict human behavior within an accounting context. This paradigm is of interest to internal and external users of accounting, producers and attesters of information, and the general public or its surrogates.

THEORIES

Cognitive Relativism in Accounting

The cognitive revolution in social psychology has created strong interest in the knowledge structure in memory, in general, and how people learn, in particular. This research paradigm also affects accounting and auditing. Given that the difference between declarative knowledge and procedural knowledge is equivalent to the difference between content knowledge and the use of that knowledge or between "knowing what" and "knowing how," W. S. Waller and W. L. Felix used the concepts to propose a model of how an ordinary person learns from experience.[7] Basically,

Its thesis is that learning from experience involves the formation and development of generalized structures that organize experience-based declarative and procedural knowledge in long term memory. Declarative knowledge is organized by categories, which depend on spatial and/or temporal relations. Procedural knowledge is organized into production systems, i.e., hierarchies of condition-action pairs.[8]

What the model implies is that schemata are developed through a gradual process of abstracting domain-specific knowledge based on experience. The difference between the expert's and the novice's knowledge structure is therefore the result of differences in experience. What is apparent from the research on novices and experts is that longer chunks of information are taken and stored by experts than novices at any point in time and for a particular task,[9,10] pieces of information are better clustered into meaningful categories within a single chunk by experts,[11] and the recall of experts is based on functional relationships.[12,13,14]

The findings in accounting so far parallel those in psychology. More specifically, R. Weber found that expert auditors clustered internal control cues according to their control categories significantly more than novices did.[15]

The notion of schemes (knowledge structures or templates) was used by Michael Gibbins to make general propositions, corollaries, and hypotheses about the psychological operations of professional judgment in the "natural" everyday settings experienced by public accountants.[16]

Professional judgment in public accounting was described as a five-component process:

1. schemas or knowledge structures accumulated through learning or experience,
2. a triggering event or stimulus,
3. a judgment environment,
4. a judgment process, and
5. a decision/action.

The list of propositions, corollaries, and hypotheses is shown in Exhibit 6.1. Although it awaits empirical validation, the list constitutes one general descriptive theory of professional judgment in public accounting (PJPA), where auditor judgment is viewed as a responsive, continuous, unconscious, instrumental process of sequentially matching cues to knowledge structures to generate preferences and responses based on experience.[17] Preliminary findings on these propositions are provided by Gibbins,[18] Gibbins and Emby,[19] and Emby and Gibbins.[20]

A model of the judgment/decision process in accounting is proposed as an exercise in social perception and cognition, requiring both formal and implicit judgment.[21] The primary input to this process is an accounting problem or phenomenon that needs to be solved and requires judgment preceding either a preference or a decision. The model, as applicable to accounting, consists of the following steps:

1. observation of the accounting phenomenon by the decision maker,
2. schema formation or building of the accounting phenomenon,
3. schema organization or storage,
4. attention and recognition process triggered by a stimulus,
5. retrieval of stored information needed for the judgment decision,
6. reconsideration and integration of retrieved information with new information,
7. judgment process, and
8. decision/action response.[22]

The essence of cognitive relativism in accounting is the presence of a cognitive process that is assumed to guide the judgment/decision process. The model shows that judgments and decisions made about accounting

Exhibit 6.1
List of Propositions and Corollaries

A. *Propositions about the routine PJPA cycle*
  A(1). *The judge's experience (accumulated learning)*
    P1: Experience produces structured judgment guides ("templates")
        C1(i): Template exists prior to event triggering its use
        C1(ii): Greater experience, more efficient memory use
        C1(iii): Template more complete for more common tasks
    P2: The templates are maintained in long-term memory
    P3: Templates' attributes are shaped by the environment
        C3(i): Some templates more ready for use than others
  A(2). *The triggering event (stimulus)*
    P4: The environment is subjectively perceived
        C4(i): Factors limiting perception also limit judgment
    P5: Templates are continuously updated
  A(3). *The judgment process*
    P6: Judgment is a continuous process
    P7: Judgment is an incremental process
        C7(i): Routine judgment responds to the short term
        C7(ii): Routine judgment avoids limits on future responses
    P8: Judgment is a conditional process
    P9: Judgment begins with a search for a template
        C9(i): Search–retrieval may use little information
    P10: Template selection depends on circumstantial fit
        C10(i): Routine template selection based on past learning
        C10(ii): Perception and search continue until template found
    P11: Routine judgment is not, and need not be, conscious
        C11(i): Explaining own judgment involves rationalization
        C11(ii): Own explanations correlate with common templates
    P12: The judgment environment is incompletely perceived
    P13: Personal characteristics affect template selection
  A(4). *The decision/action (response)*
    P14: Templates specify conscious response preferences
        C14(i): As outputs, preferences subject to imperfections
        C14(ii): Preferences based on past actions and learning
    P15: Preferences and actions are consciously bridged
    P16: The bridging process is instrumental, not probabilistic
        C16(i): Preferences, consequences instrumentally connected
    P17: The decision/action must be justifiable
        C17(i): Some information is to justify choice, not make it
        C17(ii): Justification includes some rationalization
    P18: Bridging evaluations tend to emphasize the downside
B. *Propositions about nonroutine PJPA*
    P19: Conscious judgment is a response to the circumstances
    P20: Conscious judgment strategies also guide judgment
        C20(i): Mental "red flags" prompt conscious intervention
        C20(ii): Complex responses need conscious implementation
    P21: Fully conscious professional judgment is infrequent

Source: Michael Gibbins, "Propositions about the Psychology of Professional Judgment in Public Accounting," *Journal of Accounting Research* 22 (Spring 1984): Table 1, "List of Propositions and Corollaries," 121. Reprinted with permission.

phenomena are the products of a set of social cognitive operations that include the observation of information on accounting phenomena and the formation of schemata that are stored in memory and later retrieved to enable the formation of judgments and/or decisions when needed.

Cultural Relativism in Accounting

Cultural relativism postulates that culture shapes the cognitive functioning of individuals faced with an accounting or auditing phenomenon.[23] Culture can be the brain of accounting research.

Various concepts of culture exist in anthropology, suggesting different themes for accounting research.[24]

1. Following Malinowski's functionalism,[25] culture can be viewed as an instrument serving biological and psychological needs. Applying this definition to accounting research suggests the perception of accounting in each culture as a specific social instrument for task accomplishment and the analysis of cross-cultural or comparative accounting.

2. Following Radcliffe-Brown's structural functionalist,[26] culture can be viewed as an adaptive regulatory mechanism that unites individuals with social structures. Applying this definition to accounting research suggests the perception of accounting in each culture as an adaptive instrument existing by process of exchange with the environment and the analysis of an accounting culture.

3. Following Goodenough's ethic science,[27] culture can be viewed as a system of shared cognition. The human mind thus generates culture by means of a finite number of rules. Applying this definition to accounting research suggests that accounting can be viewed as a system of knowledge that members of each culture share to varying degrees and the analysis of accounting as cognition.

4. Following Geertz's symbolic anthropology,[28] culture can be viewed as a system of shared symbols and meanings. Applying this definition to accounting research suggests that accounting can be viewed as a pattern of symbolic discourse or language and the analysis of accounting as language.

5. Following Levi-Strauss's structuralism,[29] culture can be viewed as a projection of the mind's universal unconscious infrastructure. Applying this definition to accounting suggests that accounting can be viewed in each culture as the maninfestation of unconscious processes and the analysis of unconscious processes in accounting.

Applied to accounting, culture can be viewed as accounting's medium. Culture, in essence, determines the judgment/decision process in accounting. The model postulates that culture, through its components, elements, and dimensions, dictates the organizational structure adopted, the micro-organizational behavior, and the cognitive functioning of individuals in such a way as to ultimately affect their judgment/decision process when they are faced with an accounting and/or auditing phenomenon.[30] The definition of the components of culture is provided by Hofstede[31] as four dimensions that reflect the cultural orientations of a country and explain 50 percent of the differences in value systems among countries: (1) individualism versus collectivism, (2) large versus small power distance, (3) strong versus weak uncertainty avoidance, and (4) masculinity versus feminity. These are defined next.

Individualism versus collectivism is a dimension that represents the degree of integration a society maintains among its members or the relationships between an individual and his or her fellow individuals. Although individualists are expected to take care of themselves and their immediate families only, collectivists are expected to remain emotionally integrated into in-groups that protect them in exchange for unquestioning loyalty.

Large versus small power distance represents the extent to which members of a society accept the unequal distribution of power in institutions and organizations. In large power distance societies, there is a tendency for people to accept a hierarchical order in which everyone has a place that needs no justification, whereas in small power distance societies people tend to live for equality and demand justification for any existing power inequalities.

Strong versus weak uncertainty avoidance is a dimension that represents the degree to which the members of a society feel uncomfortable with uncertainty and ambiguity. In strong uncertainty avoidance societies, people are intolerant of ambiguity and try to control it at all costs, whereas in weak uncertainty avoidance societies, people are more tolerant of ambiguity and tend to live with it.

Masculinity versus femininity is a dimension that represents the nature of the social division of sex roles. Masculine roles imply a preference for achievement, assertiveness, making money, sympathy for the strong, and the like. Feminine roles imply a preference for warm relationships, modesty, care for the weak, preservation of the environment, concern for the quality of life, and so on.

This cultural relativism model assumes that differences among these four dimensions create different cultural arenas that have the potential of dictating the organizational behavior that may shape the judgment/ decision process in accounting.

The cultural relativism model calls for own-cultural research in accounting. There are at least basic possible approaches to cross-cultural research in accounting.[32]

1. Parochial studies is the approach comprising studies of the United States conducted by Americans.
2. Ethnocentric studies comprise studies that attempt to replicate American accounting research in foreign countries.
3. Polycentric studies comprise studies that describe accounting phenomena in foreign countries.
4. Comparative accounting studies focus on identifying the similarities in accounting phenomena in cultures around the world.
5. Culturally synergistic studies focus on creating universality in accounting while maintaining an appropriate level of cultural specificity.

Each of these types of research addresses a different set of accounting questions and is based on different sets of assumptions.

Cross-cultural research in accounting is needed for the following reasons:[33]

First, it would establish the boundary conditions for accounting models and theories.[34] The model proceeds with the testing of the validity of a model or theory in another culture to determine the cultural groups where the model or theory is valid and to specify the varieties for which the model is not valid in some cultural groups. Basically, the discovery of the limits of accounting theories is an important part of accounting research.

The second reason is to evaluate the impact of cultural and ecological factors on behavior in accounting.[35] Between-cultural-group mean comparisons are used to demonstrate cultural differences in the dependent variable. If these comparisons cannot be made because of the absence of score equivalence, then the strategy should be to test the universality of an accounting model or theory. Triandis, Malpass, and Davidson made a crucial distinction between cross-cultural research aimed at proving the cross-cultural generality of a relationship or phenomena and studies that attempt to show differences in the relationship of phenomena that depend on cultural factors as follows:

The former study can be done with relatively loose methodology, since if the same finding is obtained in spite of differences in the stimuli, responses and people, it must be a strong finding. The latter requires extremely stringent controls and a multi-method approach, since there are many competing hypotheses that can account for the observed differences. The best kind of study of the second type is more likely the one where the differences have been predicted on theoretical grounds.[36]

The third reason is that although variables are often generally confounded, the confounding is not complete, as a few cultunits may present deviant cases. "Cultunits" as the object of study of some cross-cultural psychologists were defined by Naroll as "people who are domestic speakers of a common district dialect language and who belong either to the same state or the same contact group."[37] As stated by Triandis:

So, even if variables A and B are highly positively correlated, there are nevertheless a few cultunits that are high on A and low on B, and a few that are low and A and high on B. If we study the deviant cultunits we can establish whether relationships between dependent variables Y and the independent variables A and B are caused by A, caused by B, or caused by both A and B. This is information that is most valuable.[38]

The fourth reason is that cultunits act as "natural grain-Experiments" by being high or low or variables of particular interest.[39] For example, some cultures may focus on some aspects of accounting more than others. As a result, perceptual and decision styles may differ and can be traced to ecological differences.

The fifth reason is that cultures determine aspects of psychological functioning.[40] For example, some cultures may deem certain accounting functions to be useless or unnecessary for their particular context. As a result, those functions are not practiced because they are not rewarded. Triandis, Vassilion, Vassilion, Tanaka, and Shanmugam give the example of the low probability of the planning function in cultures where belief in the unpredictability of events is extremely high.[41] The study of behavior in cross-cultural accounting contexts needs to match the particular nature of the ecology with the particular nature of the participants.

The sixth reason is that the frequency of different accounting methods and behavior in different cultures need to be identified.

Behavioral Effects of Accounting Information

The idea that accounting information, in terms of its content and format, may have an impact on individual decision making, although evident and easily accepted, suggests avenues of research for the improvement of accounting and reporting system. Accordingly, research studies in this area have examined alternative reporting models and disclosure practices to assess the available choices in terms of the relevance and impact in behavior. Because a general theoretical framework has not been established, however, it is difficult to classify these studies. Several writers have attempted to provide classification schemes.[42] An exhaustive attempt by Dyckman, Gibbins, and Swieringa[43] illustrates the nature of studies of the behavioral effects of accounting information.

We can divide these studies into five general classes: (1) the adequacy of disclosure, (2) the usefulness of financial statement data, (3) attitudes about corporate reporting practices, (4) materiality judgments, and (5) the decision effects of alternative accounting procedures.[44]

Three approaches were used to examine the *adequacy of disclosure*. The first approach examined the patterns of use of data from the view point of resolving controversial issues concerning the inclusion of certain information.[45] The second approach examined the perceptions and attitudes of different interest groups.[46] The third approach examined the extent to which different information items were disclosed in annual reports and the determinants of and significant differences in the adequacy of financial disclosure among companies.[47] The research on disclosure adequacy and use showed a general acceptance of the adequacy of available financial statements, a general understanding and comprehension of these financial statements, and a recognition that the differences in disclosure adequacy among the financial statements are due to such variables as company size, profitability, and size and listing status of the auditing firm.

Three approaches were used to examine the *usefulness of financial statement data*. The first approach examined the relative importance of the investment analysis of different information items to both users and preparers of financial information.[48] The second approach examined the relevance of financial statements to decision making, based on laboratory communication of financial statement data in terms of readability and meaning to users in general.[49,50] The overall conclusions of these studies were that (1) some consensus exists between users and preparers regarding the relative importance of the information items disclosed in financial statements when making their decisions and (2) users do not rely solely on financial statements when making their decisions.

Two approaches were used to examine attitudes about *corporate reporting practices*. The first approach examined preferences for alternative accounting techniques.[51] The second approach examined attitudes about general reporting issues, such as how much information should be available, how much information is available, and the importance of certain items.[52] These research studies showed the extent to which some accounting techniques proposed by the authoritative bodies are accepted, and brought to light some attitudinal differences among professional groups concerning reporting issues.

Two approaches were used to examine *materiality judgments*. The first approach examined the main factors that determine the collection, classification, and summarization of accounting data.[53] The second approach focused on what items people consider to be material and sought to determine what degree of difference in accounting data is required before the difference is perceived as material.[54] These studies indicated that several factors appear to affect materiality judgments and that these judgments differ among individuals.

Finally, the *decision effects of alternative accounting procedures* were examined, primarily in the context of the use of different inventory techniques, price level information, and nonaccounting information.[55] The results indicated that alternative accounting techniques may influence individual decisions and that the extent of the influence may depend on the nature of the task, the characteristics of the users, and the nature of the experimental environment.

Human Information Processing

Interest in the human information processing arose from a desire to improve both the information set presented to users of financial data and the ability of these users to use the information. Theories and models provide tools for transforming accounting issues into generic information-processing issues. There are three main components of an information-processing model—input, process, and output. Studies of the information set *input* (or *cues*) focus on the variables that are likely to affect the way people process information for decision making. The variables examined are (1) the scaling characteristics of individual cues (level of measurement, discrete or continuous, deterministic or probabilistic), (2) the statistical properties of the information set (number of cues, distributional characteristics, interrelationship of cues, underlying dimensionality), (3) the informational content or predictive significance (bias, reliability or form of relationship to criterion), (4) the method of presentation (format, sequence, level of aggregation), and (5) the context (physical viewing conditions, instructions, task characteristics and feedback).[56]

Studies of the process component focus on the variables affecting the decision maker, such as (1) characteristics of judgment (personal, task-related, human or mechanical, number of judges) and (2) characteristics of decision rules (form, cue usage, stability, and heuristic).[57]

Studies of the output component focus on the variables related to the judgment, prediction, or decision that are likely to affect the way the user processes the information. The variable examined include (1) the qualities of the judgment (accuracy, speed, reliability in terms of consistency, consensus, and convergence, response biases, and predictability) and (2) self-insight (subjective cue usage, perceived decision quality, and perceptions of characteristics of information sets).[58]

The varying emphasis in any of the three components of an information-processing model led to the use of four different approaches: (1) the lens model approach, (2) probabilistic judgment, (3) predecisional behavioral, and (4) the cognitive style approach. Each approach is examined next.

The Lens Model

Brunswick's lens model allows explicit recognition of the interdependence of environmental and individual-specific variables.[59] It is used primarily to assess human judgmental situations—situations in which people make judgments based on a set of explicit cues from the environment. The model emphasizes the similarities between the environment and the subject response. The right side of the model describes the relationships between the actual criterion or event (Ye) and the level of cues (Xi). The analysis relies on a *regression model* when the cues are continuous and on an *analysis of variance* (ANOVA) *model* when cues take on categorical values. Other methods include conjoint measurement, multidimensional scaling techniques, and discriminant analysis.

Most accounting research using the lens model has been motivated by the need "(1) to build mathematical models that represent the relative importance of different information cues (often called 'policy capturing'), and (2) to measure the accuracy of judgment and its consistency, consensus, and predictability."[60] Various accounting decision problems have been examined using the lens model. These include (1) *policy-capturing* studies, which examine the relative importance of different cues in the judgment process and consensus among decision makers; (2) *accuracy of judgments* made on the basis of accounting cues; and (3) *effects of task characteristics on achievement and learning.*[61]

The policy-capturing research focused on issues related to between-judge *consensus,* the relative *importance of cues,* the *functional form* of the decision rule, and the judge's self-insight. Decision problems examined in the policy-capturing research included materiality judgments, internal control evaluation, reasonableness of forecasts, uncertainty disclosures, policy making, and loan classification.

The accuracy of judgments is very important to accountants. The research focused not only on *judgmental accuracy* but also on *judgmental consistency, consensus, and predictability.* The decision problems examined in the accuracy-of-judgment research included bankruptcy prediction, stock recommendations, and price predictions.

The effects of task characteristics in achievement and learning were examined in both the psychological and the accounting literature. In psychology, the problems examined included task predictability, the functional form of cue criterion relationships, the number of cues, cue validity distributions and intercorrelations, and feedback type. In accounting, the problems examined included the impact of accounting changes, feedback methods, the report format, and cue presentation.

Probabilistic Judgment

The probabilistic judgment approach, sometimes known as the *Bayesian approach,* focuses first on a comparison of intuitive probability judgments and the normative model. The *normative* model for probability revision, known as *Bayes's theorem,* is used as the *descriptive* model of human information processing. Basically, the a posteriori probability form of Bayes's theorem states that

$$\frac{P(H1/D)}{P(H2/D)} \quad = \quad \frac{P(D/H1)}{P(D/H2)} \quad \times \quad \frac{P(H)}{P(H1)},$$

| A posteriori probability | Likelihood ratio | A priori probability |

where $H1$ and $H2$ are the alternative hypotheses and D is the datum.

The basic question examined in the early research on probabilistic judgment is whether probabilities are revised in the direction indicated by Bayes's theorem.[62] The findings suggest that this occurs to a lesser extent than Bayes's theorem would suggest. The phenomenon has been labeled conservatism. This shifted the focus of the research to finding the sources of the observed human information-processing biases. Tversky and Kahneman reported that people rely on a number of heuristics to reduce the complex tasks of assessing probabilities and predicting values to simpler judgmental operations.[63] These heuristics include *representativeness, availability, and adjustment and anchoring.*

Representativness refers to the heuristic people use when they assess the probability of an event based on its degree of similarity, or representativeness, to the category of which it is perceived to be an example. *Availability* refers to the heuristic people use when they assess the probability of an event based on the case with which it comes to mind. Finally, *adjustment and anchoring* refer to the heuristic people use when they make estimates by starting with an initial value (anchoring) and then adjusting the value to yield the final answer.

The early literature of probabilistic judgment in accounting reached the same conclusion concerning the decision makers' use of simplifying heuristics in their processing of information, with the difference that such may be sensitive to task and situation variables. More current research has examined the choice of techniques used to elicit subjective probabilities and the departures from normative decision-making behavior.

Research on probability elicitation has attempted to assess the convergent validity of different elicitation techniques in auditing as well as their accuracy and their effect on audit decisions. No general conclusions can be derived at this stage of the research.

Research on the departures from normative decision-making behavior has focused on heuristics and biases—basically, representativeness in auditing, anchoring in auditing, anchoring in management control, and anchoring in financial analysis—and on the ability of decision makers to perform the role of information evaluators. Little, however, is known about how the information-processing capabilities of individuals interact with task structure to produce heuristics and biases.

Predecisional Behavior

Most of the experiments based on the lens model or on probabilitic judgment involve highly representative situations in which the task is well defined, the subject is exposed to the right cues, and the possible responses are prespecified. These experiments fail to deal with the dynamics of problem definition, hypothesis formation, and information search in less structured environments. In brief, they fail to explore the stages of predecisional behavior.

Predictional behavior is generally examined using *process-tracing methods*. The process-tracing method evolved from the theory of problem solving developed by Newell and Simon,[64] who argue that humans have a limited capacity to process information. They also suggest that humans have short-term memory with limited capacity and virtually unlimited long-term memory. As a result, humans tend to display "satisficing" rather than optimal responses, leading them to be adaptive. This adaptiveness, in turn, implied that the cognitive representation (nature and complexity) of the task determines the way in which the problems are solved, since the tasks tend to elicit and therefore control the behavioral responses of decision makers.

Process tracers tend to rely on four methods: (1) eye movements, (2) information search behavior, (3) information cue attending or response time, and (4) verbal "think aloud" introspective protocols.[65] Verbal protocol, the most frequently used technique in accounting, consists of asking subjects to "think aloud" into an audio or video recorder while performing a task. The protocols are then analyzed, using a particular coding strategy. Given the potential reasonableness of the verbal protocol coding strategy employed by the researchers, Payne, Bramstein, and Caroll suggest the additional use of other data-collection methods so that the results of several methods can be compared to determine their convergence.[66] Joyce and Libby add the following disadvantages:

Among the disadvantages are (1) the sheer volume of data collected in such studies, which limits the number of subjects that can be studied, and (2) the lack of objective coding techniques. This makes the analysis arduous and the communication of the results quite difficult. Reports of verbal protocol studies are usually quite long to read, even when the results from just a few subjects are presented.[67]

Very few accounting studies have relied on process-tracing methods. Issues examined include the modeling of expert financial analysts, the general strategies used by managers in performance report evaluation, and audit decision making. Although they are in the early stages of development, the accounting applications of the process-tracing approaches are promising. Some of these potentials follow:

For example, research examining the memory of experts might indicate explanations for differences between experts and novices demonstrated in prior research and might lead to the development of training aids. The role of cognitive representation in the choice of decision heuristic may provide insights into methods for redesigning management report or audit programs to lead to proper heuristic choice. Studies of the interaction of memory and information search may lead to the development of decision aids to be used at these important stages in less structured accounting situations such as variance investigation and audit client screening.[68]

The Cognitive Style Approach

The cognitive style approach focuses on the variables that are likely to have an impact on the quality of the judgments made by the decision process between stimuli and responses. Five approaches to the study of cognitive style in psychology have been reported: authoritarianism, dogmatism, cognitive complexity, integrative complexity, and field dependence:[69]

1. *Authoritarianism* arose from the focus by Adorno and others on the relationship between personality, anti-democratic attitudes, and behavior.[70] These researchers were primarily interested in individuals whose way of thinking made them susceptible to anti-democratic propaganda. Two of the behavioral correlates of authoritarianism—rigidity and intolerance of ambiguity—were reflections of an underlying cognitive style.

2. *Dogmatism* arose from Rokeach's efforts to develop a structurally based measure of authoritarianism to replace the content-based measure developed by Adorno and his colleagues.[71] Their interest was in developing a measure of cognitive style that would be independent of the content of thought.

3. *Cognitive complexity,* as introduced by Kelly[72] and Bieri,[73] focuses on psychological dimensions that individuals use to structure their environments and to differentiate the behavior of others. More cognitively complex individuals are assumed to have a greater number of available dimensions with which to construe the behavior of others than less cognitively complex persons. Decision makers are also classified in terms of two cognitive styles: *heuristic and analytic.* Based on the terms used by Huysman[74] they can be defined as follows:

Analytic decision makers reduce problem situations to a more or less explicit, often quantitative, model on which they base decisions.

Heuristic decision makers refer instead to common sense, intuition, and unqualified feelings about future development as applied to the totality of the situation as an organic whole rather than to clearly identifiable parts.

Exhibit 6.2
The U-Curve Hypothesis

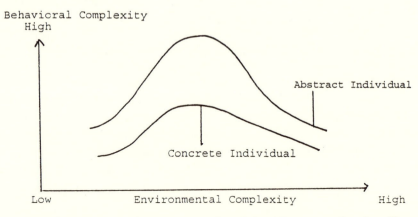

4. *Integrative complexity,* as presented by Harvey and others[75] and later expanded by Schroeder and others,[76] results from the view that people engage in two activities in processing sensory input: differentiation and integration. *Differentiation* refers to the individual's ability to employ complex rules to combine these dimensions. *Integration* refers to the individual's ability to employ complex rules to combine these dimensions. A person engaging in less of both activities is said to be *concrete;* a person engaging in more of both activities is said to be *abstract.* The continuum from concrete to abstract is referred to as *integrative* or *conceptual complexity.*

To the concept of integrative complexity is usually added the concept of environmental complexity and the level of information processing, as expressed by the U-curve hypothesis depicted in Exhibit 6.2. As the level of environmental complexity increases, the level of information processing increases and reaches a maximum level at an optimal level of environmental complexity beyond which it begins to decrease.[77] Schroeder and others extended the concept of the inverted U-shaped curve to the study of integrative complexity. The differences between the concrete and the abstract individual are also shown in Exhibit 6.2. The more abstract the individual, the higher the maximum level of information processing.

5. Finally, *field dependence,* as presented by Witkin and his associates, is a measure of the extent of differentiation in the area of perception.[78] *Field-dependent* individuals tend to perceive the overall organization of a field and are relatively unable to perceive parts of the field as discrete.

Field-independent individuals, however, tend to perceive parts of the field as discrete from the overall organization of the field, rather than as fused with it.

Accounting studies based on these five approaches to cognitive style have focused on classifying users of information by their cognitive structure and on designing information systems that are best suited to the cognitive style of the decision maker. Evidence to support a tailor-made information system is, however, rather mixed, due mainly to the failure to account for and control a host of unmeasured, intervening variables. Similarly, evidence on the impact of "information overload" on the quality of the decision is also mixed and suffers from the failure to arrive at an adequate operational definition of accounting information overload.

Linguistic Relativism in Accounting

Accounting can be represented as a language given the existance of the two components of symbolic representations and grammatical characteristics.[79] As a result early behavioral accounting research attempted to examine the connotative and denotative meaning of accounting constructs and to investigate the differences in the perception of these constructs by different uses and prepares. Most of the attempts were generally characterized by the successful use of the various methodologies used in the study of language, namely semantic differential, antecedent consequent methods, cloze procedure and multidimensional scaling techniques.[80] Some of these method attempts went beyond the mere use of the techniques to support the research questions by theoretical models from linguistics, namely the "Sapir-Whorf hypotheses" of linguistic relativism, sociolinguistics, and bilingualism. The end result is that the judgment/decision process in accounting is determined by the impact of language in behavior and attitudes, as hypothesized by the linguistics relativity hypothesis, the sociolinguistic hypothesis, and the bilingual thesis.[81] The three hypotheses are examined next.

First, according to the linguistic relativity hypotheses in accounting, the linguistic codifibility of a structure of accounting language affects the linguistic and nonlinguistic behavior of users. Four hypotheses are suggested as follows:

1. The users that make certain lexical distinctions in accounting are enabled to talk about and solve a problem that cannot be easily solved by users that do not.

2. The users that make certain lexical distinctions in accounting are enabled to perform (nonlinguistic) tasks more readily or more completely than those that do not.

3. The users that process the accounting (grammatical) rules are predisposed to different managerial genial styles or emphases than those that do not.

4. The accounting techniques may tend to facilitate or render more difficult various (nonlinguistic) managerial behaviors on the part of users.[82]

Second, according to the sociolinguistic thesis, the social roles created by different professional memberships, social claims, and education lead to different communication codes, either elaborated or restricted, that affect concept function, understanding, and decision making in accounting.[83]

Third, according to the bilingual thesis, the use of different language or directions, as in bilingualism or diglossia, provides speakers with different understandings of accounting phenomena as well as different cognitive ability.[84]

Functional and Data Fixation

Functional fixation, as it is used in accounting, suggests that under certain circumstances a decision maker may be unable to adjust his or her decision process to a change in the accounting process that supplied him or her with impact data.[85] Borrowed from the psychological literature, the phenomenon has been used in a slightly different way by accounting researchers.

Functional fixation originated as a concept in psychology, arising from an investigation of the impact of past experience on human behavior. Duncker introduced the concept of functional fixation to illustrate the negative role of past experiences.[86] He investigated the hypotheses that an individual's prior use of an object in a function dissimilar to that required in a present problem would serve to exhibit the discovery of an appropriate, novel use for the objects. This result supported the functional fixation hypothesis with regard to several common objects, for example, boxes, pliers, weights, and paper clips.

Ijiri, Jaedicke, and Knight viewed the decision process as being characterized by three factors: decision inputs, decision outputs, and decision rules.[87] They then introduced the conditions under which a decision maker cannot adjust his or her decision process to a change in the accounting process. They attributed the inability to adjust, if it existed, to the psychological factor of functional fixation. Thus, whereas psychologists are interested in functional fixation involving function or objects, accounting research, influenced by the Ijiri, Jaedicke, and Knight exploration, is interested in functional fixation involving data. Therefore accounting research should consider two forms of the functional fixation hypotheses, one focusing on function and one focusing on output or data. There lies the main difference: in the case of functional fixation, psychologists used objects such as medallions, string, and boxes to solve relatively simple tasks, whereas the data fixation experiments all used data to solve unstructured problems. One might assume correctly that most of the interest in psychology has been on functional fixation. The exceptions to this assumption were a psychological data fixation study by Knight[88] and two mixed data fixation/functional fixation studies in accounting by Barnes and Welb and Riahi-Belkaoui.[89,90]

Various concepts exist for both the function and data fixation results in accounting, namely,

The conditioning hypotheses:[91] It may be that the subjects of the experiments, mostly accounting students, have been conditioned to react to some form of accounting outputs and have failed to adjust their decision processes in response to a "well-disclosed" accounting change. The conditioning phenomenon inhibits the subjects from adopting the correct behavior, which is to adjust to the accounting change, and has led them to act as they have been conditioned to act in their previous behaviors or socialization sessions. Thus, the conditioning phenomenon is a form of functional fixation, as the subjects no longer are able to discriminate.

Prospect theory and framing hypotheses:[92] Framing occurs because the wording of a question has the potential to alter a subject's response. Functional fixation can be viewed as a result of the particular choice of framing options made by the subjects in the experiments. The formulation of the decision tasks as well as the norms, habits, and personal characteristics of the subjects affect the framing of the decision and lead to functional data fixation results.

Primacy versus recency ego involvement:[93,94] In matters of ego involvement with an accounting technique just learned, subjects will give importance to what is perceived as relevant, significant, or meaningful. This would explain some of the data fixation findings where the subjects have reverted to either the use of the first learned method (primacy) or the second learned method (recency) as to the method more clear or basic to their ego involvement.

Information Inductance

The individual is either providing or receiving information. His or her behavior is affected in both situations by the information: (1) either through information use when the individual is a user or (2) through information inductance when the individual is a producer and sender of information. By information inductance it is meant that the individual's behavior is affected by the same information he or she is required to produce and communicate.[95] In other words, the phenomenon of information inductance refers to the outcome resulting from the sender's anticipations or expectations regarding the potential use of the information produced and communicated. As stated by Prakash and Rappaport:

An individual anticipating the consequences of his or her communication might lead him or her—before any information is communicated and, hence, even before any consequences arise—to choose to alter the information, or his or her behavior, or even his or her objectives. This is the process of information inductance.[96]

Two factors seem to govern inductance. First, communication of information that is either in fact a description of the sender's behavior and is regarded as such by the information sender, or concerning which the information sender has some apprehension that it could be so regarded by the information recipient, will be strongly conducive to information inductance. Secondly, consequences that represent possible feedback effects in the information sender will be strongly conducive to information inductance. Second, consequences that represent possible feedback effects on the information sender will be strongly conducive to information inductance. We can broadly classify the feedback effects of an information sender as arising from (1) external evaluation of performance, (2) regulation and control of operations, (3) interaction with the decisions of other behavioral units, and (4) changes in the set of choices open to the information sender.[97]

Information inductance can be integrated to information use to provide an integrated theory of the impact of information involving both senders and users.

Organizational and Budgetary Slack

Slack arises from the tendency of organizations and individuals to refrain from using all the resources available to them.[98] It describes a tendency to not operate at peak efficiency. In general, two types of slack have been identified in the literature, namely organizational slack and budgetary slack. Organizational slack basically refers to an unused capacity, in the sense that the demands put on the resources of the organization are less than the supply of these resources. Budgetary slack is found in the budgetary process and refers to the intentional distortion of information that results from an understatement of budgeted sales and an overstatement of budgeted costs.

Organizational slack is a buffer created by management in its use of available resources to deal with internal as well as external events that may arise and threaten an established condition—organizational slack, therefore, is used by management as an agent of change in response to changes in both the internal and external environments. Some means of organizational slack have been suggested by various researchers. For example, Martin M. Rosner used profit and excess capacity as slack measures,[99] L. J. Bourgeois and Jitendra V. Singh refined these measures by suggesting that slack could be differentiated in an "case-or recovery" dimension.[100] Basically, they considered excess liquidity to be *available slack,* not yet earmarked for particular uses. Overhead costs were termed *recoverable slack,* in the sense that they are absorbed by various organizational functions but can be recovered when needed elsewhere. In addition, the ability of a firm to generate resources from the environment, such as the ability to raise additional debt or equity capital, was considered *potential slack.* All of these measures were divided by sales to control for company size.

Building on Bourgeois and Singh's suggestions, Theresa K. Lant opted for the following four measures:

1. Administrative Slack = (General and Administration Expense)/Cost of Goods Sold,

2. Available Liquidity = (Cash + Marketable Securities − Current Liabilities)/ Sales,

3. Recoverable Liquidity = (Accounts Receivable + Inventory)/Sales, and

4. Retained Earnings = (Net Profit − Dividends)/Sales.[101]

The literature on organizational slack shows that managers have the motives necessary to desire to operate in a slack environment. The literature on budgetary slack considers the budget as the embodiment of that environment and, therefore, assumes that managers will use the budgeting process to bargain for slack in budgets through a process of *understating revenues and overstating costs.*[102] The general definition of budgetary slack, then, is the budgeting process. A detailed description of the creation of budgetary slack by managers was reported by Schiff and Lewis in their study of the budget process of three divisions of multidivision companies.[103] They found evidence of budgetary increases in personnel requirements, establishment of marketing and sales budgets with internal limits on funds to be spent, use of manufacturing costs based on standard costs that do not reflect process improvements operationally available at the plant, and inclusion of discretionary "special projects."

Evidence of budgetary slack has also been reported by others. A. E. Lowe and R. W. Shaw found a downward bias, introduced through sales forecasts by line managers, which assumed good performance where rewards were related to forecasts.[104] M. Dalton reported various examples of department managers allocating resources to what they considered justifiable purposes even though such purposes were not authorized in their budgets.[105] G. Shillinglaw noted the extreme vulnerability of budgets used to measure divisional performance given the great control exercised by divisional performance given the reporting of results.[106]

Slack creation is a generalized organizational phenomenon. Many different organizational factors have been used to explain slack creation, in particular, organizational structure, goal congruence, control system, and managerial behavior. Slack creation is assumed to occur in cases where a Tayloristic organizational structure exists,[107] although it is also assumed to occur in participative organizational structure.[108] It may be due to conflicts that arise between the individual and organizational goals, leading managers to intentionally create slack. It may also be due to the attitudes of management toward the budget and to workers' views of the budget as a device used by management to manipulate them.[109] Finally, the creation of slack may occur whether the organization is based on a centralized or decentralized structure.[110] With regard to this last issue, Schiff and Lewis have taken the tasks of creating and managing divisional slack as the most influential in the internal allocation of slack.

Studies of budgetary slack include Onsi's investigation of the connection between the type of budgeting system and the propensities to create slack,[111] Merchant's investigation of how managers' propensities to create budgetary slack are affected by the budgeting system and the technical context,[112] Young's testing of the effects of risk and asymmetric information on slack budgeting,[113] Waller's testing of the joint effect of a truth-inducing pay scheme and risk preferences in slack in participative budgeting,[114] and Belkaoui's testing of self-esteem feedback in slack budgeting as an information distortion mechanism.[115] A theoretical framework aimed at structuring knowledge about biasing behavior was proposed by Kari Lukka.[116] It contains an explanatory model for budgetary biasing and a model for budgetary biasing at the organizational level. It draws from the management accounting and organizational behavior literature and related behavioral research to suggest a set of intentions and determinants of budgetary biasing. Budgetary biasing is at the center of many interrelated and sometimes contradictory factors with the actor's intentions as the synthetic core of his or her behavior.

In conclusion, organizational slack and budgetary slack are two hypothetical constructs to explain organizational phenomena that are prevalent in all forms of organizations. Evidence linking both constructs to organizational, individual, and contextual factors is growing and in the future may contribute to an emerging theoretical framework for an understanding of slack. Further investigation into the potential determinants of organizational and budgetary slack remains to be done. This effort is an important one because the behavior of slack is highly relevant to the achievement of internal economic efficiency in organizations. Witness the following comment: ''The effective organization has more rewards at its disposal, or more organizational slack to pay with, and thus can allow all members to exercise more discretion, obtain more rewards, and feel that their influence is higher.''[117]

Contingency Approaches to the Design of Accounting Systems

A perfect match between specific contingencies and the various characteristics of accounting systems is the objective of the method of theoretical and empirical research generally known as the contingency approach to the design of accounting systems. Research of this type dismisses the notion that universality in the design of accounting systems can be reached to accommodate all situations through a search for the factors that can best ensure the effectiveness of the accounting systems.

The contingency theory approach to the design of accounting systems assumes that a general strategy applicable to all organizations does not exist. On the contrary, it assumes that the design of various components of accounting systems depend on specific contingencies that can create a perfect match. It is then the perfect link or match between the design of accounting systems and the specific contingencies, which is the scope of contingency theory. To date, the contingency formulations have considered the effects of technology, organizational structure and theory, and the environment in attempting to explain how accounting systems differ in various situations. All of these formulations point to the accepted thesis that there is no universal, "best" design for a management accounting information system, and that "it all depends upon situational factors."[118]

These formulations adopt a general framework that links (1) some contingent variables (that is, variables that cannot be influenced by the organization) to (2) any components of an organization control package (consisting of accounting information design, other management information design, organizational design, or organizational control arrangements), and then (3) some intervening variables provide a link to (4) a measure of organizational effectiveness.[119] The formulations are either empirical or theoretical.

Participative Budgeting and Performance

Participation in budgeting entails the involvement of subordinates in the setting of standards that affect their operations and rewards. The implied benefit of participative budgeting is that it will improve attitudes, productivity, and/or performance. The results, however, have been mixed. Some studies have supported the argument that budgetary participation leads to higher job satisfaction,[120] higher motivation to achieve the budget,[121] and higher performance.[122] Other studies, however, found either a weak association between participation and performance,[123] or a negative association between the two variables.[124]

Although findings on the relationship between participative budgeting and performance have been mixed, participation in decision making has been broadly defined as the "organizational process whereby individuals are involved in, and have influence on, decisions that have direct effects on those individuals."[125]

Brownell reviewed participation in decision making and found evidence of positive effects of *antecedent moderators* on participation and positive effects of participation on outcomes conditioned by *consequence moderators*. The antecedent moderators included (1) the cultural variables of nationality,[126] legislative systems,[127] race,[128] and religion and (2) the organizational variables of environmental stability,[129] technology,[130] task uncertainty,[131] and organizational structure.[132] The consequence moderators included (1) the interpersonal variables of task stress,[133] group size,[134] intrinsic satisfaction of task,[135] and congruence between task and individual[136] and (2) the individual level variables of locus of control,[137] authoritarianism,[138] external reference points,[139] and perceived emphasis placed in accounting information.[140]

A comprehensive review of participation in decision making (hereafter PDM) was attempted by Locke and Schweiger.[141] They reached the following interesting conclusions: (1) The use of PDM is a practical rather than a moral issue; (2) the concept of participation refers to shared or joint decision making, and therefore excludes delegation; (3) there are numerous mechanisms both cognitive and motivational through which PDM may produce high morale and performance; (4) research findings yield equivocal support for the thesis that PDM necessarily leads to increased satisfaction and productivity, although the evidence for the former outcome is stronger than the evidence for the latter; (5) the evidence indicates that the effectiveness of PDM depends on numerous contextual factors; and (6) PDM is the only way to motivate employees.[142]

The view that the relationship between participation and performance holds under all conditions is known as the universalistic perspective. As we have seen, support for this view is mixed. Another view, that the relationship between participation and performance is moderated by organizational, task-related, structural, attitudinal, and personality variables, is known as the contingency perspective. This perspective accounts for the moderating effects of motivation, leadership style, task uncertainty, role ambiguity, reward structure, cognitive dissonance, authoritarianism, locus of control, and the Pelz effect. Findings on the impact of these moderating variables demonstrate the superiority of the contingency perspective in the analysis of the relationship between participative budgeting and performance. Before reviewing the findings, it is appropriate to note that the literature in participation in decision making has also identified more intervening mechanisms that mediate the effects of participation in decision making.

METHODS

Methods in the behavioral approach include field studies, natural field experiments, laboratory experiments, and simulation experiments. Field studies take place in a natural setting without any attempt to control or influence individuals. They are relatively free from any Hawthorne effects. An assessment of field studies follows:

A group of individuals who under natural conditions are available for study in the same place at the same time may be likely to be systematically homogeneous in ways that make them unrepresentative of the total population. Furthermore, because no experimental manipulation of independent variables is undertaken, it is rarely possible to interpret the direction of causal relationships in field studies. Under most circumstances field studies are particularly useful either at the very early stages of investigation of a particular issue (in order to evaluate the kinds of variables most likely to be related to the dependent variable under study, and thus most appropriate for further research) or at very late stages of investigation, when a great amount of specific knowledge about a particular kind of behavior has been accumulated and it has become desirable to test particular hypotheses or theories in natural contexts.[143]

Field experiments enable the investigation to intrude in a setting and manipulate a variable for the purpose of studying its effects on individual behavior.

Laboratory experiments take place in the laboratory under experimental conditions whereby the investigation is able to manipulate any and all of the conditions that can affect the subjects.

Simulation experiments try to reproduce the most important variables of a natural situation in an abstract and stylized way.[144]

CONCLUSION

This chapter has evaluated the nature of the behavioral approach. Most of the theses borrowed from the social sciences are used to establish a generalization about human behavior in relation to accounting information. The paradigm has gained a good measure of legitimacy in accounting research as evidenced by the large number of studies examining behavioral implications in the accounting environment. A good grounding in the social sciences is necessary for the survival of this paradigm and its eventual acceptance by policy makers.

NOTES

    1. Ahmed Riahi-Belkaoui, *Accounting Theory,* 3rd ed. (London: Academic Press, 1992), 113.

    2. C. T. Devine, "Research and Accounting Theory Formation," *The Accounting Review* (July 1960): 387–99.

    3. American Accounting Association, "Report of the Committee on the Behavioral

Science Content of the Accounting Curriculum,'' *The Accounting Review* 46 (Supplement 1971): 247.

4. Ibid., 394.

5. J. G. Birnberg, and Raghu Nath, ''Implication of Behavioral Science for Managerial Accounting,'' *The Accounting Review* (July 1967): 468–79; William J. Bruns, Jr., ''Accounting Information and Decision Making: Some Behavior Hypotheses,'' *The Accounting Review* (July 1968): 469–80; T. R. Hofstedt, and J. C. Kinard, ''A Strategy for Behavioral Accounting Research,'' *The Accounting Review* (July 1970): 38–54.

6. American Accounting Association, ''Report of the Committee on the Behavioral Science Content of the Accounting Curriculum,'' 247.

7. W. S. Waller, and W. L. Felix, Jr., ''The Auditor and Learning from Experience: Some Conjectures,'' *Accounting, Organization and Society* (June 1984).

8. Ibid., 390–406.

9. W. G. Chase, and H. A. Simon, ''Perception in Chen,'' *Cognitive Psychology* 4 (1973): 55–87.

10. H. L. Chiesi, G. J. Spilich, and J. F. Von, ''Acquisition of Domain-Related Information in Relation to High and Low Domain Knowledge,'' *Journal of Verbal Learning and Verbal Behavior* 18 (1979): 257–73.

11. A. R. Halpern, and H. G. Bowa, ''Musical Expertise and Melodic Structure in Memory for Musical Notation,'' *American Journal of Psychology* 95 (1982): 31–50.

12. B. Schneiderman, ''Exploratory Experiments in Programmer Behavior,'' *International Journal of Computer and Information Science* 5 (1976): 123–43.

13. B. Adelson, ''Problem Solving and the Development of Abstract Categories in Programming Languages,'' *Memory and Cognition* 9 (1981): 922–33.

14. B. Adelson, ''When Novices Surpass Experts: The Difficulty of a Task May Increase with Expertise,'' *Journal of Experimental Psychology: Learning, Memory and Cognition* 10 (1984): 483–95.

15. R. Weber, ''Some Characteristics of the Free Recall of Computer Control by EDP Auditor,'' *Journal of Accounting Research* (Spring 1980): 914–41.

16. Michael Gibbins, ''Proposition about the Psychology of Professional Judgment in Public Accounting,'' *Journal of Accounting Research* (Spring 1984): 103–25.

17. Michael Gibbins, ''Knowledge Structures and Experienced Auditor Judgment,'' in *Auditor Probability to the Year 2000: 1987 Proceeding of the Arthur Young,* Andrew Bailly, ed. (Reston, VA: Arthur Young, 1988), 57.

18. Ibid., 51–73.

19. M. Gibbins, and C. Emby, ''Evidence on the Nature of Professional Judgment in Public Accounting,'' in *Auditing Research Symposium 1984,* A. R. Ahdel-Khalik and I. Solomon, eds. (Champaign: University of Illinois at Urbana/Champaign, 1985).

20. C. Emby, and M. Gibbins, ''Good Judgment in Public Accounting: Quality and Justification,'' *Contemporary Accounting Research* (Spring 1988): 287–313.

21. Similar models have been proposed for the performance appraisal process. See, for example, A. S. De Nisi, T. P. Cafferty, and B. M. Meglinio, ''A Cognitive View of the Performance Appraisal Loan. A Model and Research Proportion,'' *Organizational Behavior and Human Performance* 33 (1984): 360–96; J. M. Feldman, ''Beyond Attribution Theory: Cognitive Process in Performance Appraisal,'' *Journal of Applied Psychology* 66, no. 2 (1981): 127–48.

22. Ahmed Riahi-Belkaoui, "A Model About the Psychology of Judgment in Accounting," *The Middle East Business and Economic Review* 4, no. 2 (1992): 25–31.

23. Ahmed Riahi-Belkoui, *The Cultural Shaping of Accounting* (Westport, CT: Greenwood Publishing, 1995).

24. Linda Smircich, "Concepts of Culture and Organizational Analysis," *Administrative Science Quarterly* 28 (1983): 339–58.

25. Bronislaw Malinowski, *A Scientific Theory of Culture* (Chapel Hill: University of North Carolina Press, 1944).

26. A. R. Radcliffe-Brown, *Structure and Function in Primitive Society* (New York: Free Press, 1968).

27. Ward H. Goodenough, *Culture, Language and Society* (Reading, MA: Addison-Wesley, 1971).

28. Clifferd Geertz, *The Interpretation of Cultures* (New York: Baric Books, 1973).

29. Claude Levi-Strauss, *Structural Anthropology* (Chicago: University of Chicago Press, 1983).

30. Ahmed Riahi-Belkaoui, *The Cultural Shaping of Accounting.*

31. Geert Hofstede, *Culture's Consequences: International Difference in W-Related Values* (Beverly Hills, CA: Sage, 1980).

32. Nancy J. Adler, "Understanding the Ways of Understanding: Cross-Cultural Management Methodology Reviewed," in *Advances in International Comparative Management,* Vol. I, R. Farmer, ed. (Greenwich, CT: JAI Press, 1984), 31–67.

33. Ahmed Riahi-Belkaoui, Claude Perochon, M. A. Nathews, Bruno Bernardi, and Youssef A. El-Adly, "Report of the Cultural Studies and Accounting Research Committee of the International Accounting Section, American Accounting Association, 1988–1989" *Advances in International Accounting* 4 (1991): 175–198.

34. D. Willer, *Scientific Sociology: Theory and Method* (Englewood Cliffs, NJ: Prentice-Hall, 1967).

35. F. L. Strodtbeck, "Considerations of Metamethod in Cross-Cultural Studies," *American Anthropologist* Pt. 2, 66 223 (1969).

36. Harry C. Triandis, Roy S. Malpass, and Andrew R. Davidson, "Cross-Cultural Psychology," in *Biennial Review of Anthropology 1971,* B. J. Siegel, ed. (Stanford, CA: Stanford University Press, 1972), 8.

37. R. Naroll, "The Culture-Bearing Unit in Cross-Cultural Surveys," in *Handbook of Methods in Cultural Anthropology,* R. Naroll and R. Cohen, eds. (New York: Columbia University Press, 1970–1973), 248.

38. H. C. Triandis, "Introduction to Cross-Cultural Psychology," in *Handbook of Cross-Cultural Psychology,* H. C. Triandis and W. W. Lambert, eds. (New York: Allyn and Bacon, 1980), 2.

39. Ibid., 4.

40. Ibid.

41. H. C. Triandis, V. Vassilion, Y. Tanaka, and A. V. Shanmugam, *The Analysis of Subjective Culture* (New York: Wiley, 1972).

42. Birnberg and Nath, "Implications of Behavioral Science for Managerial Accounting," 81–98; T. R. Hofstedt, "Some Behavioral Parameters of Financial Analysis," *The Accounting Review* (October 1972); "Accounting Research: References and Source

Materials,'' Section 7 of "Report of the Committee on Research Methodology in Accounting," *The Accounting Review* (Supplement 1972): 454–504.

43. T. R. Dyckman, M. Gibbins, and R. J. Swieringa, "Experimental and Survey Research in Financial Accounting: A Review and Evaluation," in *The Impact of Accounting Research in Financial Accounting and Disclosure on Accounting Practice,* A. R. Abdel-Khalik and T. F. Keller, eds. (Durham, NC: Duke University Press, 1978), 48–49.

44. Ibid.

45. Charles T. Horngren, "Security Analysis and the Price Level," *The Accounting Review* (October 1955): 575–81; id., "The Funds Statement and Its Use by Analysts," *Journal of Accountancy* (January 1956): 55–59.

46. R. D. Bradish, "Corporate Reporting and the Financial Analyst," *The Accounting Review* (October 1965): 757–66; W. W. Ecton, "Communication Through Accounting-Bankers' Views," *Journal of Accountancy* (August 1969): 79–81.

47. A. R. Cerf, *Corporate Reporting and Investment Decisions* (Berkeley, CA: Institute of Business and Economic Research, 1961); S. S. Singhvi and H. B. Desao, "An Empirical Analysis of the Quality of Corporate Financial Disclosure," *The Accounting Review* (January 1971): 129–38; S. L. Buzby, "Selected Items for Information and Their Disclosure in Annual Reports," *The Accounting Review* (July 1974): 423–35; A. Belkaoui and A. Kahl, *Corporation Financial Disclosure in Canada,* CCGAA Research Monograph No. 1 (Vancouver: Canadian Certified General Accountants Association, 1978).

48. H. K. Baker, and J. A. Haslem, "Information Needs of Individual Investors," *Journal of Accountancy* (November 1973): 64–69; G. Chandra, "A Study of the Consensus in Disclosure Among Public Accountants and Security Analysts," *The Accounting Review* (October 1974): 733–42; A. Belkaoui, A. Kahl, and J. Peyrard, "Information Needs of Financial Analysts: An International Comparison," *Journal of International Education and Research in Accounting* (Fall 1977): 19–27; A. Belkaoui, "Consensus on Disclosure," *The Canadian Chartered Accountant Magazine* (June 1979): 44–46.

49. H. Falk and T. Ophir, "The Effect of Risk on the Use of Financial Statements by Investment Decision Makers: A Case Study," *The Accounting Review* (April 1973): 323–28; id., "The Influence of Differences in Accounting Policies on Investment Decision," *Journal of Accounting Research* (Spring 1973): 108–16; R. Libby, "Accounting Ratios and the Predictions of Failure: Some Behavioral Evidence," *Journal of Accounting Research* (Spring 1975): 475–89.

50. F. J. Soper, and R. Dolphin, Jr., "Readability and Corporate Annual Reports," *The Accounting Review* (April 1964): 358–62; J. E. Smith, and N. P. Smith, "Readability: A Measure of the Performance of the Communication Function of Financial Reporting," *The Accounting Review* (July 1971): 552–61; A. A. Haried, "The Semantic Dimensions of Financial Statements," *Journal of Accounting Research* (Autumn 1972): 376–91; id., "Measurement of Meaning in Financial Reports," *Journal of Accounting Research* (Spring 1973): 117–45; B. L. Oliver, "The Semantic Differential: A Device for Measuring the Interprofessional Communication of Selected Accounting Concepts," *Journal of Accounting Research* (Autumn 1974): 299–316; A. Belkaoui, "The Interprofessional Linguistic Communication of Accounting Concepts: An Experiment in Sociolinguistics," *Journal of Accounting Research* (Fall 1980): 362–74.

51. K. Nelson, and R. H. Stawser, "A Note on APB Opinion No. 16," *Journal of Accounting Research* (Autumn 1970): 284–89; V. Brenner, and R. Shuey, "An Empirical Study of Support for APB Opinion No. 16," *Journal of Accounting Research* (Spring 1972): 200–208.

52. R. M. Copeland, A. J. Francia, and R. H. Strawser, "Students as Subjects in Behavioral Business Research," *The Accounting Review* (April 1973): 365–74; L. B. Godurn, "CPA and User Opinions in Increased Corporate Disclosure," *The CPA Journal* (July 1975): 31–35.

53. S. M. Woolsey, "Materiality Survey," *Journal of Accountancy* (September 1973): 91–92; James W. Patillo and J. D. Siebel, "Materiality in Financial Reporting," *Financial Executive* (October 1973): 27–28; J. Dyer, "A Search for Objective Materiality Norms in Accounting and Auditing," Ph.D. Dissertation, Lexington, KY: University of Kentucky, 1973; J. A. Boastsman, and J. C. Robertson, "Policy-Capturing on Selected Materiality Judgments," *The Accounting Review* (April 1974): 342–52.

54. J. Rose, W. H. Beaver, S. Becker, and G. H. Sorter, "Toward an Empirical Measure of Materiality," *Journal of Accounting Research* 8 (Supplement 1970): 138–56; J. W. Dickhaut and I. R. C. Eggleton, "An Examination of the Process Underlying Comparative Judgments of Numerical Stimuli," *Journal of Accounting Research* (Spring 1975): 38–72.

55. Charles T. Horngren, "Security Analysts and the Price Level," *The Accounting Review* (October 1955): 575–81; R. E. Jensen, "An Experimental Design for the Study of Effects of Accounting Variations in Decision Making," *Journal of Accounting Research* (Autumn 1966): 224–38; John L. Livingstone, "A Behavioral Study of Tax Allocation in Electric Utility Regulations," *The Accounting Review* (July 1967): 544–52; Advellatif Khemakhem, "A Simulation of Management-Decision Behavior: 'Funds' and Income," *The Accounting Review* (July 1968): 522–24; T. R. Dyckman, *Accounting Research Study No. 1, Investment Analysis and General Price-Level Adjustments: A Behavioral Study* (Sarasota, FL: American Accounting Association, 1969); id., "On the Investment Decision," *The Accounting Review* (April 1976): 258–95; M. E. Barrett, "Accounting for Intercorporate Investments: A Behavioral Field Experiment," *Journal of Accounting Research* 9 (Supplement 1971): 50–92; N. Elias, "The Effects of Human Asset Statements on the Investment Decision: An Experiment," *Journal of Business* 10 (July/Supplement 1977): 334–42.

56. R. Libby, and B. L. Lewis, "Human Information Processing Research in Accounting: The State of the Art in 1982," *Accounting, Organizations, and Society* (December 1982): 233.

57. Ibid.

58. Ibid.

59. E. Brunswick, *The Conceptual Framework of Psychology* (Chicago: University of Chicago Press, 1952).

60. Libby and Lewis, "Human Information Processing Research in Accounting: The State of the Art in 1982," 233.

61. Ibid., 234.

62. W. Edwards, "Conservatism in Human Information Processing," in *Formal Representations of Human Judgment,* B. Kleinmutz, ed. (New York: John Wiley & Sons, 1968).

63. A. Tversky, and D. Kahneman, "Judgment Under Uncertainty: Heuristics and Biases," *Science* 185 (1974): 1125–31.

64. A. Newell, and H. A. Simon, *Human Problem Solving* (Englewood Cliffs, NJ: Prentice-Hall, 1972).

65. J. N. Payne, M. L. Braunstein, and J. S. Caroll, "Exploring Predecisional Behavior: An Alternative Approach to Decision Research," *Organization Behavior and Human Performance* (February 1978): 17–44.

66. Ibid.

67. E. J. Joyce, and R. Libby, "Behavioral Studies of Audit Decision Making," *Journal of Accounting Literature* (Spring 1982): 115.

68. Libby and Lewis, "Human Information Processing Research in Accounting: The State of the Art in 1982," 279.

69. K. R. Goldstein, and S. Blackman, *Cognitive Style: Five Approaches and Relevant Research* (New York: John Wiley & Sons, 1978), 12–13.

70. T. W. Adorno, E. Frenkel-Brunswick, D. J. Levinston, and R. N. Sanford, *The Authoritarian Personality* (New York: Harper & Row, 1950).

71. M. Rokeach, *The Open and Closed Mind* (New York: Basic Books, 1960).

72. G. A. Kelly, *The Psychology of Personal Constructs* (New York: W. W. Norton, 1955).

73. J. Bieri, "Cognitive Complexity and Personality Development," in *Experience, Structure, and Adaptability*, O. J. Harvey, ed. (New York: Springer Publishing, 1966).

74. J.H.B. Huysman, "The Effectiveness of the Cognitive Style Constraint in Implementing Operations Research Proposals," *Management Science* (September 1970): 94–95.

75. O. J. Harvey, D. E. Hunt, and H. M. Schroeder, *Conceptual Systems and Personality Organizations* (New York: John Wiley & Sons, 1961).

76. H. M. Schroeder, M. J. Driver, and S. Steufert, *Human Information Processing* (New York: Holt, Rinehart & Winston, 1967).

77. Ibid., 37.

78. H. A. Witkin, R. B. Dyks, H. F. Faterson, D. R. Goodenough, and S. A. Karyn, *Psychological Differentiation* (New York: John Wiley & Sons, 1962).

79. Ahmed Belkaoui, "Linguistic Relativity in Accounting," *Accounting Organizations and Society* (October 1978): 97–124.

80. Ibid.

81. Ahmed Riahi-Belkaoui, *The Linguistic Shaping of Accounting* (Westport, CT: Greenwood Publishing, 1996).

82. Ahmed Belkaoui, "Accounting and Language," *Journal of Accounting Literature* 8 (1989): 281–92.

83. Ahmed Belkaoui, "The Interprofessional Linguistic Communication of Accounting Concepts: An Experiment in Sociolinguistics," *Journal of Accounting Research* (Fall 1980): 362–74.

84. Janice Monti-Belkaoui, and Ahmed Belkaoui, "Bilingualism and the Perception of Professional Concepts," *Journal of Psycholinguistic Research* 12, no. 2 (1983): 111–27.

85. Ahmed Belkaoui, *Behavioral Accounting: The Research and Practice Issues* (Westport, CT: Greenwood Publishing, 1989).

86. K. Dunker, "On Problem Solving," *Psychological Monographs* 58, no. 5 (1945).

87. Y. Ijiri, R. K. Jaedicke, and K. E. Knight, "The Effects of Accounting Alternatives on Management Decisions," in *Research in Accounting Measurement*, R. K. Jaediclse, Y. Ijiri, and O. Nielsen, eds. (Sarasota, FL: American Accounting Association, 1966), 186–99.

88. K. E. Knight, "Effect of Effort on Behavioral Rigidity in Luchins/Water Jar Task," *Journal of Abnormal and Social Psychology* (Fall 1960): 192–94.

89. Paul Barnes, and John Welb, "Management Information Changes and Functional Fiscation: True Experimental Evidence from the Public Sector," *Accounting, Organizations and Society* (February, 1986): 1–18.

90. Ahmed Riahi-Belkaoui, "Accrual Accounting, Modified Cash Basis of Accounting and the Loan Decision: An Experiment in Functional Fiscation," *Managerial Finance* 18, no. 5 (1992): 3–13.

91. Robert R. Sterling, "On Theory Construction and Verification," *The Accounting Review* (July 1970): 433.

92. D. Kahneman and A. Tversley, "Prospect Theory: An Analysis of Decision Under Risk," *Econometrica* (March 1979): 263–91.

93. Ahmed Belkaoui, "Learning Order and the Acceptance of Accounting Techniques," *The Accounting Review* (October 1975): 897–99.

94. Ahmed Belkaoui, "The Primacy-Recency Effect, Ego Involvement and the Acceptance of Accounting Techniques," *The Accounting Review* (July 1977): 252–56.

95. P. Prakash, and A. Rappaport, "Information Inductance and Its Significance for Accounting," *Accounting, Organization and Society* (December 1982): 33.

96. Ibid., 38.

97. Ibid.

98. Ahmed Riahi-Belkaoui, *Organizational and Budgetary Slack* (Westport, CT: Greenwood Press, 1994).

99. Martin M. Rosner, "Economic Determinant of Organizational Innovation," *Administration Science Quarterly* 12 (1968): 614–25.

100. L. J. Bourgeois, and Jitendra V. Singh, "Organizational Slack and Political Behavior within Top Management Teams," working paper, Graduate School of Business, Stanford University, Stanford, CA, 1983.

101. Theresa K. Lant, "Modeling Organizational Slack: An Empirical Investigation," Stanford University Research Paper, No. 856, Stanford, CA, July 1986.

102. Michael Schiff, and Arie Y. Lewin, "The Impact of People on Budgets," *The Accounting Review* (April 1970): 259–68.

103. Michael Schiff, and Arie Y. Lewin, "Where Traditional Budgeting Fails," *Financial Executive* (May 1968): 51–62.

104. A. E. Lowe, and R. W. Shaw, "An Analysis of Managerial Biasing: Evidence from Company's Budgetary Processing," *Journal of Management Studies* (October 1968): 304–15.

105. M. Dalton, *Men Who Manage* (New York: John Wiley & Sons, 1961), 36–38.

106. G. Shillinglaw, "Divisional Performance Review: An Extension of Budgetary Control," in *Management Controls: New Directions in Basic Research*, C. P. Bonini, R.K. Jaediclse, and H. M. Wagner, eds. (New York: McGraw-Hill, 1964), 149–63.

107. C. Argyris, *The Impact of Budgets on People* (New York: Controllerships Foundation, 1952), 25.

108. E. H. Caplan, *Management Accounting and Behavioral Science* (Reading, MA: Addison-Wesley, 1971).

109. Argyris, *The Impact of Budgets on People.*

110. Schiff and Lewis, "Where Traditional Budgetary Fails," 51–62.

111. Mohamed Onsin, "Factor Analysis of Behavioral Variables Affecting Budgetary Slack," *The Accounting Review* (July 1973): 535–48.

112. K. A. Merchant, "Budgeting and the Prosperity to Create Budgetary Slack," *Accounting, Organization and Society* (May 1985): 535–48.

113. Mark S. Young, "Slack in Participative Budgeting: The Effects of Risk Aversion and Asymmetric Information in Budgetary Slack," *Journal of Accounting Research* (Autumn 1985): 829–42.

114. W. S. Waller, "Slack in Participative Budgeting: The Joint Effect of a Truth Including Pay Scheme and Risk Preferences," *Accounting, Organization and Society* (December 1987): 87–98.

115. Ahmed Belkaoui, "Slack Budgeting, Information Distortion and Self-Esteem," *Contemporary Accounting Research* (Fall 1985): 111–23.

116. Kari Lukka, "Budgetary Biasing in Organization: Theoretical Framework and Empirical Evidence," *Accounting, Organization and Society* (February 1988): 281–301.

117. Charles Perrow, *Complex Organizations: A Critical Essay* (Glenview, IL: Scott, Foresman and Co., 1972), 140.

118. D. T. Otley, "The Contingency Theory of Management Accounting: Achievement and Prognosis," *Accounting, Organization and Society* (December 1980): 413–28.

119. Ibid., 420–21.

120. Hofstede, *The Game of Budget Control* (NY: Van Nostrand, 1967); D. Searfoss and R. Monczla, "Perceived Participation in the Budget Process and Motivation to Achieve the Budget," *Academy of Management Journal* (December 1973): 541–54.

121. R. J. Swieringa, and R. H. Moncur, *Some Effects of Participative Budgeting on Managerial Behavior* (New York: National Association of Accountants, 1974).

122. K. W. Milani, "The Relationship of Participation in Budget-Setting to Industrial Supervisor Performance and Attitudes: A Field Study," *Accounting Review* (April 1975): 274–85.

123. I. Kenis, "Effects of Budgetary Goal Characteristics on Managerial Attitudes and Performance," *Accounting Review* (October 1979): 707–21.

124. A. C. Stedry, *Budget Control and Cost Behavior* (Englewood Cliffs, NJ: Prentice-Hall, 1960); J. F. Bryan and E. A. Locke, "Goal Setting as a Means of Increasing Motivation," *Journal of Applied Psychology* (Fall 1967): 274–77.

125. P. Brownell, "Participation in the Budgeting Process: When It Works and When It Doesn't," *Journal of Accounting Literature* (Spring 1982): 124–53.

126. Industrial Democracy in Europe International Research Group, "Participation: Formal Rules, Influence and Involvement," *Industrial Relations* (Fall 1979): 273–94; L. Coch, and J. R. P. French, Jr., "Overcoming Resistance to Change," *Human Relations* (August 1948): 512–32; J. R. P. Frech, Jr., J. Israel, and D. Ho, "An Experiment on Participation in a Norwegian Factory: Interpersonal Discussions of Decision-Making," *Human Relations* (February 1960): 3–19.

127. C. D. King, and M. van de Vall, *Models of Industrial Democracy* (New York: Mouton, 1978).

128. S. Melman, "Managerial vs. Cooperation Decision in Israel," *Studies in Comparative International Development* 6 (1970–1971).

129. P. R. Lawrence and J. W. Lorsch, *Organization and Environment* (Cambridge, MA: Harvard University Graduate School of Business Administration, 1967).

130. J. D. Thompson, *Organization in Action* (New York: McGraw-Hill, 1967).

131. Jay Galbraith, *Designing Complex Organizations* (Reading, MA: Addison-Wesley, 1973).

132. W. J. Burns, Jr., and J. H. Waterhouse, "Budgetary Control and Organizational Structure," *Journal of Accounting Research* (Autumn 1975): 177–203.

133. A. W. Halpin, "The Leadership Behavior and Combat Performance of Airplane Commanders," *Journal of Abnormal and Social Psychology* 20 (1954): 19–22.

134. H. H. Meyer, "The Effective Superior: Some Surprising Findings," in *The Failure of Success*, A. J. Marrow, ed. (New York: Amacom, 1972).

135. R. J. House, A. C. Pilley, and S. Kerr, "Relation of Leader Consideration and Initiating Structure to R. D. Subordinates' Satisfaction," *Administrative Science Quarterly* (March 1971): 19–30.

136. R. W. Griffin, "Relationships among Individual, Taste Design, and Behavior Variables," *Academy of Management Journal* (December 1980): 665–83.

137. P. Browenell, "Participation in Budgeting, Locus of Control and Organizational Effectiveness," *Accounting Review* (October 1981): 844–60.

138. V. H. Broom, *Some Personality Determinants of the Effects of Participation* (Englewood Cliffs, NJ: Prentice-Hall, 1960).

139. Hofstede, *The Game of Budget Control.*

140. P. Brownell, "The Role of Accounting Data in Performance Evaluation, Budgetary Participation and Organizational Effectiveness," *Journal of Accounting Research* (Spring 1982): 12–27.

141. E. A. Locke, and D. Schweiger, "Participation in Decision-Making: One More Look," in *Research in Organizational Behavior,* B. M. Staw, ed. (Greenwich, CT: JAI Press, 1979), 1–325.

142. Ibid.

143. John W. McDavid, and Herbert Harari, *Psychology and Social Behavior* (New York: Harper & Row Publisher, 1974), 15.

144. Ibid., 27.

REFERENCES

Adler, Nancy. "Understanding the Ways of Understanding: Core-Cultural Management Reviewed." In *Advances in International Comparative Management,* Vol. 1, edited by R. Farmer, 31–67. Greenwich, CT: JAI Press, 1984.

Belkaoui, Ahmed. "Learning Order and the Acceptance of Accounting Technique." *The Accounting Review* (October 1975): 897–99.

Belkaoui, Ahmed. "The Primacy-Recency Effect, Ego Involvement, and the Acceptance of Accounting Technique." *The Accounting Review* (January 1977): 252–56.

Belkaoui, Ahmed. "Linguistic Relativity in Accounting." *Accounting, Organization and Society* (October 1978): 97–124.

Belkaoui, Ahmed. "The Interprofessional Linguistic Communication of Accounting Concepts: An Experiment in Sociolinguistics." *Journal of Accounting Research* 1 (Fall 1980): 362–74.

Belkaoui, Ahmed. "Slack Budgeting, Information Distortion and Self-Esteem." *Contemporary Accounting Research* (Fall 1985): 111–23.

Belkaoui, Ahmed. "Accounting and Language." *Journal of Accounting Literature* 8 (1989): 281–92.

Belkaoui, Ahmed. *Behavioral Accounting: The Research and Practical Issues.* Westport, CT: Greenwood Publishing, 1989.

Bourgeois, L. J. "On the Measurement of Organizational Slack." *Academy of Management Review* 6, no. 1 (1981): 29–39.

Gibbins, Michael. "Proprosition about the Psychology of Professional Judgement in Public Accounting." *Journal of Accounting Research* (Spring 1984): 103–25.

Ijiri, Y., R. K. Jaedicke, and K. E. Knight. "The Effects of Accounting Alternatives as Management Decisions." In *Research in Accounting Measurement* edited by R. K. Jaedicke, Y. Ijiri, and O. Nielsen, 189–99. Sarasota, FL: American Accounting Association, 1966.

Locke, E. A., and D. Schweiger. "Participation in Decision-Making: One New Look." In *Research in Organizational Behavior* edited by B. M. Staw, 1–325. Greenwich, CT: JAI Press, 1979.

Monti-Belkaoui, Janice, and Ahmed Belkaoui. "Bilingualism and the Perception of Professional Concepts." *Journal of Psycholinguistic Research* 12, No. 2 (1983): 111–27.

Perera, M. H. B., and M. R. Mathews, "The Cultural Relativity of Accounting and International Patterns of Social Accounting." *Advances in International Accounting* 3 (1990): 215–51.

Prakash, P., and A. Rappaport. "Information Inductance and Its Significance for Accounting." *Accounting, Organizations and Society* (Feburary 1977): 29–38.

Riahi-Belkaoui, Ahmed. "A Model About the Psychology of Judgment in Accounting." *The Middle East Business and Economic Review* 4, No. 2, (1992): 25–31.

Riahi-Belkaoui, Ahmed. *Organizational and Budgetary Slack.* Westport, CT: Greenwood Press, 1994.

Riahi-Belkaoui, Ahmed. *The Cultural Shaping of Accounting.* Westport, CT: Greenwood Publishing, 1995.

Riahi-Belkaoui, Ahmed. *The Linguistic Shaping of Accounting.* Westport, CT: Greenwood Publishing, 1996.

Riahi-Belkaoui, Ahmed, Claude Perochon, M. A. Mathews, Bruno Bernardi, and Youssef A. El-Adly. "Report of the Cultural Studies and Accounting Research Committee of the International Accounting Section of the American Accounting Association, 1988–1989." *Advances in International Accounting* 4 (1991): 175–98.

Index

Accountants: professional value system for, 24–25; societal role of, 24–25

Accounting: cross-cultural research in, 155; evaluation of market-based research in, 135–41; functionalist view in, 10–11; interpretive view in, 11–12; linguistic relativism in, 165–66; as multiple paradigm science, 22–24; radical humanist view in, 12–13; radical structuralist view in, 13–14; as social science, 1–4; and theory of scientific revolutions, 19–22

Accounting foundations: marginal-economics-based, 5–6; political-economy, 6–8

Accounting information, 157–58

Accounting regulation, 136

Accounting research: framework of nature of, 8–10; ideography vs. nomothesis approaches in, 15–19; using lens model, 159–60

Accounting researchers, 25–27

Accounting systems design, 171–72

Accounting theory: normative-deductive approach to construction of, 65; and value system, 24

Adverse selection, 42

Agency theory, 50

Alexander, Sidney S., 66

Allport, Gordon, 15, 18

Altman, E. I., 99, 100, 102

American Accounting Association, 148, 149

Analytic decision makers, 163

Analytical-agency paradigm: and agency relationship, 42–44; exemplars of, 42; and positive-agency paradigm, 41–42

Antecedent moderators, 172

Anthropological/inductive paradigm: and analytical-agency paradigm, 41–44; and earnings management research, 53–55; evaluation of, 55, 58–59; exemplars of, 35–37; and income smoothing, 36, 44–48, 50–51; and information/economics paradigm, 38–41; overview of, 35; and positive theory of accounting, 48–50; and research, 52; and subject matter, 38

Arbitrary pricing theory (APT), 126–27

Arrow, K. J., 43

Artificial smoothing, 47–48

Authoritarianism, 163

Baiman, Stanley, 43
Bank lending decisions, 111–12
Barnes, Paul, 110
Bayesian random coefficient model
    (BERAB), 129–30
Bayes's theorem, 160–61
Beerman, K. B., 103
Behavioral accounting. *See* Decision use-
    fulness/decision maker/individual user
    paradigm
Behling, Orlando, 16
Belkaoui, Ahmed, 23, 106, 110
Beta estimation, 130–31
Bilderbeek, J. B., 102
Bond ratings, 104–8
Bondford, M. D., 108
Bontemps, P. O., 103
Bourgeois, L. J., 169
Budgetary slack, 169–71
Bunge, Marie, 4
Burrell, Gibson, 9–10, 15–16

Capital maintenance, 68–69
Capital-asset pricing model, 126, 127
Capital-market efficiency, 52
Castagna, A. D., 102
Chambers, R. J., 93–94, 108
Classificatory smoothing, 48
Coase, R. H., 42
Cognitive complexity, 163
Cognitive relativism, 150–51, 153
Cognitive style approach, 163–65
Collongues, Yves, 103
Committee on Behavioral Science Con-
    tent of the Accounting Curriculum,
    148, 149
Conditioning hypotheses, 167
Consequence moderators, 172–73
Contingency theory approach, 171–72
Contracting cost theory, 50
Cooper, D. J., 6, 7, 13–14
Corporate restructuring, 108–11
Cultural relativism, 153–56
Current values, 69

Dalton, M., 170
Data fixation, 166–67

Davidson, Andrew R., 155
Davis, T. R., 17
Decision usefulness/decision maker/aggre-
    gate market behavior paradigm: and ar-
    bitrary pricing theory, 126–27; and
    beta estimation, 130–31; and capital-
    asset pricing model, 126, 128; and effi-
    cient market hypothesis, 125–26, 135;
    and efficient market model, 123–24;
    and equilibrium theory of option pric-
    ing, 127–28; and event study method-
    ology, 131–32; exemplars of, 121–22;
    explanation of, 121; and information
    content of earnings, 133; and market
    model, 128–30; and Ohlson's valuation
    model, 132; and price-level balance
    sheet valuation models, 132–33; and
    relation between earning and return,
    133–34; subject matter of, 122–23
Decision usefulness/decision maker/indi-
    vidual user paradigm: and behavioral
    effects of accounting information, 157–
    58; and cognitive relativism, 150–51,
    153; conclusions regarding, 174; and
    contingency theory, 171–72; and cul-
    tural relativism, 153–56; exemplars of,
    149; explanation of, 147–48; and
    functional and data fixation, 166–67;
    and human information processes, 158–
    65; and information inductance, 168;
    and linguistic relativism, 165–66;
    methods in, 173–74; and organizational
    and budgetary slack, 168–71; and par-
    ticipative budgeting and performance,
    172–73; subject matter of, 149
Decision usefulness/decision model para-
    digm: and bond premiums and bond
    ratings, 104–8; conclusions regarding,
    115; and corporate restructuring behav-
    ior, 108–11; and credit and bank
    lending decisions, 111–12; and distress
    prediction, 98–104; exemplars of, 93–
    95; explanation of, 93; and forecasting
    financial statement information, 112–
    14; methods of, 114–15; subject matter
    of, 96–97; and time-series properties of
    reported earnings, 97–98

Decision-theory model, 40
Deductive paradigm. *See* True income/deductive paradigm
Default risk, 104
Demand-revlation model, 41
Devine, C. T., 147
Dispersion of forecast errors, 112–13
Distress prediction, 98–104
Dogmatism, 163
Dopuch, N., 122

Earnings: information content of, 133; and relation between return, 133–34; time-series properties of reported, 97–98
Earnings management. *See* Income smoothing
Economic income, 67–68
Efficient market hypothesis, 125–26, 135
Efficient market model, 123–24
Equilibrium theory of option pricing, 127–28
Ethnography, 17–18
Event study methodology, 131–32
Expected value of error (EVE), 113

Fama, E. F., 42, 123, 124
Felix, W. L., 150
Field dependence, 164–65
Financial capital maintenance, 68–69
Financial reporting, 136–41
Financial statement information forecasting, 112–14
Fisher, Irving, 67
Fisher, L., 104
Framing hypotheses, 167
Functional fixation, 135–36, 166–67
Functionalist view, 10–11

Gebhardt, G. L., 103
General price-level adjusted, historical cost accounting, 76–79
General price-level adjusted, net realizable value accounting, 81–82
General price-level adjusted, replacement cost accounting, 79–81
Gibbins, Michael, 150

Gonedes, N. J., 121, 122
Gordon, M. J., 36, 37, 44, 45
Gort, Michael, 108
Gramsci, Antonio, 12–13
Griffin, P. A., 113–14

Hagstrom, W. O., 21
Hayes, S. L., 108
Hemmpel, C. G., 3
Heuristic decision makers, 163
Hicks, J. R., 68
Historical cost accounting: general price-level adjusted, 76–79; principles of, 71–73
Human information processes: and cognitive style approach, 163–65; components of, 158–59; and Lens model, 159–60; and predecisional behavior, 161–63; and probabilistic judgment and, 160–61
Hypotheses: arising from statistical or tendency laws, 4; confirmation of, 3–4; refutable, 3–4

Ideographic approach, 15–19
Ijiri, Yuji, 35–36, 38
Income: concept of, 67–68; definitions of, 67
Income determination models: alternative, 69; evaluation criteria for, 70; list of, 70; and main asset valuation, 71
Income smoothing: and anthropological/inductive paradigm, 36, 38–41, 44–48; dimensions of, 47–48; empirical tests in, 37; methods in research, 50–52; motivations of, 45–47; nature of, 44–45
Information inductance, 167
Information/economics paradigm: disciplines providing insight to, 40–41; exemplars of, 38–39; subject matter of, 39–40
Informational-evaluation-decision-maker model, 40–41
Integrative complexity, 164
Interactionism, 11

Interest-rate risk, 104
Interpretive view, 11–12

Jensen, M. C., 42, 48
Joyce, E. J., 162
Jung, C. G., 26

Kilman, R. H., 27
Kinglit, R. M., 102
Kuhn, Thomas, 19–20, 22

Lant, Theresa, 169
Lavallee, M.T.R., 102
Lens model, 159–60
Libby, R., 162
Lindhal, E., 67
Linguistic relativism, 165–66
Littleton, A. C., 36
Lowe, A. E., 170
Lukacs, George, 12
Lukka, Kari, 171
Luthans, F. T., 17

Maanen, John Van, 18
Mader, F. R., 103
Malpass, Roy S., 155
Marginal-economics-based accounting, 5–6
Market model, 128–30
Marketability risk, 104
Marris, R. N., 108
Matobesy, Z. P., 102
Mautz, R. K., 2
May, G. O., 94
McCann, H. Gilman, 20
Mean square error (MSE), 112
Meckling, J.W.H., 42
Meeks, G., 109
Merton, R. K., 21–22
Mitroff, I. I., 27
Money income, 67
Moral-hazard problem, 42–43
Morgan, Gareth, 9–10, 15–16
Mueller, D. C., 109–10

Net realizable value accounting: characteristics of, 75–76; general price-level adjusted, 81–82
Nomothesis approach, 15–19
Nonzero agency costs, 52

Objectivism, 11
Ohlson, J. A., 103
Option pricing, equilibrium theory of, 127–28
Organizational slack, 169, 171

Palepu, K., 109
Paradigm: accounting as science of multiple, 22–24; concept of, 19–20, 22, 23; as political phenomenon, 22–23
Participation in decision making (PDM), 173
Paton, W. A., 65–66
Phenomenology, 17, 18
Physical capital maintenance, 68, 69
Policy-capturing studies, 160
Political-economy accounting: background of, 6–7; explanation of, 7; features of, 7–8
Positive theories: evaluation of, 55, 58–59; explanation of, 48–50; methods in research, 52. *See also* Anthropological/inductive paradigm
Positive-agency paradigm: assumptions that characterize, 52; and tension between analytical-agency paradigm, 41–42
Prakash, P., 168
Predecisional behavior, 161–63
Predictive-ability criterion: advantages of, 96–97; origins of, 94–95
Price change models, 82–86
Price-level balance sheet valuation model, 132–33
Primacy, 167
Prisoner's Dilemma, 43
Probabilistic judgment, 160–61
Process tracers, 162
Professional judgment in public accounting (PJPA), 151
Prospect theory, 167

Psychic income, 67
Purchasing-power risk, 104
Puxty, Tony, 87

Radical humanist view, 12–13
Radical structuralist view, 13–14
Rappoport, A., 168
Real smoothing, 47
Recency ego involvement, 167
Replacement cost accounting: characteristics of, 74–75; general price-level adjusted, 79–81
Ritzer, George, 22, 23
Rochester School of Accounting, 48
Rosner, Martin M., 169

Samuels, J. M., 108
Scientific method, 25
Scientific revolutions, theory of, 19–22
Scott, J., 98–99
Shaw, R. W., 170
Sherer, M. J., 7
Shillinglaw, G., 170
Singh, Jitendra, 169
Slack, 168–71
Smith, Adam, 67–68
Social science: accounting as, 1–4; assumptions about, 8
Society, assumptions about, 9
Sommer Report (Securities and Exchange Commission), 138
Spiegelberg, Herbert, 18
Sterling, R., 95, 96
Survival of the efficient, 52
Syndicate-theory model, 40

Taussig, R. A., 108
Team-theory model, 41

Time-series analysis, 97–98
Tinker, Anthony, 5, 87
Trade-credit analysis, 111
Triandis, Harry C., 155
Triangulation, 19
True income/deductive paradigm: and concept of capital maintenance, 68–69; and concept of income, 67–68; conclusions regarding, 88; exemplars of, 65–66; and falsity of desirability, 86–87; and historical cost accounting, 71–73, 76–79; and income determination models, 69–71; and market for excuses, 87–88; net and realizable value accounting, 75–76, 81–82; and replacement cost accounting, 74–75, 79–81; subject matter of, 66; and taxonomy of price chance models, 82–86
Tzoannos, J. T., 108

U-curve hypothesis, 164

Valuation model (Ohlson), 132
Value system, of academic accountants, 24–25
Van Fredrikslust model, 102–3
Vance, J. S., 108

Waller, W. S., 150
Watts, R. L., 36, 37, 58
Weber, R., 150
Weibel, P. F., 103
Wells, M. C., 24
Wenrich, G. T., 103

Zeff, Stephen A., 87
THE ZETA CREDIT RISK, 100–101
Zimmerman, J. L., 36, 37, 58
Z Score, 99–101

About the Author

AHMED RIAHI-BELKAOUI, is Professor of Accounting at the College of Business Administration, University of Illinois at Chicago. A prolific author of journal articles and scholarly and professional books and textbooks, he serves on the editorial boards of numerous prestigious journals in his field and is known for his unusual, often groundbreaking research and analysis.

ISBN 1-56720-048-6

90000>

EAN

9 781567 200485

HARDCOVER BAR CODE